Late Republican–Early Imperial Regional Italian Landscapes and Demography

Peter de Graaf

BAR International Series 2330
2012

Published in 2016 by
BAR Publishing, Oxford

BAR International Series 2330

Late Republican-Early Imperial Regional Italian Landscapes and Demography

ISBN 978 1 4073 0913 2

© P de Graaf and the Publisher 2012

The author's moral rights under the 1988 UK Copyright,
Designs and Patents Act are hereby expressly asserted.

All rights reserved. No part of this work may be copied, reproduced, stored,
sold, distributed, scanned, saved in any form of digital format or transmitted
in any form digitally, without the written permission of the Publisher.

BAR Publishing is the trading name of British Archaeological Reports (Oxford) Ltd.
British Archaeological Reports was first incorporated in 1974 to publish the BAR
Series, International and British. In 1992 Hadrian Books Ltd became part of the BAR
group. This volume was originally published by Archaeopress in conjunction with
British Archaeological Reports (Oxford) Ltd / Hadrian Books Ltd, the Series principal
publisher, in 2012. This present volume is published by BAR Publishing, 2016.

Printed in England

PUBLISHING

BAR titles are available from:

          BAR Publishing
          122 Banbury Rd, Oxford, OX2 7BP, UK
EMAIL   info@barpublishing.com
PHONE +44 (0)1865 310431
  FAX   +44 (0)1865 316916
          www.barpublishing.com

Table of Contents

1 Introduction 3
2 Field Survey Challenges 6
3 Survey Based Demographic Modelling 12
4 Settlement and Market Theory 16
5 Ethnographic Analogies: The Empty Landscape of Cisalpine Gaul 30
6 Urban or Rural? The Potenza Valley Survey 39
7 Demographic Modelling: The *Suburbium* of Rome 50
8 The Land Systems of the Pontine Region 65
9 Peopling the Rural Landscape: The Biferno Valley 80
10 Discussion and Conclusions 87
Abstract 93
Bibliography 94

1 Introduction

In the last decade Roman history and archaeology saw a stream of publications that focused on town and country, especially on the reconstruction of settlement patterns, settlement hierarchy, and the development of crude demographic models for the Late Republican to Early Imperial core of the Roman Empire. The work of ancient historians on Roman Italy centred on the development of a better understanding of the impact of the Gracchan land reforms, the nature and extent of agricultural production, and the interpretation of Roman census figures leading to population estimates, with a focus on total population growth or decline, suggesting economic growth or crisis, using literary sources (De Ligt and Northwood 2008).[1] Archaeological attention has, since the 1980's, been on intensive field surveys aimed at reconstructing regional rural landscapes and society over a multi-millennium time span: from the Neolithic to the Modern era, strongly influenced by the *Annales* School. Although period and region of study overlap, roughly modern-day Italy, the nature of the research and the associated theoretical and methodological framework are different. Nevertheless, archaeological research has been trying to answer those questions that are dominating historical debates, often using literary sources as a final touchstone, whereas it has the potential to study sites and aspects of society that are not part of known historical sources. In this quest, the absence of hard evidence is the norm, and ancient sources are typically elite writings that are descriptive and ambiguous. This means that a range of different approaches, methodologies and primary sources are needed for researching this topic. Archaeologists have invested much time and effort into improving site visibility and recovery, while optimizing sampling procedures and developing improved pottery typologies, under the assumption that more or more accurate data would lead to new insights. Awareness of these presuppositions and their implications can help Roman archaeology to better define the aims of future research and the reassessment of older surveys.

In this study, published intensive field surveys, from different regions on the Italian peninsula, are revisited from a range of different methodological and theoretical perspectives. Witcher has suggested that the presuppositions that are underlying survey archaeology have led to a focus on processes, land, and a drive to uniformity, whereas people, landscape as a medium of social relations, and the variability of the past, and thus the archaeological record, are very often underrepresented in publications (Witcher 2006a, 41-8). The outcome of this research should lead to a better understanding of comparative regional differences, in terms of settlement patterns and hierarchy, demography, urbanisation processes, and how society could have functioned. Much has been published in the literature on the additional insights that can be obtained by taking a regional view and the value of comparing regions, but practical case studies are often lacking or very crude. This study precisely wants to build on these thoughts of regional variations and bring them into better focus. For the theoretical and methodological framework, models and interpretive schemes will be assessed originating from archaeology, social geography and ethnography using archaeological evidence. The field surveys or regions that will be subject to study and comparison cover the Potenza Valley (University of Ghent), the 'extended' *suburbium* of Rome (Tiber Valley Project), the Pontine region (Groningen University) and the Biferno Valley (figure 1.1). These surveyed regions have high quality published data available that allow a comparative study. A sidestep will be made to Cisalpine Gaul to clarify an argument and to highlight and explain differences. The emphasis will be on the Late Republican to Early Imperial period.

Research will focus on answering the following questions: (1) Can *intensive field surveys* be used for making a case for regional variations? What are the problems when comparing published field survey results? What are the boundaries or limitations of making reconstructions? How can these issues, in quality, quantity or theoretical framework be addressed, for example in future research designs? (2) Are *ethnographic* and *historical analogies* helpful heuristic devices in reconstructing town and country? Finally, (3) what regional variations can be found via the study of the published surveys, and are these variations leading to *new or better knowledge and insights*?

The development of a better understanding of comparative regional differences in demography and settlement patterns might appear to be straightforward, but is highly problematic. The challenges not only relate to disagreements on interpretations, but also to the source data. Literary and archaeological sources are both highly incomplete and ambiguous. This has led to scepticism among ancient historians on the contribution that field surveys can make to the debate, and the ability to agree on a high-level view on the demography of Italy during the Late Republic to Early Principate. In recent years, the verification of high-level reconstructions and interpretations for the size of the population living on the Italian peninsula during the Late Republican period has been the object of peer rivalry and competing models. This scientific attention not only resulted in high quality publications, but leaves limited uncovered ground. These unresolved areas are dealing with highly speculative elements, such as regional differences in population, the size of the rural population and lower order nucleated settlements. Regional comparative studies rely more heavily on archaeological evidence than the before

---

[1] I am very grateful to Prof. dr. L. de Ligt for inviting me to the *VICI* conference '*Peasants, Citizens and Soldiers*', held on June 28-30, 2007 at Leiden University, the thorough introduction to the demography debate, and the exposure to the work of leading historians and archaeologists, whose publications and views are well represented in this study.

Figure 1.1: Approximate locations of regions discussed in this study (after Boatwright et al. 2004, appears as the backpaper).

mentioned high-level reconstructions, which use Roman census data as a starting point and extrapolate numbers to cover the whole population of the peninsula.

There are two different traditions to demographic estimates that catch the eye when studying the relevant literature. The first one is minimalistic, and potentially historicising in approaching the demographic challenge, which has literary sources at the basis of research. Within this tradition, archaeological evidence provides valuable insights, but needs to be studied with great care, especially if there are no references in the literary sources that allow validation of the archaeological evidence. A strongly self-reflexive archaeological community has very well captured its own *Quellenkritik* in publications, often in the form of detailed theoretical, methodological and interpretive shortcomings and challenges to archaeological practice and evidence. Analogies, from more recent periods, are considered as a valid surrogate for these shortfalls. The situation during the Early Modern period is often chosen because of the higher quality and quantity of literary sources. Attention is concentrated at the top of the settlement hierarchy of both periods and the size of the rural population is estimated by analogy to later periods. An alternative view recognizes that literary *and* archaeological evidence are limited and ambiguous. A thorough understanding of these elements is required to fully appreciate the nature of the trade-offs that can be made in population reconstructions of past societies. These can make use of elements that build on models from the social sciences on organisation and social behaviour, with clearly articulated assumptions, that suggest a proposition on how to view the past and how past society could have been structured and organised. Analogies are a useful heuristic device that supplement contemporary archaeological evidence, but are secondary at best.

This study will consider the complete settlement hierarchy and includes villages, road stations, hamlets and rural settlements, as these are important for understanding variations and the socio-economic structure of a region.

2 Field Survey Challenges

The use of published field surveys as the basis for research is very challenging. These publications contain not only at least three levels of interpretation that need to be assessed and deconstructed, but the research aims of the authors can be completely different, in both scope and depth. The levels of interpretation are: (1) by individual team members during field walking, (2) during pottery reading and consequent entry into a GIS database and (3) during interpretation and synthesis into a publication. Individual team members already pre-select data when field walking and give a first interpretation during field campaigns that results in an archaeological sample of collected artefacts, architectural and landscape features. A presupposition in field surveys is that the archaeological sample has a certain relationship to the sampled and target population, which in its turn has a specific relationship to past human behaviour and the human activities that generated the assemblage (Haselgrove 1985, 8-14). Archaeologists are confronted with complex multivariate systems that result in a certain visible and sampled ceramic scatter to which the survey team gives meaning, leading to a proposition on how the past landscape, settlement pattern and hierarchy, land-use, ancient economy, and demography could have looked (figure 2.1). In the past few decades, archaeologists have taken necessary processual steps and further refined collection procedures and developed methods for determining recovery factors that are needed to manage statistical inference and to better understand, and reduce, data noise that historically hindered interpretation (Van Leusen 2002). Moreover, a lot of effort and attention has been given to distinguishing permanent and temporary sites from off-site areas based on sherd distributions in the landscape, except for the general lack of attention to separating site cores from 'haloes' (Bintliff et al. 2007). Off-site scatters do not significantly affect population estimates. Sites that are of importance to population reconstructions, such as farms and *villae* leave an archaeological imprint that can be resurveyed as long as they exist with sufficient visibility, in the archaeological record.

Discard patterns
The recognition and interpretation of discard patterns represent a challenge. The highly complex pottery record and associated methodological issues have been approached via inductive and deductive methods. The model for the formation of the pottery record by Peña is an example of a deductive approach (Peña 2007). He modelled the actions that governed the formation of the pottery record, the pottery life-cycle, in terms of manufacture, distribution, prime use, reuse, maintenance, recycling, discard and reclamation for *dolia*, *amphorae*, lamps and cooking wares, table wares and utilitarian wares and how they moved from the systemic (the human behavioural) system to the archaeological context. Moreover, he studied in which part of the life-cycle the majority of the pottery of a certain functional class could end up in the archaeological record (figure 2.2). The outcome of his study was a pottery typology of the

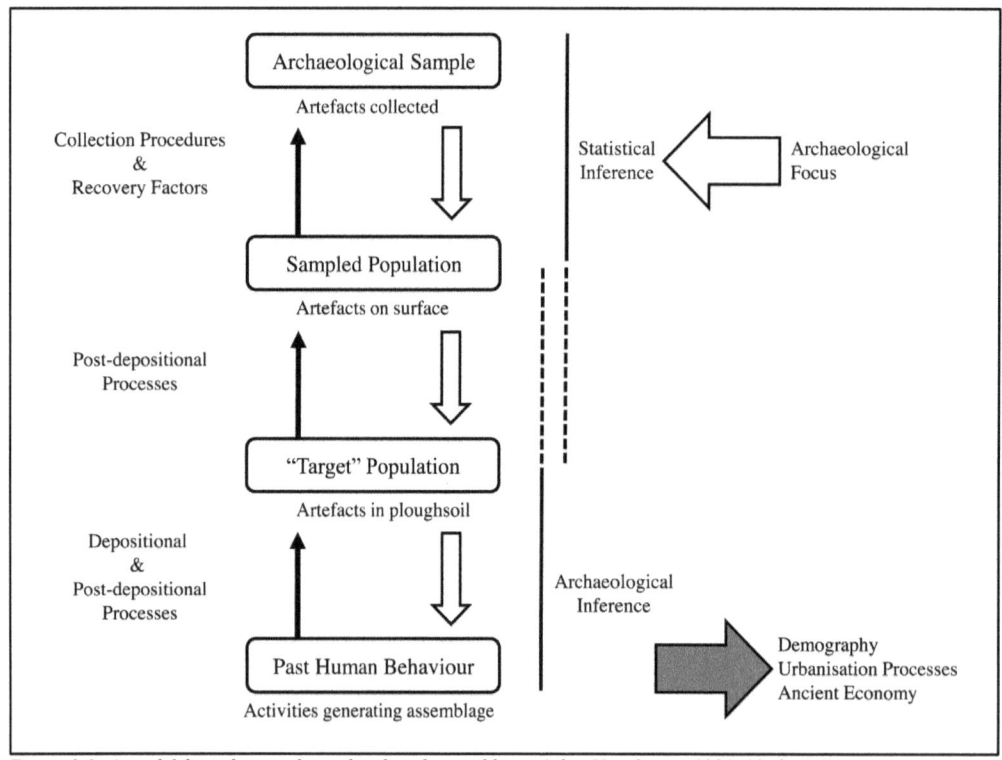

Figure 2.1: A model for inference from plough soil assemblages (after Haselgrove 1985, 10, fig 1.1).

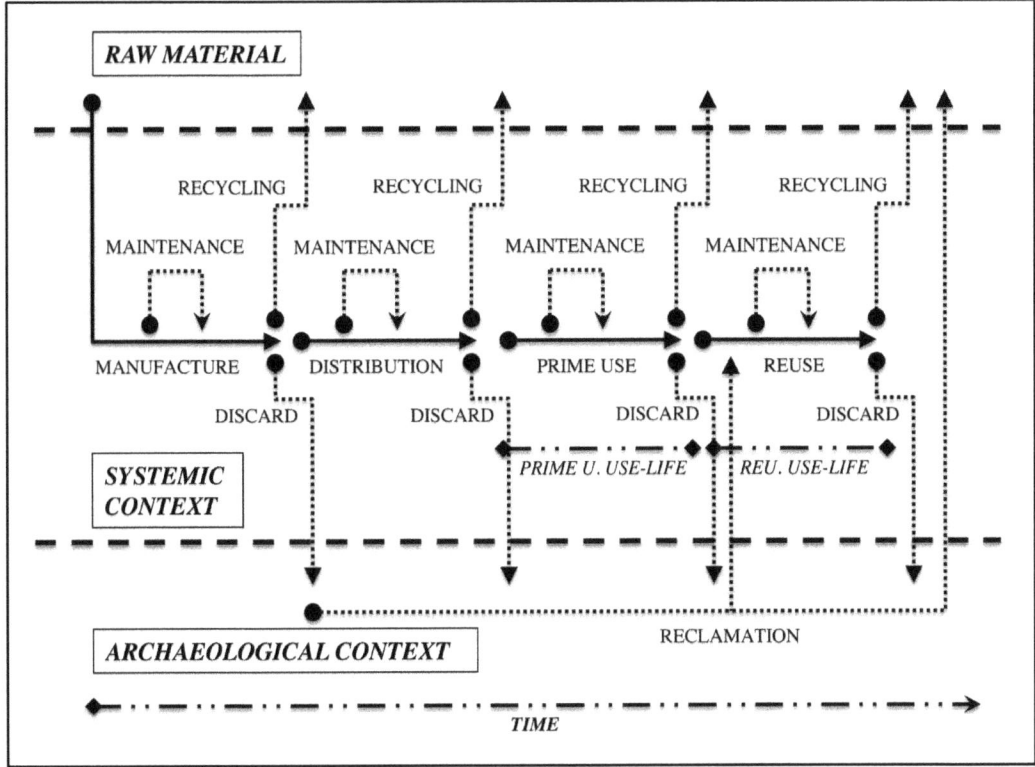

Figure 2.2: The life-cycle of Roman pottery (Peña 2007, 9, fig 1.2).

different types of deposits that could be used for determining the activities for which the specific pottery deposit is indicative (Peña 2007, 337-9). The team of the Boeotia Survey followed an inductive approach, taking the sherd scatter as a starting point. They demonstrated the value of what they call 'statistical weighting' in a recent publication on the fieldwork around the ancient town of Thespiai (Bintliff *et al.* 2007, 9-11, 15-37). The archaeological inference involves the process of establishing what activities resulted in the deposition of a material and when it happened, after which meaning is given, for instance via a functional analysis, to observations.

Site recovery

The recovery ratio of sites, which is the assessment of how many sites have been found relative to the total number of sites present in the archaeological record, is important in the interpretation of intensive field surveys. This recovery ratio affects estimates of the size of the

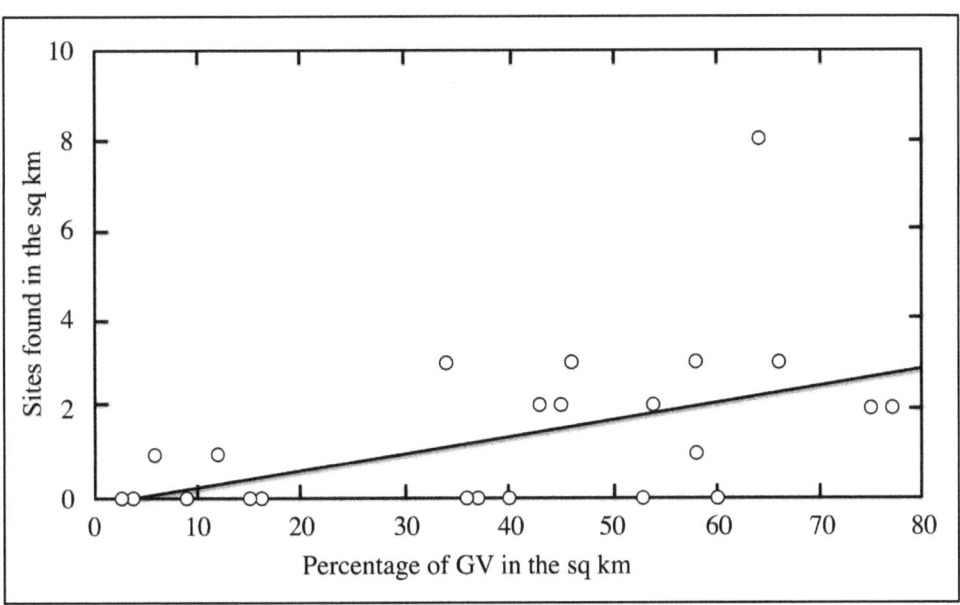

Figure 2.3: Relationship between ground visibility (GV) and the number of sites/km² for the Cecina Valley in the Hellenistic period (after Ammerman and Terrenato 1996, 104, fig 8).

rural population. Recovery ratios can be refined and studied by methodological improvements, such as survey intensity, survey coverage, sample strategy, or by geomorphological, geophysical or geochemical studies (Sbonias 1999, 4). The size of the total population that is sampled represents the big unknown that drives uncertainties in debates. Another valid question is to what extent differences in survey strategy result in valid reconstructions and represent past variations (Witcher 2008b, 289) or that intensity, methodology, geomorphology and (post-) depositional effects skew results and cause low visibility. Ammerman and Terrenato tried to quantify the relationship between visibility and site recovery for the Cecina Valley, located in central Italy, and suggested a method for correcting this problem. Their analysis is based on the classification of transects into four categories of groundcover; ploughed land, harrowed land, light vegetation cover, and heavy vegetation cover (figure 2.3). They concluded that '*It is no longer a sound practice simply to assume that the sites found during the course of survey work provide a full or adequate representation of the sites that are actually present in the area examined.*'(Ammerman and Terrenato 1996, 91-6, 106). The estimated site recovery ratio for the Cecina Valley Survey has been estimated at ca. 50%. The reassessment of the results of the Keos Survey confirmed their conclusion, demonstrating an even better correlation. They find it plausible that in the case of the coastal plain at Cecina only half of the sites have been recovered, however uniformity in site density and distribution as a function of visibility, but also for different regions, cannot be assumed, but requires testing (Ammerman and Terrenato 1996, 106-7). The percentage of sites identified in the Albegna Valley and the *ager Cosanus* during the Late Republican period, based on an estimate of the expected number of sites, derived from literary sources, and the actual material evidence found during survey work, has been estimated to vary between 20 and 33% (Cambi 1999, 117-22). A preliminary observation is that the translation of field survey data into site and regional demographic developments, especially when chronological depth is needed, is a Herculean effort!

Survey intensity
Intimately linked to recovery ratio and visibility is survey intensity. Cherry demonstrated, based on mapping Greek surveys that the number of sites increases when the inter-walker distance and size of walked transects decreases (Cherry *et al.* 1991). More efforts per unit of area (person/day per km^2), result in the identification of more sites. Van Leusen extended the plot that Cherry made for Italy by adding intensive local and extensive regional surveys that have been done in the Pontine region (figure 2.4) (Van Leusen 2002, ch 4, 12-3). Small-scale excavations can offer one way of getting closer to those activities that generated the archaeological record and can, aside from obtaining a better understanding of post-depositional processes, help in the understanding of the correlation between the artefacts in the plough soil and the archaeological sample; surface versus sub-surface. The raw data that field survey archaeologists' work with consist primarily of ceramic scatters from plough soils and landscape features. How do archaeologists currently handle and interpret their primary data?

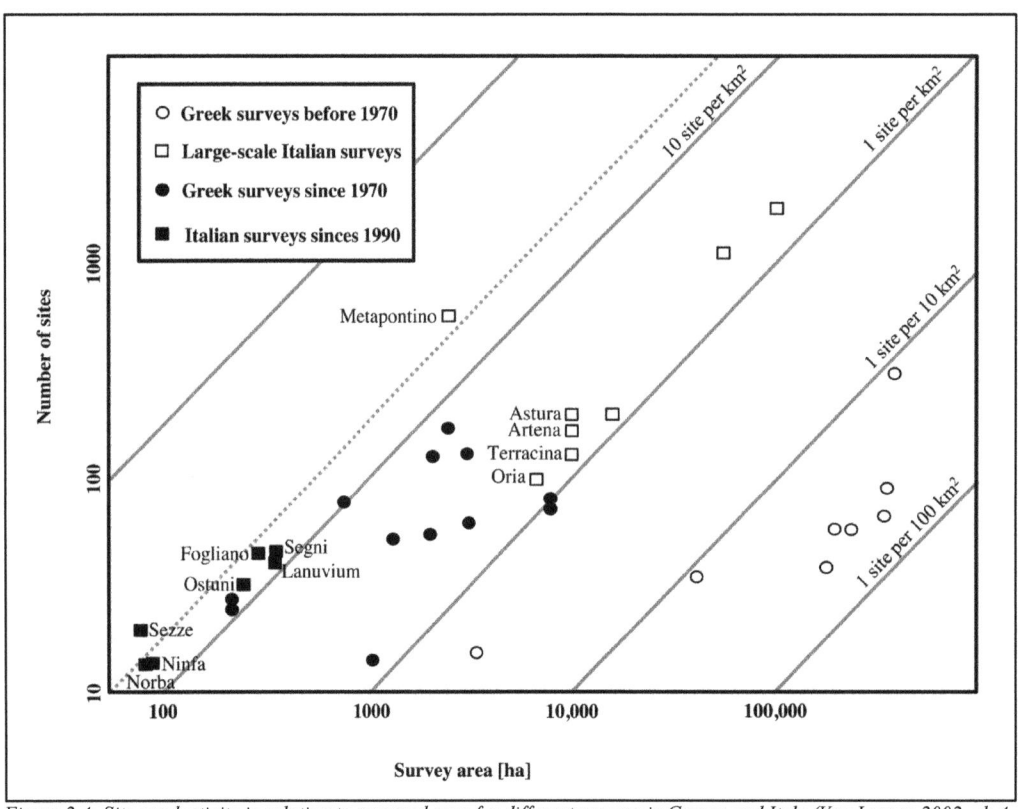

Figure 2.4: Site productivity in relation to surveyed area for different surveys in Greece and Italy (Van Leusen 2002, ch 4, 12, fig 1).

Site classification
Site classifications are not always objective and are an interpretative construct made by archaeologists, based on background and training, their own perceptions and the raw data coming from the survey. One of the many challenges in field surveys is the identification of smaller sites. Site visibility and the identification of small farms, hamlets and small villages, especially from the Republican period have often been perceived as a mission impossible. It was suggested by Pelgrom that traditional research has focused too much on plough soils and not on more difficult accessible marginal terrains, such as uplands, highlands, marshes, coastal margins, and changes in the landscape (Pelgrom 2008, 341-54). Another area of attention is the classification of hidden landscapes, which exceed the archaeologist's view from the ground and their interpretation (Bintliff *et al.* 1999). The underlying assumption is that the archaeological record is structured, at least partially, according to landscape parameters, and records processes like erosion and deposition, and can be used to inform archaeologists on the suitability of the landscape, i.e. for agriculture and housing. Surface assemblages are classified into site types, and it may be obvious that changes, or different classifications, can affect interpretations and models. Classification can be based on distinctions made by the Romans, such as *tugurum, casa, villa, vicus, forum, statio, municipium* and *colonia*. The recognition of subsidiary buildings and features belonging to larger estates also adds complexity to site definition and typology. Examples are accommodation or resting places for permanent or seasonal workers, compost heaps or manure pits, buildings for housing and storing equipment, stables, storage for agricultural produce and huts temporarily occupied by for instance shepherds (Ikeguchi 1999, 10-1). Archaeologists often create fuzzy or overlapping classes, depending on the material remains available, which influence their conclusions, and make comparisons between field surveys highly problematic. A generally accepted classification of sites has not been agreed on and will hinder comparative studies (Gkiasta 2008, 221-2). At the basis of small site typology, based on field survey data, is the size of the pottery scatter and architectural components like marble, painted plaster, tile and stone debris that would then be used for assigning the label hut, farm or *villa*. However, the relationship between floor plan versus the size of the scatter is problematic and the site halo is rarely measured. Bintliff and Snodgrass first explored the existence of these haloes of dense pottery scatter during the Boeotia Survey (Bintliff and Snodgrass 1988; Bintliff *et al.* 2007).

Rathbone expressed his concern for the typology of small sites, focusing in his publication on what seems to be a broad spectrum of different sizes of farms and *villae*. He uses the reports from excavated sites to argue that the division into two distinct and unitary categories is unjustified and not helpful. Nevertheless, he came up with broad ranges in which sites with a floor plan below 250 m^2 are classified small; medium for a floor plan in the range of 400-600 m^2 and large for large buildings above 1000 m^2. Especially for the medium range sites, it is not clear if these are farms owned by prosperous farmers, using limited slave labour, or small *villae* owned by a non-resident owner as slave-staffed estates (Rathbone 2008, 306-22).

Dating
The dating of sites, in field surveys primarily by pottery, is needed to establish chronology and occupancy history. Statistically it can be expected that small sites do not contain full, representative assemblages, and often these sites have been interpreted as impoverished. Fabric analysis helps archaeologists to create broad categories that allow a significant percentage of sherds with diagnostic features to be dated. Potter developed a chronological framework for pottery types (figure 2.5) based on the South Etruria Survey (Potter 1979, 16-7), which was at the basis of later refinements. The subsequent re-evaluation of the 90,000 artefacts from approximately 2,500 sites from the South Etruria Survey has resulted in an improved chronological resolution needed for redating sites. These improvements include the reassessment of the classes of grey bucchero, early almond rim vessels and internal slipware. The first has been redated to the sixth century BC and the later types to after 300 BC, so the Late Republican period (Patterson *et al.* 2004, 3, 7). The principal dating evidence for the period 80 BC-250 AD is based on three types of fine wares. Late black glazed pottery, also referred to as Campana ware, was in use until the Augustan period. Campana A ware, which can be recognised by its purple-red and hard metallic gloss, was made in the Naples region from 200-50 BC, and is found on Roman Republican sites across the western Mediterranean.

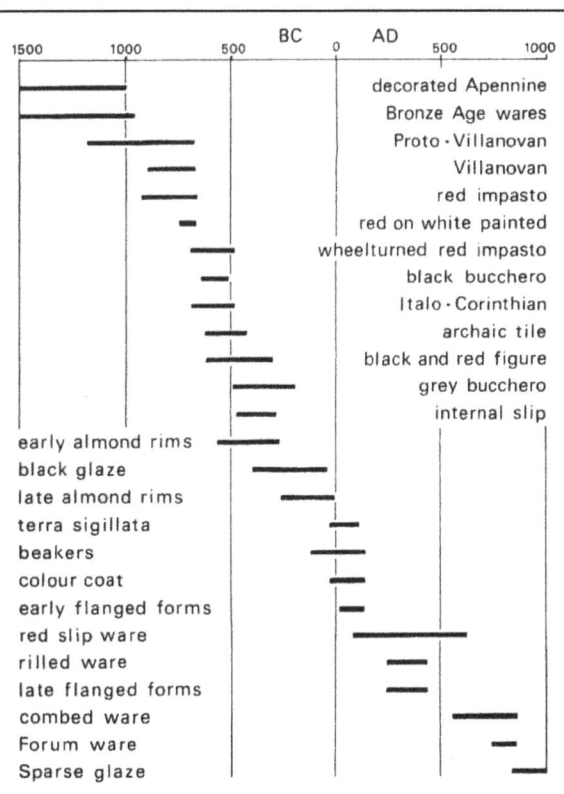

Figure 2.5: Main pottery types in South Etruria (Potter 1979, 17, tab 2).

Campana B ware developed from 150 BC and has the approximate same end period of 50 BC as Campana A ware. Campana B ware can be recognised by delicate roulette bands and some stamps, and introduces the large flat-floored plate as a common shape. By 50 BC, black glazed wares lost their popularity and were gradually replaced by red glazed successors. In the first century BC, also grey wares appear with Campana C ware as example (Hayes 1997, 37-8). Red gloss *sigillata* from northern Etruria, known as Arretine ware, started to circulate locally from 40 BC, and different variations developed and are known as Italian *sigillata* ware.

Three regional patterns of production and consumption of Italian *sigillata* have been identified, and production and consumption carried on well into the second century AD. One pattern focuses on the northern and western part of Roman Italy, a second on the northern-eastern regions of the Po area, and the third on the eastern part of the peninsula. It goes into too much detail to elaborate on the differences between the three styles, but they are important for establishing chronology in the field survey regions that are used as case histories. Finally, from the late first century AD, red gloss *terra sigillata* was replaced by a less sophisticated ware from North Africa known as African Red Slip ware. This ware stayed in use until the late Roman period (Hayes 1997, 41-6). Slightly different transition dates for the different wares are in use, based on local typologies developed during field campaigns. A good chronological resolution, based on a solid typology is required to avoid overestimating the number of small sites, which can have a short history of occupancy (Ikeguchi 1999, 12-3). If methodology and the interpretation of an individual field survey are considered problematic, can field survey results be compared at all?

Consensus on a high-level approach and trade-offs for such comparative research are required. This could relate to the erratic spatial coverage of rural surveys, the in- and exclusive selection of settlements, chronological and dating challenges, and the development of best practices for field surveys.

Case history: comparative study

An interesting perspective on how field survey results can be synthesised into a bigger picture of differences in regional settlement patterns has been offered by Mattingly and Witcher. The distribution of Early Imperial settlements identified by fourteen field surveys was studied (figure 2.6). A key aim of their paper was '*to contribute to a radically different cartographic vision of the ancient world*' (Mattingly and Witcher 2004, 173). Within this cartographic tradition, the Barrington Atlas (Talbert 2000) being the prime example, the results of regional surveys have been largely ignored leading to a distorted representation of settlement patterns in favour of towns, small towns, road stations and sanctuaries, creating blank areas on maps that could have been populated, and thus underrepresenting the importance of widespread small nucleated centres.

Mattingly and Witcher experimented with weighting survey results for varying survey intensity, doubling densities from medium intensity surveys, and using a multiplier of 1.5 for the high intensity surveys, to make them all comparable to the very high intensity surveys. Finally, they added the urban density by counting the urban centres mapped in the Barrington Atlas (figure 2.7). The smallest settlement type that is denominated urban is the road station, excluding villages and hamlets (Mattingly and Witcher 2004, 181-2). Based

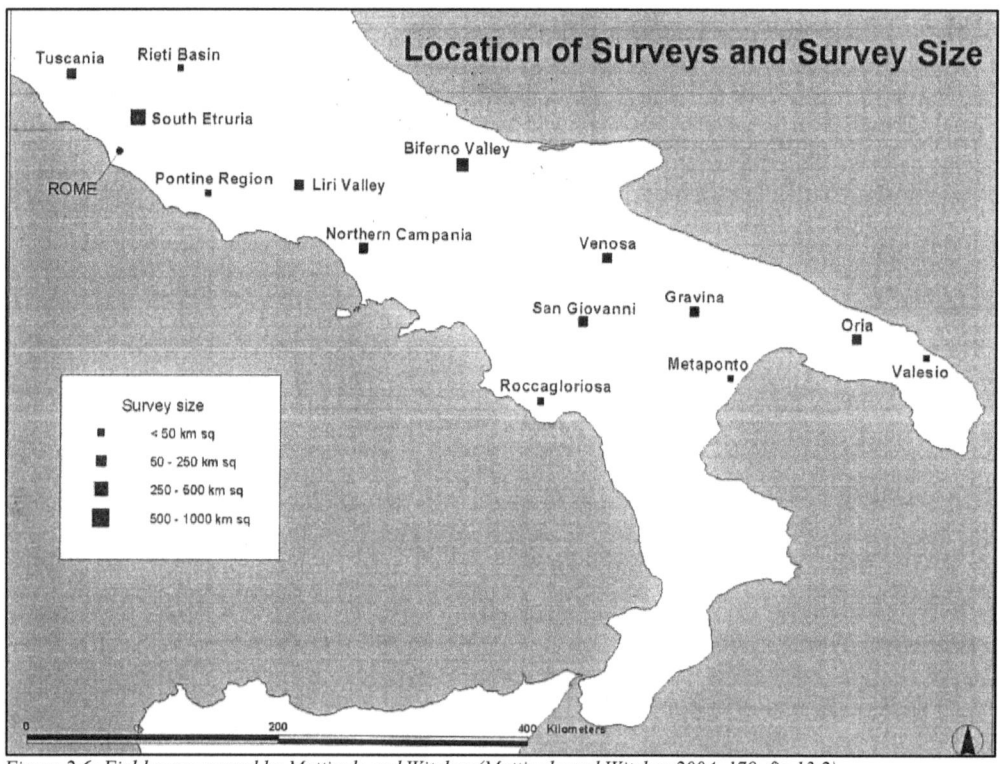

Figure 2.6: Field surveys used by Mattingly and Witcher (Mattingly and Witcher 2004, 179, fig 13.2).

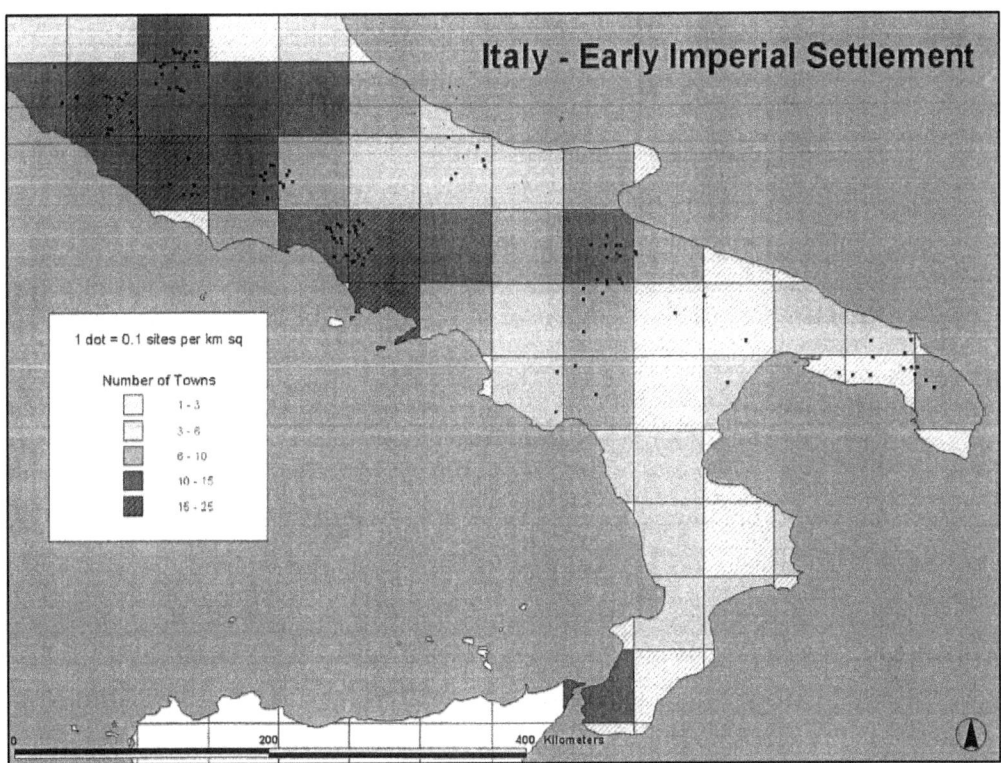

Figure 2.7: Calculated density of Early Imperial period sites and urban settlement pattern (Mattingly and Witcher 2004, 183, fig 13.6).

on their analysis, they suggest that areas of high urbanisation also demonstrate dense rural settlement (Campania, Etruria and Lazio) in contrast to areas of limited urbanisation that also have lower densities of dispersed rural settlement, such as Lucania and Northern Puglia. This preliminary assessment goes well with their expectation that urban centres require a certain surplus from their hinterland. A mixed picture has emerged from the Salento peninsula, which could be explained by the widely identified presence of *vici* (the smallest unit of Roman municipal administration; in the context of this study a village) that had an important functional role in that region. The challenge is to validate any teleological elements in their synthesis, especially the possible relationship between the number of urban centres and the density of rural sites, and the survey intensity multiplier, which can be interpreted as an alternate way of incorporating site recovery ratio into the analysis. This relationship suggests a constant rate of urbanisation and ignores the size and function of an urban settlement. This analysis opens up an interesting aspect that can be looked at further, as several of the surveys used in this analysis are also parts of this study.

3 Survey Based Demographic Modelling

Survey based population reconstructions use a mathematical approach in which site types per period are multiplied by standard site populations for farms and *villae*, and persons per hectare for nucleated settlements such as towns and villages. Issues with this approach include site visibility, chronological resolution, site typology and defining standard site populations and population densities. Recovery ratios are a function of site size leading to the underestimation of small sites. Material impoverishment or population nucleation could also be the cause of fewer visible sites. Moreover, dating for small sites is more difficult as there is less material to date, if any diagnostic material at all! If this is the case, how can surveys be compared, and in the case of future research design, how 'intensive' should a survey be? In the ideal scenario, all variables, including reliable census figures from literary sources, are known with a high degree of certainty, making the calculation of an estimated population for a certain chronological period static, but a relatively easy exercise! The contrary is however true. The limited literary and archaeological sources direct archaeologists and historians to making trade-offs, which results in highly speculative alternate mathematical constructions that extrapolate from archaeological evidence and literary sources, and make use of spatial (geographical) and temporal (chronological) analogies. Although demographic models can be expressed as equations, most historians and archaeologists prefer to be descriptive. De Ligt exposed the underlying mathematical reality (equation 3.1) in a recent publication on the population of Cisalpine Gaul in the time of Augustus by the explicit use of equations (De Ligt 2008, 140).

In publications, the words 'population estimates' have slowly been substituted by 'educated guesses', which comes closer to reality, and academic disclaimers on the validity and uncertainties of the reconstruction are the rule. However, in the absence of better alternatives these models are part of the debate and are discussed in terms of likelihood relative to competing demographic numbers. Hansen coined the mathematical methodology in the nineteen-eighties as the *'The Shotgun Method'* (Hansen 2006, 1). This analogy describes the nature and limitations of the method strikingly well. Different scholars developed variations on the theme, but the core of the logic has remained unchanged for almost three decades. Many historians and archaeologists think that there should be sliding scales in the metrics leading to population estimates, not only for nucleated settlements (large, medium and small), but also for rural sites. The latter is based on observations that the population size for farms and *villae* depends on landscape features, demographic pressure and the associated size of the agricultural plot resulting in a certain family size that can differ regionally. Hansen further refined population density as a function of settlement size, the size of the hinterland, the ratio of private versus public space and the size of houses (Hansen 2006, 35-63).

The underestimation of small sites, but also villages, has led to a focus on the top of the settlement hierarchy, where the chance of missing a site is relatively low; with the important benefit that, although fragmented, literary and archaeological evidence are available. This approach requires an estimate of the urbanisation ratio that can be calculated with the help of an historical ethnographic analogy or a unique contemporary case for which the size of the settlement and population, both rural and urban is believed to be known, resulting in a multiplier for establishing the size of the rural population. Therefore, the focus is on larger urban centres for which the estimated urban population is the outcome of the multiplication of size in hectares times the population density. This approach is not without problems. Within this line of reasoning, the smaller urban centres are considered not significant to the argument because large settlements function as population sinks (Morley 2008, 122). A low site recovery of small sites thus has limited impact on a reconstruction as long as the analogy is valid. The use of an urbanisation ratio in a demographic model underrepresents the function and nature of settlements of lower rank, and raises the issue on the criteria that determine if a settlement and its population are classified as urban or rural. Criteria that use settlement population and size thresholds, architectural features, juridical and administrative, or economic criteria like occupational structure can result in different reconstructions. Regardless of criteria used, each one has falsifiable and debatable elements. These challenges cannot be resolved in this study, but scholars are quite aware that settlement typology has a big impact on settlement and demographic reconstructions. This is especially valid for the distinction between settlement type 'town' and type 'village' that provides a boundary case, which is equated with urban and rural (De Ligt 1990, 27-30) and can tip the balance in a reconstruction when urbanisation ratios are part of the equation. Instead of reasoning in lines of typologies and creating an artificial urban-rural dichotomy, an alternative view of settlements is one of a continuum of sites and functions.

Ethnoarchaeologists have studied the archaeological implication of the use of ethnographic studies to describe the organisation of space, settlement pattern, settlement hierarchy, and crude demographic models of past pre-industrial societies. The majority of these studies have their settings in the Near East (Sumner 1989) and Mesoamerica (Kolb 1985). The focuses of these studies

$$Population = (100 : \%Urbanisation\ Ratio) \times \sum Hectare_{urban} \times Avg.\ Population\ Density$$

(equation 3.1)

are on crafts, workshop organisation and small communities, which are different from using analogies in demographic estimates and urbanisation processes. Can a historical, or contemporary, analogy be successfully used for making population estimates? Ethnographic studies can give valuable insights into the past demography for a region, but the validity of the analogy needs to be investigated before projections are made. A comparison needs to be carried out in terms of political and socio-economic organisation and differences in landscape and ecologies. What may sound common sense for a certain period and place may not be valid for another. Limited data can exist on both sides of the analogy equation. Assuming that the data of the reference case are present in enough quantity and quality to be scrutinised, the question remains if a one-on-one projection of the 'incomplete' past can be made. The criteria for making the comparison are not clear and are not well articulated in the case of Roman Italy.

A key presupposition in modelling Roman demography is that agricultural, pre-industrial societies have certain traits in common. Seldom challenged is the assumption that the majority of the population lived in a rural setting and that urbanisation ratios most likely did not exceed the levels found in Medieval and Early Modern societies prior to the industrial revolution (figure 3.1). Moreover, often early nineteenth century AD census figures, prior to the mechanisation of agriculture, are used as a ceiling for the maximum population density. This can be misleading, as the case of Classical Boeotia demonstrates. The population reconstruction by Bintliff and Snodgrass hints to a population of 150-200,000. In 1889, the region that corresponds to ancient Boeotia had a population of approximately 40-43,000 persons (Bintliff and Snodgrass 1985). The assumption that the processes behind demographic development and urbanisation are comparable implies that Late Medieval and Early Modern period sources can be used to build a case for earlier periods. The issue thus focuses on the identification of these processes and demographic drivers. Greek archaeology, and especially the work of Ruschenbusch and Bintliff, has demonstrated that the level of urbanisation can also follow a different trajectory to the above orthodoxy, which is counter intuitive to the assumption made by most scholars on how pre-industrial agricultural societies are organised (Ruschenbusch 1985; Bintliff 1997b). A study of seven field surveys (the Keos, Argolid, Asea, Methana, Melos, Metapontium and Laconia surveys) indicates that the majority of the ancient Greeks lived in the *polis* centre and a minority in its hinterland (Bintliff 2006, 22; Hansen 2006, 64-71). Moreover, ca. 80% of all *poleis* had a territory of max. 200 km^2 and a population of a few thousands (Hansen 2006, 29, 64-76), enforcing that the Greeks from the Archaic and Classical periods must have been farmers that lived in the centre and walked every morning to their fields in the hinterland, meaning that there was no town and country dichotomy (Bintliff 1997b; Bintliff 2002a). The implication is that the concept of the ancient town as consumer city has become hard to maintain for the majority of *poleis* (Hansen 2004). Exceptions are the large *poleis* with consequent large hinterland that would require a larger number of the total population to live in the countryside. The socio-political organisation of the *polis* was exported to *Magna Graecia*, which brings the discussion to the Italian peninsula. Population in these *poleis* declined sharply under Roman control suggesting a change in the socio-political and economic organisation. Garnsey concluded from a study of Latin *coloniae* and the reported number of colonists, that their modest size, the estimated size of the hinterland and the extent of centuriated areas indicated that the majority of their population lived outside of the main centre (Garnsey

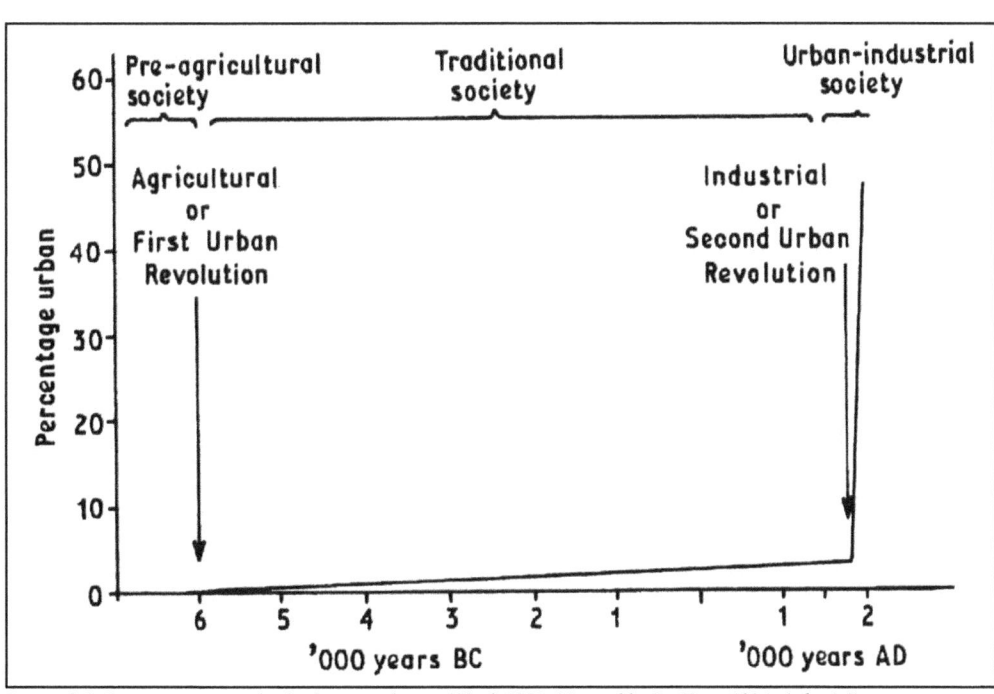

Figure 3.1: Progressive growth of urban population (Clark 1982, 82 cited by De Vries 1984, 6, fig 1.1).

1998, 123-6). It will thus be very interesting to compare the nature of Greek versus Roman urbanism and the associated town and country relationship based on published field surveys.

A causal connection is often assumed between the growth and size of towns and economic development, which is projected onto Roman Italy. The presence or absence of centres, comparable to Early Modern Europe, then becomes critical. A typical Italian town during the Roman period, with a population of a few thousands, would not qualify as a city in studies of Early Modern urbanisation. The use of a threshold population of 10,000 by De Vries, which is used by ancient historians, gives the impression that a like-for-like comparison can be made (De Vries 1984, 4, 21-2). De Vries selected a population threshold of 10,000 based on the available dataset for Early Modern Europe. This threshold allowed him to systematically study a substantial number of cities, based on historical evidence. This does not mean that he considers settlements below 10,000 as rural. He estimated the number of smaller settlements, what he calls the 'unobserved' urban subset, via extrapolation of the dataset for settlements above the 10,000 population threshold, using the rank-size rule. The rank-size rule will be discussed in detail in the next chapter. A lower population threshold, for instance 2,000-3,000 could be considered, but requires checks-and-balances via literary sources and especially a good understanding of the occupational attributes of these smaller settlements is needed for determining the urban-rural split. A simple comparison of levels of urbanisation is inadequate for describing the underlying social and economic processes, and requires more investigation into the settlement density (number of cities) and the range of urban functions (De Vries 1984, 22, 53, 152). The urban Roman landscape offers a practical challenge. Information on the non-agricultural occupational structure of settlements that could be classified as urban is anecdotal at best, and based on epigraphic evidence and urban architecture. This evidence does not reveal what percentage of the population was actually active in non-agricultural professions. In the majority of cases only the approximate urban area of a settlement, regional settlement density and a few literary sources are available. These factors have contributed to a focus on the top of the settlement hierarchy and the use of arbitrary population or settlement size threshold values, as well as the assumption that these large settlements must have had a differentiated crafts and services labour base.

Comparative studies between the two periods, and the two different societies are rare, especially on the relationship between town and country and assumptions on the percentage of the population that lived in the countryside. Morley identified the problems posed by the use of a population threshold and the typological approach to the definition of the city and its relationship to the hinterland (Morley 2008, 124-6). An artificial dichotomy is created by which a given centre is (or is not) a proper urban centre, on what is a continuum of urban forms and functions. The assumption that a town suddenly becomes urban, or economically progressive when it reaches a certain population level produces a certain type of exaggerated narrative. Moreover, it takes the Early Modern European city as a benchmark and a template for other periods (Horden and Purcell 2000, 92-101).

In current reconstructions, it is difficult to relate the process of the expansion of cities, changes in their nature and function, to other processes of social and economic change. The typology of urban settlements can, according to De Vries, be based on different quantifiable dimensions that help to categorize settlements. These characteristics are population size, the density of settlement, the share of non-agricultural occupations and the diversity of non-agricultural occupations. These criteria are continua, which result in highly debatable threshold values for each dimension, to which a settlement has to conform to be qualified urban. A settlement must score '*sufficiently high*' in all four of these criteria to be a city. What De Vries means with sufficiently high remains obscure, outside of the demographic dimension, in which he describes urbanisation as a process of population concentration in more and/or bigger cities. He recognizes that each phase of urbanisation can be viewed as having distinct demographic, behavioural and structural dimensions. Behavioural urbanisation refers to people demonstrating urban behaviour, modes of thought and types of activities, and structural urbanisation to changes in the way society is organised and nourishes the concentration of people and activities at central places (De Vries 1984, 11-3). These last elements can be related to the concept of the 'corporate community' which can begin to operate from as few as 500-600 people in a nucleated settlement (Bintliff 1999).

De Ligt questions if the levels of peasant demand, of village production and of urban-rural distribution that are observed in Antiquity really differ that much from their Late Medieval counterparts (De Ligt 1990, 25). Comparisons that focus on differences, especially the contrast between the ancient consumer city and the medieval producer city, and the rise of the capitalist system can lead to the neglect of essential similarities (De Ligt 1991, 59-62). Jongman constructed a model in which there is a causal link between a high urbanisation ratio and a consistent pattern of landowning elite residence in towns, which is in line with the findings of medievalists, who noticed that the habit of Italian landowners to live in cities was a key driver in late-medieval urbanisation (Jongman 1988, 192-8). However, the prosperity of the North Italian towns in the Late Medieval and Early Modern period, was intimately linked to the rise of merchant capitalism, a system in which the elite has its basis in trade, banking and eventually local (city-state) politics and created a continuous influx of wealth driving local and regional prosperity. Wealth in Roman Italy was primary based on the ownership of land and the presence of a healthy peasant class. In addition, the social basis was different, as elite *euergetism* was a Roman phenomenon and concentrated on towns where the elite resided. In Medieval Italy, neighbouring cities were frequently close rivals or even enemies, hindering a smooth flow of trade between them, whereas during the

Early Modern period towns were more inhibited from effective protectionism and stimulated to participate in the movement of goods within and between regions of the country. De Ligt not only envisions a town based elite, but also a primarily urban market and a smaller extra-urban outlet for urban goods. On the other side of the equation, he argues for a constant peasant demand and the need for cash for paying taxes and rents. Therefore, the question has more to do with the nature of urban-rural relations, not only on a local, but also a regional level, and their impact on urbanisation and demography. De Ligt further suggests that the ancient and medieval economies have the important contribution of rural, especially village-based, manufacturing in common, which raises further issues regarding the town-village dichotomy (De Ligt 1991, 64-5, 75).

An area for which ethnography is very well suited is the study of the nuclear family. Historical sources on the typical size of a Roman household and 'site' demography are scarce. Valid information is essential as the size of a family works as a multiplier in any mathematical demographic model. Reference to the size of a typical family of five members consisting of a married couple, two children and a slave is assumed or a comparison to Roman Egypt is used as a contemporary analogy. The former is considered speculative (Osborne 2004, 167-8) and the latter as a good starting point for demographic estimates. In Roman Egypt the average size of households, based on census figures was 5.31 and a sample of 167 families, was between 4.3 and 5 (Bagnall and Frier 1994, 66-8, 138-9). The population structure of Egypt is thought to be similar to that of Italy (De Ligt 2008, 149). Hansen beliefs that the family size was in the 5 to 6 person range on average (Hansen 2006, 60).

The use of analogies can be viewed as a surrogate for missing data and will always be debatable. This puts method and personal judgement at the forefront of the discussion. One could argue that this reduces the arguments largely to a language construction by the author, debates on opinions and likelihood, thus the ability to make a plausible case in front of peers. Perceptions and views are difficult to test, but can be deconstructed and individual elements can be challenged. The reliance of demographic models for averages and ranges for the variables is a significant weakness. Ethno-archaeological studies have demonstrated the uniqueness of sites in terms of properties and dynamics. Demographic models are static whereas society is dynamic and fluid, where movement of people and adjustments to ecological and subsistence challenges created a flux in demography that is impossible to capture accurately. Morley points to the problem of evidence and the margins of error that are a result of variations. The key examples that he mentions are the degree of variation in population estimates for sites like Rome, Pompeii, Ostia, and assumptions on the overall level of urbanisation (Morley 1996, 181-2).

Because the size of a population is mathematically determined, a propagation of errors occurs in the calculations. Two broad categories of uncertainties theoretically exist. Systematic errors can result from the method and/or personal judgement, and can be a constant or proportional value. Secondly, a random error comes from uncertainties that are unknown and not controlled. Traditional statistics can capture this error. The implications of the propagation of errors to the outcome of demographic reconstructions can be significant, as a small hypothetical example using equation 3.1 demonstrates. A region that has a total urban hectarage between 180 and 220, an urbanisation ratio between 15-25% and a population density in the range of 150-200 persons/ha will have a calculated population that can range from 108,000 to 293,000, which is a factor of 2.7 difference between the minimum and maximum. Estimates will be required for settlements for which the size and urban make-up are not known. These errors can further propagate when family size and recovery ratio are included.

4 Settlement and Market Theory

Historians and archaeologists have been using concepts and models from social geography to improve their understanding of settlement hierarchy, spatial patterning and demography. These are simplifications of a possible past reality and do not have predictive value in a positivist sense. Of special interest are the rank-size rule, the isolated state model, central place theory and locational analysis.

Rank-size analysis
Rank-size analysis provides a method for determining the level of economic and political integration of a society and characterizes the distribution of population across the settlements in a region (Falconer and Savage 2003, 39). The original form, known as Zipf's Law, suggests that in a well-integrated, mature settlement hierarchy, the population of the nth-ranked settlement can be estimated by dividing the size of the population (P) of the largest settlement by n, resulting in a log-linear empirical correlation (figure 4.1a). Zipf suggested that the rank-size relationship was the result of two different forces, the force of unification and the force of diversification. These forces act to either encourage settlement in single centres of production and consumption or disperse it throughout a region in the form of autonomous communities located near raw material sources. When these two forces are in balance, the settlement system conforms, according to Zipf, to the rank-size rule (Falconer and Savage 1995, 39; Savage 1997, 233). The precise rank-size relationship is often determined empirically using linear regression analysis (equation 4.1) (Johnston *et al.* 2000, 672). The slope of the linear correlation, represented by *k*, can be indicative for the size of the population of the region and can be estimated by the integration of the area under the empirically obtained relationship.

Because rank-size theory has been used in archaeology a few critical notes need to be made before discussing these examples and what they could imply. Conformance to the rank-size rule was first noticed for the urban system of the United States and five European countries (Caroll 1982). Because of the advanced market economy of the United States, geographers thought that the rank-size rule was one of the regularities or desired norm for modern urban systems. A link between the growth of an urban system and the position and growth of its centres requires theories on how urban systems evolve, how they are maintained, interurban dependencies and the growth of individual cities. The discussion requires a closer investigation of the economy; the speed and flow of goods, industry, services, and the productive hinterland, as well as the general socio-political characteristics of the society. The rank-size rule does not explain the spatial distribution and does not consider landscape. A large number of studies have tried to explain deviations from the rank-size rule for the twentieth century AD, trying to classify countries and their urban systems according to their economy and population spread (Sheppard 1982). Sheppard has suggested that the rank-size relationship should be treated as a derivative concept in which patterns depend on specific processes of urbanisation and development. Moreover, comparisons can be misleading because the same pattern could be caused by different situations, including the underlying economic system. (Sheppard 1982, 149).

Archaeologists have tried to fit data to rank-size graphs, but it remains debatable what they are capturing and how the relationship, or lack of correlation, should be explained. If the assumption that towns are partly or wholly interdependent with other towns in the urban system is removed then market and central place concepts, landscape and micro-regions become more important factors than the dominance of economic hierarchical integration. The implications will be discussed in the second part of this chapter. The archaeological applications of rank-size analysis are generally derived from the manner and degree to which rank-size distributions depart from a log-linear correlation (figure 4.1a), and are expressed in terms of hierarchical economic relations (flow of goods), political integration (level of centralization), and social complexity of a society (Harrison 1997; Falconer and Savage 2003, 39). Different discourses derived from rank-size analysis can be interpreted as alternative expressions of urbanisation. None of the large sites dominates the settlement system in a convex distribution (figure 4.1b), in which several large settlements have approximately the same population size. A convex pattern can be indicative of a low level of integration or the existence of a heterarchical settlement system (Harrison 1997, 3). In a heterarchical settlement system, many aspects of the economy were probably self-organized by autonomous communities, more influenced by resource structure, crafts, and land-use strategies than by hierarchical elite regulation. It avoids the assumption that complexity must take a tiered hierarchical form (King and Potter 1995). A convex pattern can also be the result from pooling of two or more settlement systems or from the absence of a primate centre belonging to the settlement system (Falconer and Savage 1995, 40). A primate distribution contains fewer intermediate and large places than predicted by the rank-size rule, or in which the first ranked settlement has a considerably larger population than expected (figure 4.1c). Primate patterns may be indicative for an extraordinary centralization of political or economic functions. Artificial primate distributions may arise when the entire extent of a settlement system has not been identified, and the primate settlement has a role or function that exceeds its regional hinterland

$$\log P_n = \log P_1 - k (\log n) \qquad \text{(Equation 4.1)}$$

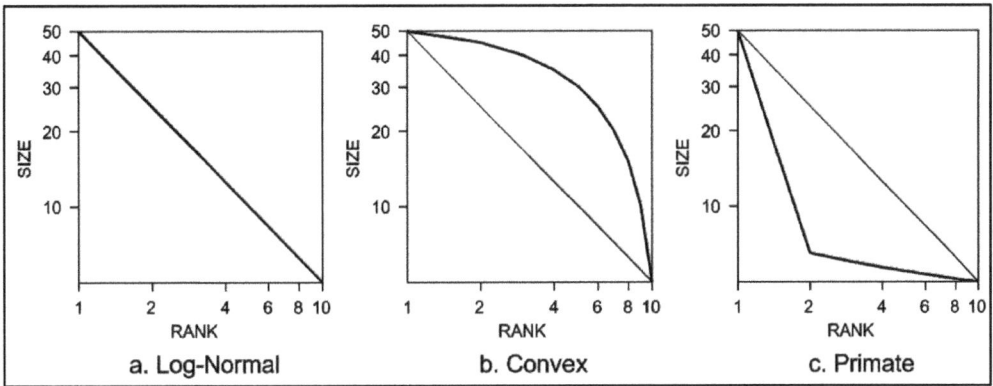

Figure 4.1: Examples of rank-size graphs with different shapes (after Drennan and Peterson 2004, 534, fig 1).

(Falconer and Savage 1995, 40). The obvious example would be the position of Rome in an Italian centric rank-size analysis. When the number of small settlements is lower than expected based on a regular rank-size relationship, it has also been explained as a demarcation between urban and rural settlements, but this suggests that there is a kind of internal definition of the urban threshold. Changes in rank-size distribution over time could signal a change in the character of settlements (De Vries 1984, 54-5). Studies of early Neolithic Thessaly point towards a threshold population of 150-200 people for small-scale communities at which level either village fission or the formation of proto-urban villages of 500-600 persons occurs (Bintliff 2007, 52). The latter number could even be taken as a cut-off point in rank-size analysis, equalling to a ca. 3-5 ha village.

Traditional rank-size methods do not consider the effects of archaeological sampling, especially the lower recovery ratio of small towns and villages, which often define the shape of the rank-size distribution. Moreover, samples are taken from an unknown sample population and the area of a site often reflects the extent of the largest occupation phase. An assessment of the recovery ratio can be used to estimate the number of sites in the hierarchy (Falconer and Savage 1995, 42-3). Data can be checked versus literary sources for the historical period, but in the absence of written sources, the interpretation of rank-size data is problematic. The choice between partial and total survey strategy can have important implications when rank-size analysis is considered. The field walking of preselected transects that are considered representative for the total study area is done when time, people,

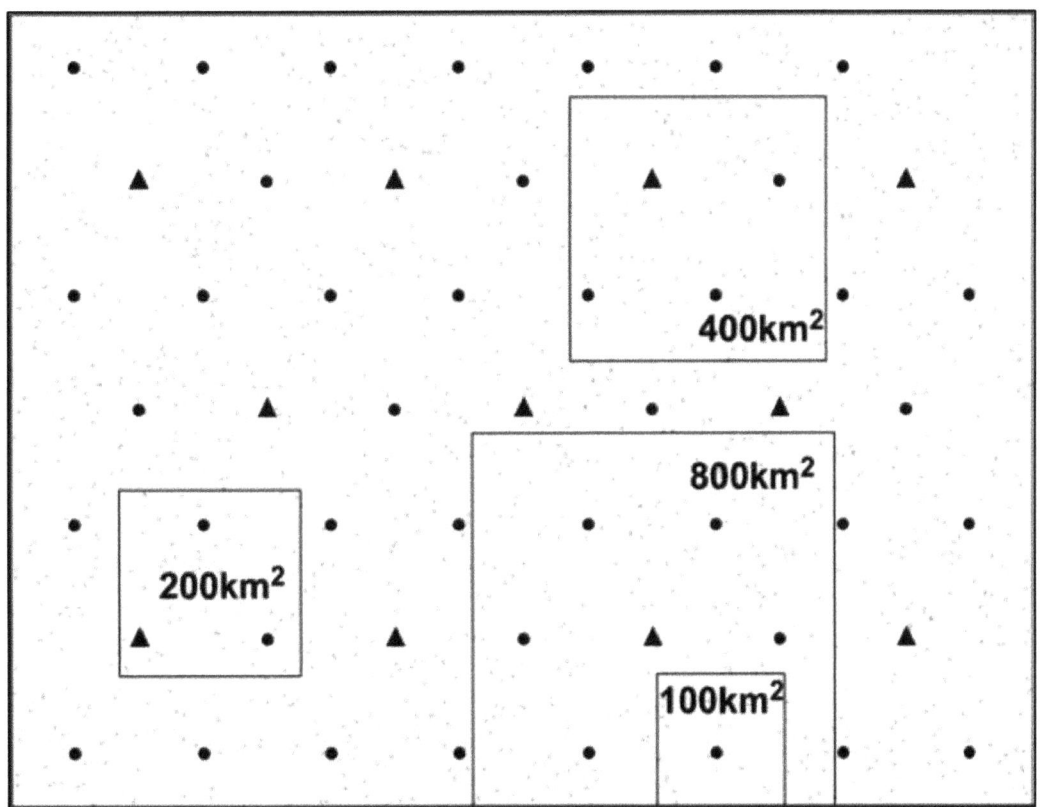

Figure 4.2: Hexagonal lattice of two levels of centres (black triangles and black circles) and a computer generated distribution of lower order settlements represented by the grey dots (Drennan and Peterson 2004, 538, fig 6).

financial resources and access to the survey area are limited.

Drennan and Peterson took a pragmatic approach and evaluated the impact of spatial scale and size of the sample transect for which the coordinates have been randomly determined. This was done on a hexagonal lattice of two levels of centres superimposed on a computer-generated population of lower order settlements (figure 4.2). The top-rank centres ranged from 22-81 ha and the second level centres from 6.2-46 ha (Drennan and Peterson 2004, 537-8). Sample blocks of rising size were independently evaluated. The A-value in the rank-size graphs (figure 4.3) is a measure of divergence from the log-normal line expressed as a coefficient based on the measurement of areas on both sides of the log-normal line. A positive value is indicative for a convex pattern and a negative value for a primate settlement distribution. The rank-size graph for the total settlement system (figure 4.3a) suggests a convex pattern. However, this pattern shifts towards a log-normal settlement distribution when smaller blocks are considered (figure 4.3b and figure 4.3.c), The example tries to demonstrate the importance of making transects in the study area not too small, as there is a risk that the sample is not representative for the total study area. In this case, using a 100 km^2 transect resulted in not finding any of the highest order settlements. If literary sources are absent then an incomplete settlement pattern can lead to different conclusions compared to a full coverage survey. A potential weakness in their analysis is that the small sites are randomly generated by the computer, whereas social science research suggests that people would tend to base their decision on where to settle based on socio-political, economic and environmental factors.

Drennan and Peterson suggest that regional or chronological differences in rank-size pattern can signal changes in the organization of a society (Drennan and Peterson 2004, 535). They revisited publications that contain analyses of archaeological settlement data and a chronological comparison of rank-size pattern is made suggesting periods of development leading to centralisation (primate pattern) and periods with a more decentralized organisation, like autonomous clusters (convex pattern), using the deviation from a theoretical Zipf log-normal line (A-factor) and statistical confidence levels to explore underlying socio-political processes. One of the case histories discussed is for the Susiana Plain in Uruk times (3900-3200 BC). The overall trend (figure 4.4) is a decrease in convexity and a fundamental and gradual shift in underlying settlement dynamics towards centralization from Terminal Susa A to late Uruk (Drennan and Peterson 2004, 543-4).

Completeness of survey coverage can be a vital component in rank-size analysis, however full coverage is seldom achieved in the majority of the field surveys. The extrapolation of discrete transects or, as in the case of Roman archaeology, the study of a limited number of settlements known from literature, to the whole area of study is currently the norm. Cavanagh and Laxton suggest that settlements in a survey area are part of a larger set of interrelated settlements, so self-similar. Their working hypothesis is that '*the whole is, to a reasonable degree of approximation, a scaled-up representation of its parts*' (Cavanagh and Laxton 1995, 334). This hypothesis is based on Mandelbrot's description of the irregularities and fragmented patterns in nature that he named *fractals* (Mandelbrot 1982, 1-19). Cavanagh and Laxton wanted to explore if fractal theory could be used for analysing settlement hierarchy and patterns. A key element in their analysis is the determination of the slope of a manually best-fit linear correlation through a rank-size scatter plot. They suggest that this fitting should be done based on the data from the middle rank settlements, as opposed to the top or bottom end of the ranking. The slope of the rank-size line for a self-similar subset of a selected region should be very similar to that for the whole of which the region is a subset. The data for one region can be superimposed on the graph for the wider area via a multiplier, which leads to the importance of what is referred to as the *fractal* or *scaling* dimension.

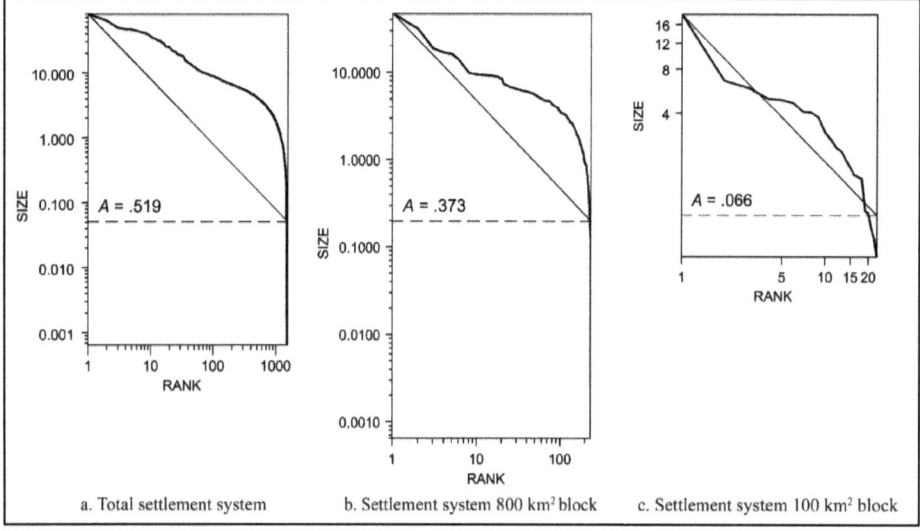

Figure 4.3: Rank-size graph for artificial population of settlements with an hexagonal lattice of centres (after Drennan and Peterson 2004, 538-9, fig 7-9).

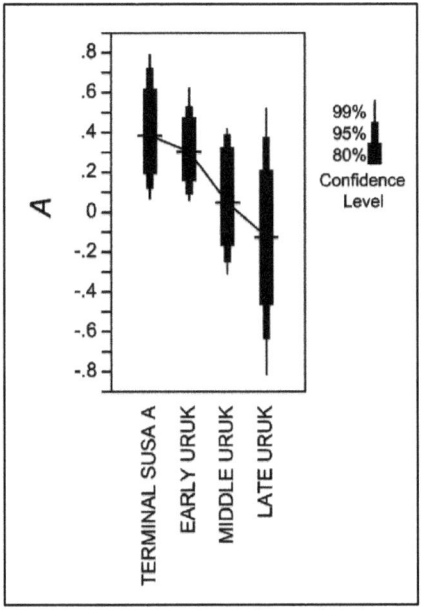

Figure 4.4: 'A' values for Uruk period rank-size patterns (Drennan and Peterson 2004, 544, fig 16).

The scaling dimension means that that the degree of irregularity and/or fragmentation of fractals is identical at all scales. The fractal dimension, being a measure of the slope in the case of a log-normal rank-size distribution, will be a constant if all the population (or the distribution of settlement areas) in the system increases or decreases in the same proportion. Non-constant scaling would be indicative for economic or social changes (Cavanagh and Laxton 1995, 331-9). The fractal dimension that Cavanagh and Laxton explored is expressed as the D-factor, which is the negative reciprocal value of the slope (k-value) of the ideal curve according to Zipf's rule, which is 1 (Mandelbrot 1982, 37; Cavanagh and Laxton 1995, 338). A fractal dimension of 1 has been interpreted as implying a perfect balance between the distribution of the population and the carrying capacity of a given catchment. A D-factor above 1 would indicate that the settlements are too close to each other and a value below 1 suggests that the settlements are too far apart (Cavanagh 2009, 417-8). This interpretation of the slope is derivative from the geographers' original description highlighted in the beginning of this chapter.

This methodology was applied on the dataset from the intensive Laconia field survey that covered an area of 70 km^2 east of the edge of Sparta. This area equates to 0.8% of the 8,500 km^2 occupied by the Lakedaimonians in the Classical period. The fractal dimension has been used for chronological analysis. The settlement pattern of the Bronze Age did not result in a linear correlation, whereas the four stages in the intermediate period, roughly Classical antiquity, show a good linear correlation for the middle sized sites in each set, generating almost identical slopes and D-values (k ≈ 1.4, D ≈ 0.7) (Cavanagh 2002, 421-37). The common slopes are graphically shown in the rank-size graph for these periods (figure 4.5) and suggest continuity throughout classical antiquity, which is remarkable because Spartan society underwent great structural change from the Archaic to Late Roman period.

However, several of the sites could be multi-period, resulting in a similar slope. This is possibly misleading because the sites probably varied in size from period to period (Bintliff *et al.* 2007). The Byzantine period also shows good linear correlation for the middle-sized sites, but generates a different slope, thus fractal dimension. The latter is close to the 'classic' dimension of D=1 and is often observed in the Early Modern period and seems to imply a distribution of population in which settlements compete for economic resources. A deviation from the 'classic' dimension would thus suggest a departure from the competition model. Cavanagh suggested for the dataset of the Laconia with a steeper slope (k>1 or D<1) that this is indicative for an additional influence, or a politico-economic establishment, which matched population to resources differently. The same can be valid for the opposite scenario. The explanation from Cavanagh focuses on the landholding elite and how they exploited their land in a regime that did not aim to optimise resources, possibly because of other social imperatives (Cavanagh 2002, 428). To which social imperatives he is referring is not clear. Of special notice in Cavanagh's analysis is the use of artefact scatter as a proxy for settlement size. The size scatters, in the range of 0.1 ha, represent most likely individual farms or huts with a scatter radius of ca. 15 metres and not nucleated settlements. The tail-end for the Classical antiquity rank-size graphs starts at an artefact scatter of 0.001 ha (10 m^2) and 0.01 ha (100 m^2) for the Byzantine scatters. These very small scatters are suspect and could be non-permanent structures. Rank-size analysis offers a methodology for describing an urban system and not individual rural sites. Only a few sites would qualify if a threshold value of 500-600 people, or a 5 ha nucleated settlement is applied. An alternative explanation considers different size ranges for artefact scatters representing farms and small farms and has been highlighted in figure 4.5 by ovals. The points in the middle of the graphs are in the same ballpark scatter size, but this type of analysis does not provide insight into the spatial distribution of these small sites. Possible explanations for the banding could be due to differentiated social and economic processes affecting each group, for example wealth differences, functional differences, variable surface evidence and variations in recording.

De Vries noticed that departure from log-linear correlation for a certain settlement system over time, could be indicative for changes in the character of the settlements, and potentially influence population threshold levels in relation to the urban-rural distribution. This observation could suggest differences in urban dimension over time and care should be taken to use one absolute population threshold for different periods. Another key issue in analysing settlement pattern and hierarchy is the establishment of appropriate boundaries for the system that is studied. For the Early Modern and Modern periods, the obvious choice is based on the boundaries of countries, but these consist of regional subsystems and sub-regions. In Italian field surveys the boundaries of these subsystems and sub-regions tend to be defined by landscape features, such as mountains,

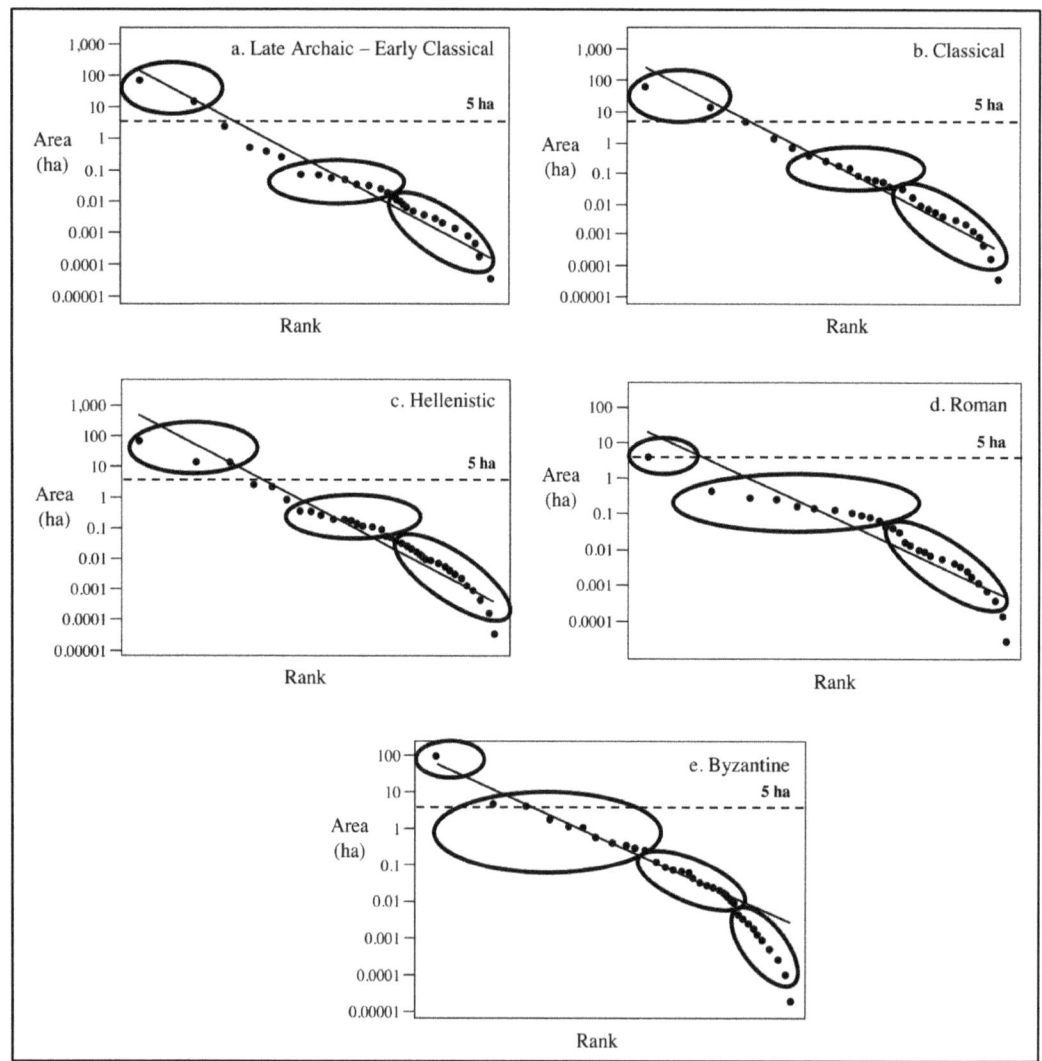

Figure 4.5: Laconia Survey: size ranking of artefact scatter per period (after Cavanagh 2002, 427-9, fig 9.3-7). Areas expressed in hectares and ovals added by the author.

valleys and plains, so-called 'national regions', but can also be based on (periodic) market circuits or extended rural hinterlands. In most cases, the historian or archaeologist selects the boundaries of the area, based on specific research questions. De Vries sees the dangers of misinterpretation coming from the temptation to examine the urban system out of context, in particular from such data as society size, economic structure, number of cities, and level of urbanisation. Over-interpretation can happen if too much importance is given to rank-size distributions, and the potential for the existence of different urban networks, without looking at the way the system functions (De Vries 1984, 54-5, 82-3, 92-5).

Whereas the rank-size rule directs historians and archaeologists to focus on the top of the settlement hierarchy (top-down approach); the isolated state model and central place theory start with basic surplus selling at local markets and take a more nuanced functional view.

Isolated State Model

The Isolated State Model, developed by Von Thünen (Von Thünen 1875), assumes that the distance from the market would be the prime determinant in the decision of which crops to grow, where prices, production costs, and yield are constant in all directions, resulting in the highest net returns to the farmer. In the simplest form only transport costs vary, where the rates per unit are the highest for bulky and/or perishable goods, and it predicts a zonal pattern of land use organization around the market (Johnston *et al.* 2000, 895-6). The model has the potential to be used to compare signs of structured land use around regional and market centres. Bintliff hypothesised a zone of market gardening in the immediate hinterland of Classical Athens based on increased village *deme* density (Bintliff 1994). Frayn (Frayn 1993) explored the isolated state model to describe idealised patterns of trade for Roman Italy that makes sense from an economical perspective (figure 4.6). However, the figure is too scaled to apply to a typical Roman town and the density of towns of Roman Italy.

The market and the mode of transport might vary according to the nature of the goods. The most perishable foods, like fresh vegetables and flowers, would come from the immediate hinterland of a settlement. The produce that could withstand a journey, but was not worth more than a day's absence from the farm would

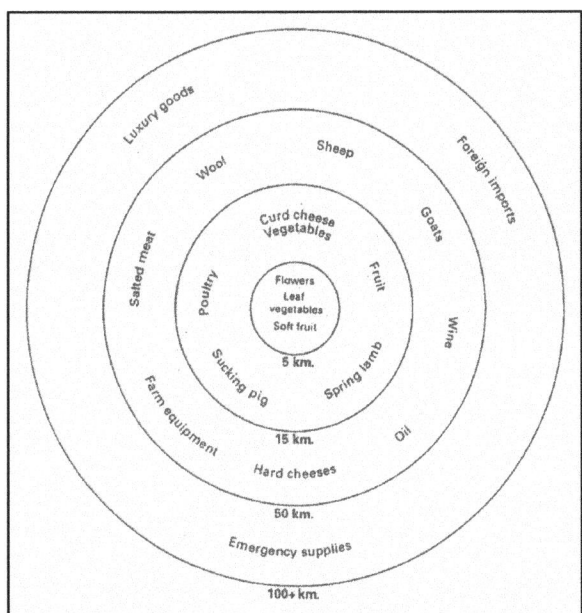

Figure 4.6: Idealised patterns of trade for Roman Italy (Frayn 1993, 77, fig 7).

come from farms and smallholdings not more than 10-15 km away. The distance was limited by the proximity of competing sources of supply, mainly other markets, and the logistics of peasant movement (Bintliff 2002a). The same conditions would apply whether the trade took place within Italy or involved imports from abroad. More valuable goods such as wine and oil were worth transporting further, and their containers made them a suitable cargo to send by sea or river. This brings up the issue of the importance of dispersed hinterlands and access to rivers that can be navigated and port settlements. Hinterlands are thus not per definition concentrically organized around a settlement. The geographical position of market centres and the distance between them can be used to discover how far the market produce had to be carried. Kron suggest that the classification of crops based on rural economics or mono-cropping rejects the possibility of intensive mixed farming, which represents a better survival strategy for the rural population in which they do not depend on a single or a few crops or animal husbandry exclusively (Kron 2008, 73-9, 108-10). Depending on the level of market sophistication and efficacy, specialisation on high-value crops and mono-cropping, as suggested for the area around Athens, can be envisioned for Rome, but perhaps not for typical market towns.

Central Place Theory

Central place theory is a theoretical attempt to explain the spatial arrangement, size and number of settlements within an urban system. The theory is associated with Walter Christaller, who wrote about the traditional settlements in Southern Germany (Christaller 1933). His studies showed that there were a large number of very small settlements, or hamlets, that he called first order settlements. Slightly larger settlements, villages or small towns, would grow up every few kilometres, and at even greater distances, cities would develop. He noticed that towns of a certain size had approximately the same interdistance, suggesting regularity. By examining and defining the functions of the settlement structure and the size of the hinterland, he found it possible to model the pattern of settlement locations. The basic premise of central place theory is that small-scale settlements in a settlement hierarchy will tend to cluster around a central settlement that supplies certain goods and services to these smaller settlements and extracts certain goods and services in return, resulting in a reciprocal economic relationship (Harrison 1997, 3). The theory shows what might appear under idealized circumstances and suggests that for every good or service there is a maximum distance a buyer is willing to travel. Sellers want to be as close to their customers as possible, minimizing the costs to acquire and travel time for the buyer, while maximizing their own turnover. The second basic concept of central place theory is threshold, which is the minimum population that is required to bring about a provision of certain goods or services. Markets and shops are thus centrally located within their hinterlands in settlements that meet the threshold population for a certain good or service. If the population is uniformly distributed and movements in all directions are not impeded, then meeting this centrality requirement produces a hexagonal network of market and shop locations in central places (Johnston *et al.* 2000, 72). Central places are competing with other centres resulting in a hierarchy of settlements. Centres of lesser order have functions of lesser range and higher order settlements have the same functions plus functions with a greater range for the hinterland, thus a higher degree of centrality. Christaller established the average population, their interdistance and the size and population of their tributary areas based on his study of the settlement patterns in Southern Germany (table 4.1) (Ullman 1941). Most of the centres of Southern Germany that Christaller studied were historic towns with medieval foundation and represent also pre-modern developments.

Central place theory has three orders or principles in which a hierarchical spatial structure can be organized. The number of settlements serving an area is minimised in the model known as the marketing principle. The number of settlements at each level of the hierarchy below the second is three times the number at the next highest (1, 2, 6, 18, and 54). Centres are placed amidst nested hexagons. In the transport principle, the length of the roads is minimised. Each settlement is centrally located on each side of a hexagon, at the boundary of two rather than central to one hinterland. The number of settlements is thus greater than in the marketing principle and creates the sequence 1, 2, 8, 32, and 128. This spatial system suggests a model region with a single dominant city, linked to all its lower hierarchy settlements and to the outer world along major radial transport routes. Finally, the administrative principle is the last system in which each lower order hinterland is nested exclusively within that of a single higher order central place only (1, 6, 42, and 294). In such a settlement network, every settlement forms the centre for a territory and in turn offers services to it. Up to the single regional city, all the

Table 4.1: Settlement hierachy according to Central Place Theory for Southern Germany (Ullman 1941, 857, tab 1).

Central Place	Towns		Tributary Areas	
	Interdistance (km)	Population	Size (km²)	Population
Market Hamlet (*Marktort*)	7	800	45	2,700
Township Centre (*Amtsort*)	12	1,500	135	8,100
County Seat (*Kreisstadt*)	21	3,500	400	24,000
District City (*Bezirksstadt*)	36	9,000	1,200	75,000
Small State Capital (*Gaustadt*)	62	27,000	3,600	225,000
Provincial Head City (*Provinzhauptstadt*)	108	90,000	10,800	675,000
Regional Capital City (*Landeshauptstadt*)	186	300,000	32,400	202,5000

other lower-order settlements and their territories form cellular clusters around higher-order centres (Johnston *et al.* 2000, 72-3).

Kunow has studied the applicability of central place theory for Roman Germania Inferior and concluded that the northern sector, along the *limes*, approaches Christaller's transport principle. The pattern of central places provided a defence network and transport routes. The southern part had a more nested distribution of central places that had its antecedents in the Bronze Age and this conforms rather to the marketing principle. The Northern region before Roman control was less urbanised (Kunow 1988, 58-65). Bintliff theorized under what type of conditions a certain organization of central places would emerge. The transport principle could apply to an early state system where political or military control dominate the location of all significant settlements, or where regional surplus production was commercialised so that settlement location was predicted on access to long-distance transport links. The administrative principle would potentially fit a scenario of a mature regionally developed agricultural society with well-developed segregation of servicing into at least four levels of central-places (Bintliff 2002a, 215-6). If a region is organised according to the administrative principle then this results in a dense landscape of settlements with a high level of infill between the larger sites, which would be very noticeable for third and fourth order centres. This pattern fits the perception of several scholars on Roman Italy, but statements of a general nature ignore the possible presence of regional variations. An empirical correlation of importance to market theory is the presence of spatial regularities between different levels of the settlement hierarchy. A radius of 15 km (2-3 hours travel) as catchment for a regional market settlement, which is associated with a day-return for farmers wanting to sell their surplus and conduct other transactions, is reported in literature for different regions and periods. Bintliff argued that constraints in mobility might have moulded early settlement hierarchies so that a strong influence of a day-return logistics may be apparent in their spatial parameter even where social and political services were as important as economic. Similar central-place catchments to those established under later, purely commercial peasant-to-market settlement systems might be expected during antiquity (Bintliff 2002a, 216-8).

Whereas rank-size analysis can be considered linear and one dimensional, Christaller's central place theory has two dimensions. Instead of city interdependence within an urban system, a banding-servicing view can be hypothesised in which a rank-size relationship could reflect different levels of servicing governed by geography, politics and historical trajectories of the central places.[2] The degree of ranking can be envisioned to work in bands and represents different ranges of services for local, sub-regional and regional centres. A hypothetical settlement system that is a hybrid between rank-size and central place theory can be modelled.

According to the marketing principle, the number of settlements at each level of the hierarchy below the second is three times the number at the next highest. The assumption is made that the size of the population for each level is constant and can be calculated by dividing the size of the population of the first order settlement by the order (group) instead of the rank of each individual centre. If the population for the first order centre is 5,000 people and the centre 33 ha in size then bandwidths for population and size can be established for the central places in each order of the settlement system (table 4.2). Starting at a first order settlement of 33 ha, representing a Roman *municipium*, the lower order settlements are approaching size ranges that are difficult to distinguish by archaeological investigation. This potentially, together with the often incomplete archaeological identification of lesser settlements, clouds the identification of market systems that could have existed. The lack of size differentiation results in a rank-size graph with a slope of -0.20 when a linear best-fit correlation is established (figure 4.7). A primate pattern with a dominant town at the top of the hierarchy and a low level of economic and political integration would be a traditional rank-size interpretation.

Morley studied the regional market system of Campania, based on *nundinae* tablets and created, based on central place theory, an abstract model of the relationship between the market centres of Campania (Morley 1996). He constructed a schematic representation of the Campanian market system, in which major centres are at

---

[2] The concept of a banding–services view was developed following discussions with Prof. dr. J.L Bintliff on how to interpret rank-size data in a central place context.

Table 4.2: Degree of ranking and services for a hypothetical settlement system.

Order	Population	Size (ha)	Number of Centres	Size Band (ha)	Population Band
1	5,000	33	1		
2	2,500	17	2	14 - 25	2,083 - 3,750
3	1,667	11	6	10- 14	1,458 - 2,083
4	1,250	8	18	8 - 10	1,125 - 1,458
5	1,000	7	54	6 - 8	917 - 1,125
6	833	6	162	5 -6	774 - 917

the core of the each hexagon and where minor centres are shown as dots (figure 4.8). This scheme would fit a representation of the market system based on the transport principle, as minor centres are centrally located on each side of a hexagon, at the boundary of two rather than three hinterlands, which minimizes the road length. The Campanian market system is, according to Bintliff and Morley, not as fully developed and well integrated compared to for instance Late Medieval England, and the market towns do not have a dense series of overlapping access catchments for rural producers. In addition, the sequence of the market days is not logical for visiting merchants to efficiently bulk-up local surplus (Bintliff 2002a, 229-30). Morley sees the local market town as primarily serving local peasantry, suggesting a system where the majority of the rural surplus is consumed within the region, rather than distant markets. Major producers would be attractive enough for merchants to consider travelling directly to purchase at the farm-gate, and some landowners might be in a position to control their own channel to market. This is confirmed by the presence of substantial rural estate-centres around Roman towns associated with the more fertile agricultural zones.

Little signs of hierarchical ranking in terms of size suits a network of local centres of consumption and servicing rather than a network articulated around a vertical stacking of hierarchical market foci serving to bulk-up surplus for export out of the region, or even the district of each small town (Bintliff 2002a, 234-5). Morley identified however a tendency to hierarchy for Capua and its associated major port of the *ager Campanus* Puteoli. He concluded that a lack of detailed knowledge of the volume and nature of exchange in each market and of the interaction between market centre and hinterland are hindering a more complete reconstruction of the market hierarchy (Morley 1996, 166-74).

Laurence did a reassessment of the role of transport by land in comparison to transport by river or sea. He argues that there are competing interpretations of the sources possible when the cost of goods and cost of transport are analysed separately, and a combination of transport by land and river or sea, which is often required, is taken into consideration (Laurence 1998). The traditional interpretation of transport cost is based on Cato's *De Agricultura* (22.3), in which he discusses the cost of buying and transporting an olive-oil mill overland, and

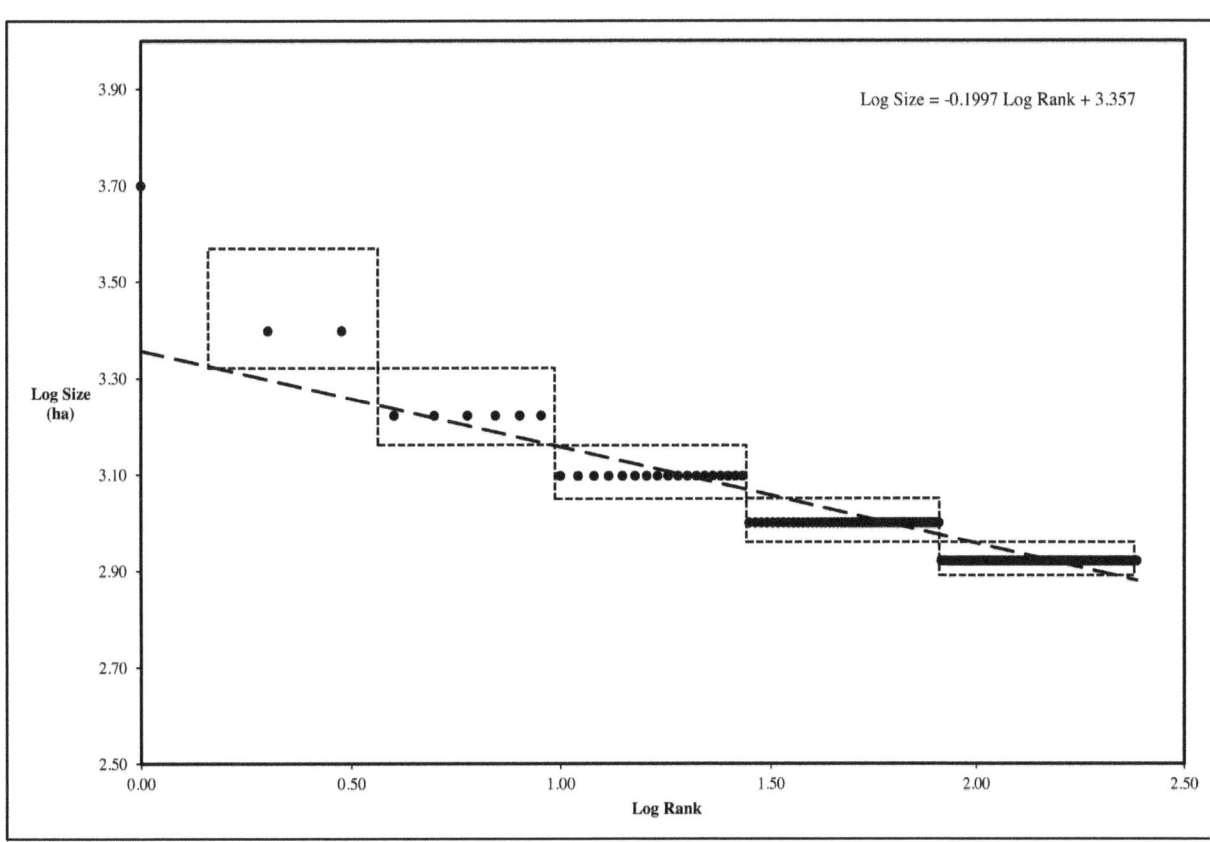

Figure 4.7: Rank-size analysis of hypothetical settlement system with banding-servicing windows.

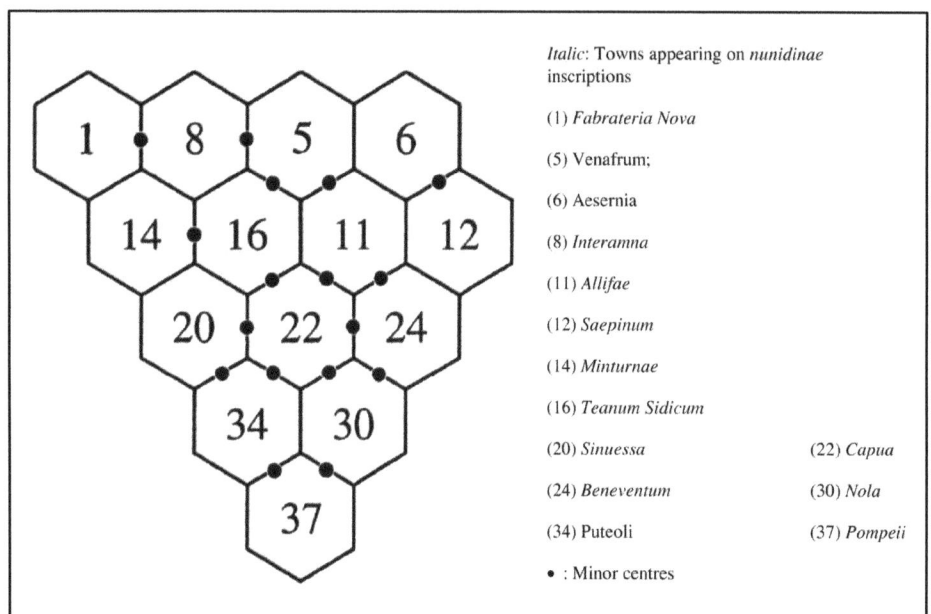

Figure 4.8: Condensed version of the Campanian market system based on Central Place Theory (after Morley 1996, 172, fig 4).

Diocletian's Price Edict, which provides a cost ratio of sea to land transport of 1:31. Laurence suggest that land transport complemented transport by river and sea, either by necessity, i.e. the goods need to be transported from and to the harbour, or because sea transport was not practical from October to April. Moreover, an issue that is of influence to the transport cost is the question if the means of transport and the labour involved need to be hired or can be resolved with one's own resources. He suggests that the Roman economy needs to be described in terms of interrelated centres of production and consumption. He sees the development of the road system and large estates as a reduction in temporal distance. Transport was an important factor in the successful economic integration of the *villa* into the Roman economy. The construction of private roads leading from the estate to the main road seems to have been common practice (Laurence 1998, 130-43).

The limited literary and material evidence inhibits the description of Roman settlements in terms of centralized functions, and often functions need to be assumed based on the official status in the Roman hierarchy of settlements and through inscriptions. Bekker-Nielsen studied urban density as a function of geography and developed a typology of towns (table 4.3) in the Western Roman Empire (Bekker-Nielsen 1989). His analysis is based on the list of official towns, *municipia* and *coloniae*, and cities allowed to keep civic status by the Romans. Of interest for the settlement system on the Italian peninsula and this study are type A and B. Primitive towns are characteristically the long-established city-state form of town with a radius of control of 5.5-8 km only. The dominant exploitation of the associated territory is agricultural. These settlements are both the residence of and focus for farming populations, as a small-scale market centre, social and religious focus, and might have had an administrative function, leading to a status as *municipia*. Colonial towns are represented by Roman *coloniae* and with control radii of 10.5-18.5 km and are well within the parameters suitable for district marketing on a day-return basis. This means that the town would be a residence of farmers as well as craft and trade populations and the associated rural population of its territory could be serviced by the town. The dominant role is the agricultural exploitation of the hinterland (Bekker-Nielsen 1989, 30).

The presented inter-urban distances per Augustan regions of Italy suggest the presence of regional variations in urban density (table 4.4). The primitive towns would go well with an organic settlement pattern that relied on the administrative principle and a colonial landscape that would come closer to the transport principle. A convergence of spatial properties for colonial towns arises around the distance covered by a one-day military march and a half a day market radius.

Table 4.3: Typology of towns in the Western Roman Empire (after Bekker-Nielsen 1989, 28-9, Tab 5.5 and 5.7).

Type	Description	Avg. Inter-urban distance	Geographical Distribution	Type of Exploitation	Radius of the hinterland (range)	Time- Distance
A	Primitive	13.1 km	Central Italy, *Via Aemilia*, Apulia	Agriculture	8 km	1/4 day
B	Colonial	29.8 km	Northern and Southern Italy	Agriculture	19 km	1/2 day
C	Civitas	58.5 km	Southern and Nortern Gaul	Fiscal	37 km	1 day
D	Civitas	105.7 km	Central and Western Gaul, Rhineland	Fiscal	66 km	> 1 day

Table 4.4: Inter-urban distances per Augustan region (Bekker-Nielsen 1989, 25, Tab 5.3).

Regiones		Number of Towns	Avg. Distance (km)	Range (km)
VIIIa	Via Aemilia corridor	14	15.3	6 - 20
VIIIb	Aemilia remainder	8	24.9	19 - 39
IX	Liguria, Cispadana	16	26	14 - 56
X	Venetia	19	35.7	20 - 60
XI	Transpadana	12	35.6	24 - 55
I	Latium, Campania	71	11	5 - 10
V	Picenum	19	13.6	7 - 25
VIIa	Southern Etruria	23	13.5	8 - 28
VIIb	Northern Etruria	16	30.8	10 - 49

Locational analysis

Locational analysis of settlement systems offers the possibility to treat place and region as results of processes of interaction between sites, to evaluate catchment areas (Conolly and Lake 2006, 209), and to provide insight into the socio-political organisation of the settlements in a given region. A simple way of providing a notional territorial division for a settlement pattern is via the construction of Thiessen polygons (figure 4.9). These polygons are obtained by sketching connecting lines between a centre and its nearest neighbours, and then drawing boundaries that bisect these connecting lines. If this process is repeated for a region then a network of polygons emerges. However, when the analysis is limited to the large centres then networks of smaller communities can be overlooked (Falconer and Savage 2003, 32). Moreover, the division of space by Thiessen polygons ignores cost of transport, the size of the centre, civic functions and cultural factors (Conolly and Lake 2006, 212).

One method that partially overcomes this issue is weighted Thiessen polygons. These are based on gravity modelling in which it is assumed that the intensity of interaction between locations is proportional to some quantitative value, such as population size, which can be translated to a certain distance from the settlement. This means that large population centres will have a larger immediate hinterland than smaller population centres. The next step has been the use of cost-weighted distance analysis, using GIS software that has been elaborately used by Farinetti in her PhD study in which she analyses the archaeological datasets of ancient Boeotia (Farinetti 2009).

Renfrew and Level developed a method which recognises that not only weighting is required, but that the dominance of one centre over another needs to be considered. The XTENT model offers this functionality (Renfrew and Level 1979, 147). If *municipia* and *coloniae* are considered autonomous polities under the umbrella of Rome, each having a dominant position for a region, then the sphere of influence, and in this specific case jurisdiction, will include lower order settlements. This methodology requires a discrete separation between the settlements that make up the settlement hierarchy and assumes that the political influence of a centre is a function of its size, and declines linearly with distance.

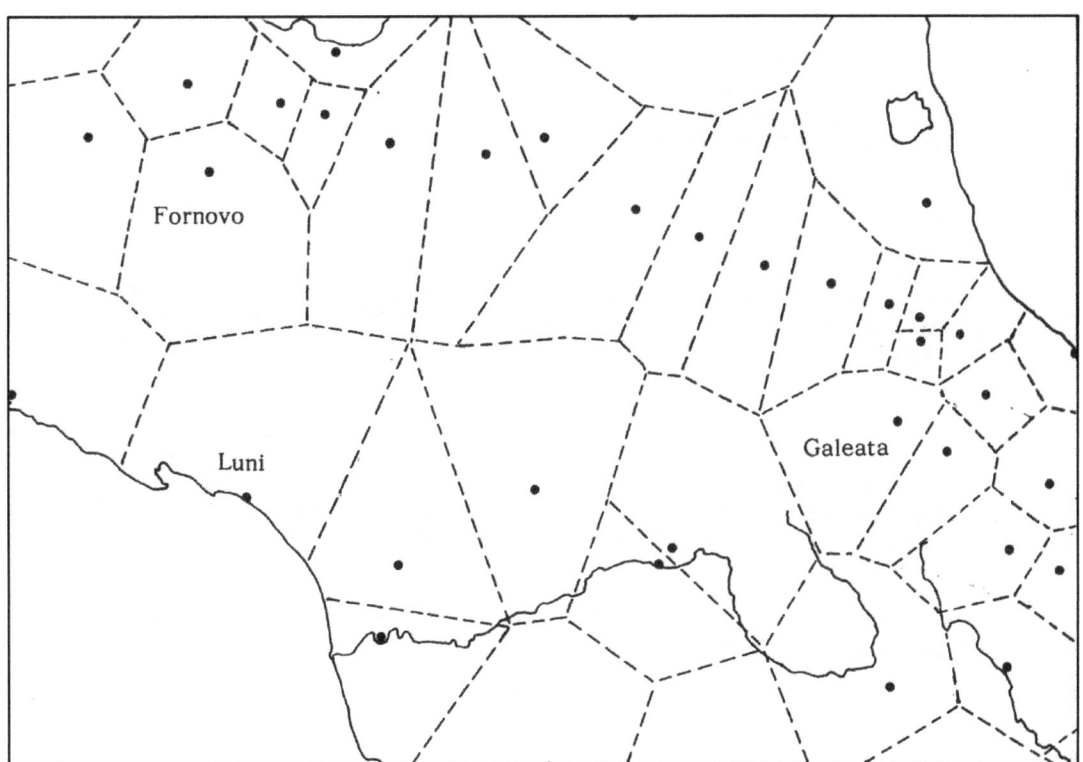

Figure 4.9: Theoretical hinterlands in the northern Apennines of Roman Italy based on Thiessen polygons (Bekker-Nielsen 1989, 12, fig 3.4).

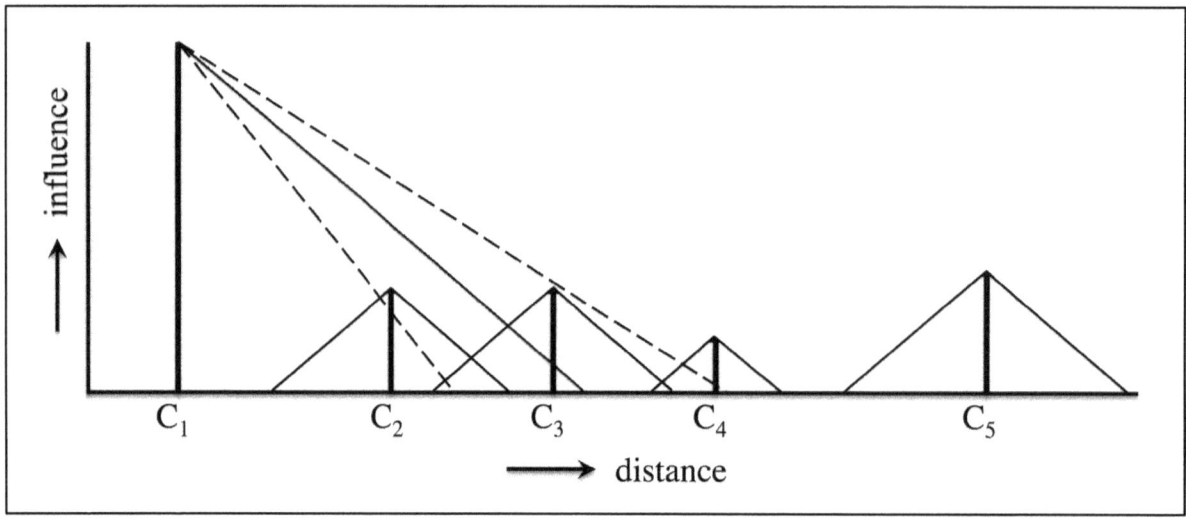

Figure 4.10: XTENT model. Influence of different slopes(Renfrew and Level 1979, 150, fig 6.4).

The slope of the 'tent' represents the fall-off of influence (figure 4.10). Renfrew and Level suggest that the value for the slope needs to be empirically determined. The distance from the settlements, which is taken as linear, can also be transformed into travel time to incorporate varieties in terrain. The model has the ability for creating hypothetical political landscapes, using the order and size of settlements as input, creating political divisions that can be analysed for validity (Renfrew and Level 1979, 148-151). The model does not look at how towns function, but at the power relation versus the main dominant centre, and does not remove the need to analyse the position and function of regional centres, as there would still be a need for market and administrative functions at regional centres.

The model was tested against a case where real political boundaries are accurately known. The authors analysed the political boundaries created by the analysis of the 117 cities in Europe that had a population exceeding half a million in 1960, assuming in the analysis that they are autonomous centres, using the XTENT model. Different values for the slope generated interesting theoretical boundaries, which depending on the point in history, medieval, modern or most recent history make sense. In their 1979 publication, before the fall of the Iron Curtain and the collapse of the USSR, the authors noted a distortion in the tendency toward autonomy of a number of areas in the former USSR, especially Georgia, Azerbaijan and Armenia, when a slope of 0.01 is used. A picture strongly representing the medieval situation for Western Europe emerges when the slope parameter is 0.02. The two maps that are closest to the political reality of 1979 are generated with a slope of 0.014 and 0.01 (figure 4.11). Applying this retrospective view on the recent past, in which sources are abundant, does not cover the issues that this methodology can be difficult to apply for the prehistoric period when political boundaries cannot be derived from written sources or the historic period with limited source material.

Ecological history

In *The Corrupting Sea*, Horden and Purcell challenge researchers to study the landscape in terms of the productive opportunities and human interactions as opposed to following traditional typologies that define town and country in a narrow sense (Horden and Purcell 2000, 80, 90-2). Within their ecological framework, words like town or urban should only refer to their architectural distinctiveness or their legal status. This approach, a history of the region that starts from its countryside, is especially valid where doubt exists on the degree of urbanisation. They put special emphasis on the study of geographical and chronological variety, meaning that different kinds of settlements have coexisted within a very short distance of one another and settlements have slipped in and out of artificial categories, emphasising the spatial and temporal dynamics of settlements (Horden and Purcell 2000, 90-101). Intensive field surveys have the potential to facilitate the study of geographical and chronological variety, but is the archaeological record detailed enough, and are methods and theories advanced to such a degree that they capture these variations to facilitate dynamic demographic reconstructions? Horden and Purcell made a successful case for diversity in environments, so called micro-ecologies, and the survival strategies pursued by the local population. Each micro-ecology has its specific physical characteristics, in terms of landscape, soil properties, rainfall and hydrology, which consequently could translate into differences in settlement hierarchy and patterns, and urbanisation in general. The existence of discrete hinterlands for settlements has been disputed in recent years and dispersed hinterlands provide a better response to the environment, stimulating intense regional and inter-regional connectivity (Horden and Purcell 2000, 115-22). The development of marketing, specialisation, manufacturing and services all require a better understanding of connectivity with both the immediate and dispersed hinterland, in the sense highlighted by Horden and Purcell, and are vital ingredients in understanding urbanisation, outside of traditional political history. An ecological approach is very much compatible with market theory and diverts attention away from long-

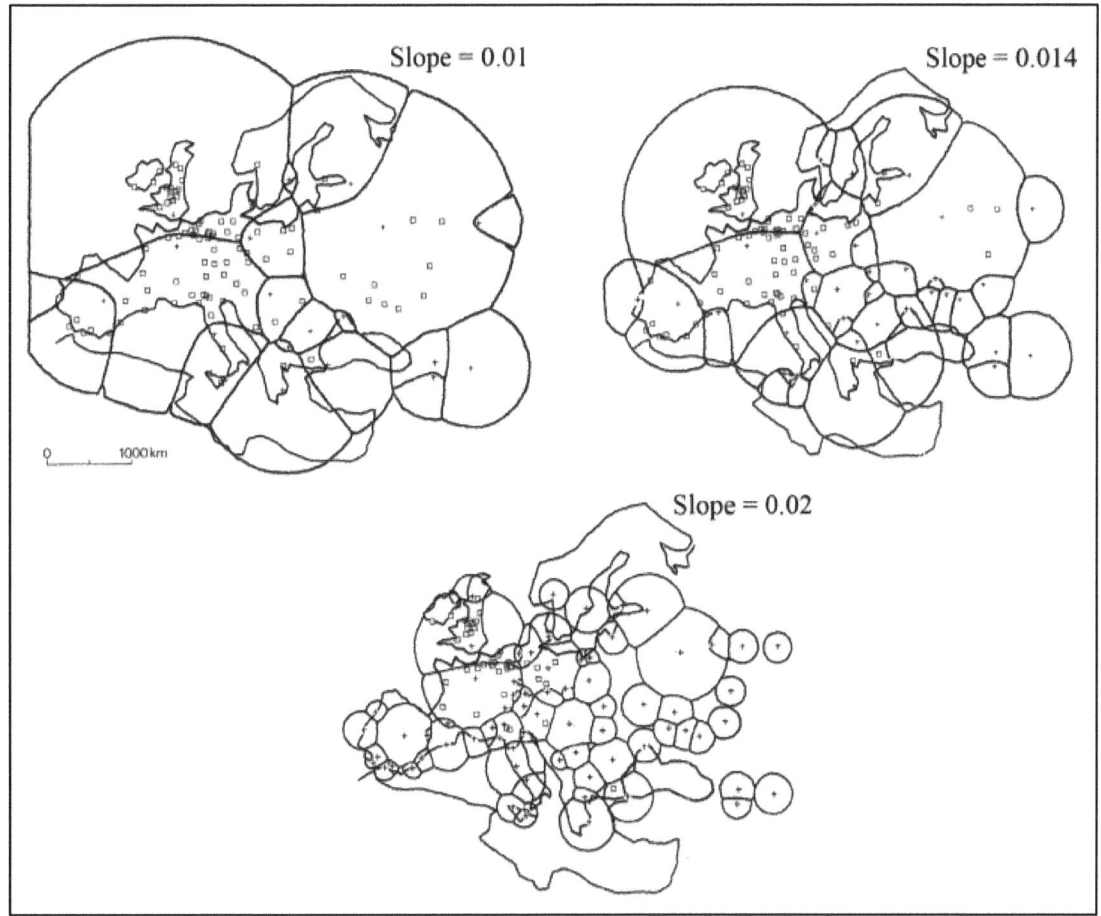

Figure 4.11: XTENT locational analysis for Europe (Renfrew and Level 1979, 160-1, fig 6.9).

distance trade and elite goods to everyday local and regional activities. The traditional focus of Roman historians and archaeologists has been on the rise of the slave run *villa*-system, the production and trade of cash crops, and how the elite created and maintained wealth and political power. There is a difference between this world of elite controlled production and trade, and the world associated with peasant farmers, small merchants, peddlers, and the small regional markets, the *nundinae* (Morley 1996). An ecological approach is compatible with marketing theory as it focuses on survival strategies people would pursue, which would translate into mixed farming, and where possible, cash-crops and trade. It can however be argued that a rigid settlement hierarchy and spatial patterning is actually what an ecological approach is disputing.

Under Early Roman rule everybody had to go to market for obtaining cash to pay tax. Marketing of goods, both foodstuff and manufactured, could take place at various locations in towns and villages as well as in the countryside. The traditional location for marketing is the central area of the larger settlement, the forum, but expanded during the Republican period to *macella* (daily markets), *nundinae* (held every eight days) and *tabernae* (shops where foodstuff and manufactured goods were sold). The people of the town primarily visited the shops, whereas peasants would use the *forum*, markets and fairs for their transactions. Several *macella* have been archaeologically identified, as they are held in permanent buildings, and must have been functioned as a daily provision market. The distribution of *macella* across Roman Italy suggest that they were only required or sustainable in larger settlements, which might relate to a correlation between elite spending power and the presence of these potentially exclusive fixed daily markets. The surviving examples of *macella* suggest that there was no standard architectural design, and many are relatively small compared to the size of the settlement. Such a market could not have formed a general meeting place for inhabitants, as *fora* in earlier periods. In Roman Italy eleven *macella* have been identified. All except for two are rectilinear and the *macellum* at Aeclanum has a round floor plan. At Alba Fucens and at Herdonia there is a circular courtyard within this. The *macella* were often in districts where cash crops were grown, but the *macellum* at Saepinum forms an exception (Frayn 1993, 42-4).

The *nundinae* created the opportunity for farmers to sell or exchange their agricultural surplus and to participate in social life. These periodic markets provided the means for entrepreneurs to make a living on produce for which insufficient demand existed to justify settling in one place, or to buy-up surpluses that were available only periodically. For small merchants it was more economical to collect surpluses at these regional markets compared to visiting a large number of different small farms, a practice that was not uncommon in the trade of cash crops from slave run estates (Morley 1996, 167). Small traders and peddlers were quite capable of dealing in a variety and quantity of goods to meet the needs of the majority of the population. The *nundinae* included all the temporary structures used for buying and selling on that particular day. These markets provided country dwellers a place to buy goods cheaply, and to buy alternative types of merchandise, not available in every *vicus*. Another opportunity for trade occurred at *tabernae*. The word refers to the type of accommodation and not to its function, which could have been the sale of merchandise, services, including cooked food, wine and bread. These shops were typically integrated into domestic houses or *insulae*, often contained a counter open to the street, and included a living and possibly storage space, or a workshop. Where *tabernae* appear along a number of adjacent streets, and built against residential property, they could have been part of a market quarter (Frayn 1993, 1-7, 35).

Evidence for *nundinae* comes from a series of market calendars, the *indices nundinarii*, of which four, dating from the first century AD, have survived and been subject to study. Marble tablets, into which a metal peg could be fixed, indicated the day of the market in a particular listed town (Frayn 1993, 38). Most of the settlements listed on these tablets are located in southern Latium, Campania or Samnium, and several mention the actual market day sequence, which allows the reconstruction of old trade routes. The routes that trade would follow would depend

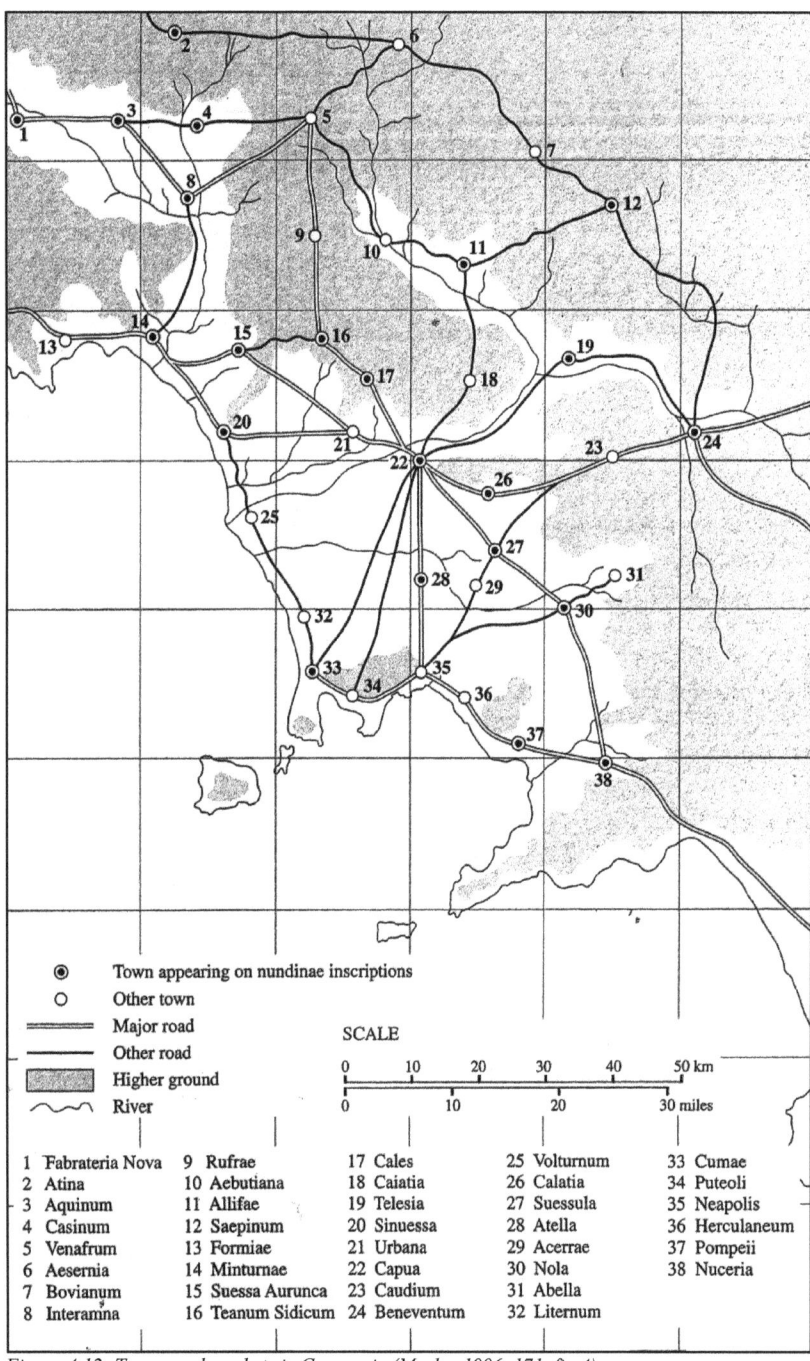

Figure 4.12: Towns and markets in Campania (Morley 1996, 171, fig 4).

on how the settlements were interconnected, the cost involved in transport and the expected market value on the far-away market. Special products were acquired from greater distances, like tunics, togas, cloaks, shoes, but also ploughs and yokes, which is very much as suggested by central place theory. Roads, but also harbour settlements played an important role in the redistribution of goods and functioned as gateway settlements within this network. The movements of goods across short distances, by sea, river or road, with frequent overnight stops, a dense and mutable pattern of movements, and the redistribution of a great variety of goods played an important and significant role in the economy of Roman Italy. The *nundinae* tablet from Campania demonstrates that towns across the Apennines in Apulia played a role in trade between the coastal regions and the highlands, thus confirming connectivity of micro-ecologies and the diversity of survival strategies (Morley 1996, 169-74). It is clear from the indices that a town could be an important market centre without having a *macellum* (Frayn 1993, 42-4).

The most complete Campanian tablet contains the following list of places: Aquinum, in vico, Intermna, Minturnae, Rome, Capua, Casimum and Fabrateria. It is not clear to which site 'in vico' refers to, but it could simply indicate 'the one in our region'. There was another list of the same length opposite, but these names have not survived (Frayn 1993, 39). Frayn and De Ligt suggest that this particular tablet implies that a market can be held in a *vicus* of a town or city as well as in its main market place (De Ligt 1991, 53). This opens up the possibility of linking large and smaller settlements in networks of trade. These lists would have been most useful to traders using the markets in these localities to sell their goods. This can be seen as evidence that travelling salesmen or local smallholders visited the towns of Roman Italy and set up temporary stalls on the *nundinae*. They are also evidence of interurban trade and of the existence of well-established *ius commercii* (Roman citizens with the right to make legal contracts and to hold property). Morley shows a lack of integrated market days so that that traders could move around the region in a weekly circuit (Morley 1996). Seaport settlements offer another important variation of the pattern of trade. In these towns the number of trade contacts by sea (Frayn 1993, 39, 88-9) balanced commerce on the landward side. There has been one inscription found at Ariminum, located on the coast between Ravenna and Ancona, thus coming from significantly north. Only one name is recognizable and that is Sestinum, located 46 km from Ariminum. One would expect Ariminum to have figured on such a tablet. The following settlement names are listed on the *Indices Nundinarii*: Aquinum, Atella, Atina, Beneventum, Calatia, Cales, Capua, Casinum, Cumae, Fabrateria, Interamna, Luceria, Minturnae, Nola, Nuceria, Pompeii, Puteoli, Saepinum, Sinuessa, Suessa, Suessula, Teanum and Telesia. All of these towns, except Suessula and Casinum were Roman colonies. This suggests that colonies are associated with increased trade (Frayn 1993, 40-6).With the exception of Rome and Luceria, the market towns are located at intervals of 30-50 km (figure 4.12). This is above the range of a day-return trip for a farmer going to market. This means that only parts of the countryside could have made it to the key markets and went to local *vici*. However, Morley shows for Campania that parts of the hexagons were rugged terrain and thinly settled so that part of the Thiessen network may not be relevant to market catchment (Morley 1996). All the Campanian towns were located on Roman roads and the *Via Latina* and the *Via Appia* linked the settlements of Latium to the Campanian centres. Beneventum and Luceria are the most remote settlements found on the same tablet fragment and connected with Campania via Aecae. This *colonia* is located on a junction of two major roads, but does not show up on the market lists. (Frayn 1993, 40-1). It could be that the goods they offered did not differ much from what was available in more closely located towns. The listing of Luceria on the tablet highlights the presence of a specialized market that would bring buyers into an area where livestock and products of sheep farms, like wool and sheepskins, would have been available in quantity. Five Roman roads met at Beneventum the *Via Appia*, the road leading to Brundisium via Canusium, roads leading to Saepinum, Telesia, and Salerno (Frayn 1993, 41-2, 50).

Summary

Central place concepts play a dominant factor in the development of settlement patterns of towns and market centres in the pre-modern world. Central place theory provides a more accurate description of the settlement system then rank-size analysis that depends on dominance of interdependence (market integration). A banding-servicing view could be envisioned for the towns and market centres that could reflect different levels of servicing for local, sub-regional and regional centres.

5 Ethnographic Analogies: The Empty Landscape of Cisalpine Gaul

A compelling case for the reconstruction of the size of the population of Cisalpine Gaul in the time of Augustus (figure 1.1) has been put forward by De Ligt (De Ligt 2008). Although not field survey based, the study uses data on the settlement system, based on high quality literary and archaeological sources. De Ligt took a top-down approach and explored ranges for key parameters, such as urban hectares, population density, built environment, the degree of urbanisation and the ramifications for the size of the population. This demographic approach explicitly does not consider the function and nature of the ancient city.

The objective for this chapter is to broaden the discussion to include a wide range of settlements that have a central place function in common, creating a functional landscape, and secondly, to have a closer look at the historical and contemporary analogies that have been used by De Ligt. Moreover, was the landscape of Cisalpine Gaul as 'empty' as historical sources are suggesting? Brunt was very explicit when he summarized the geographical considerations and socio-economic position of this region: *'(...) the country was very largely cut off from trade with other parts of Italy, Gaul, or the Mediterranean at large; more important, there was far more forest and marsh than in later times; inundations were a serious danger, and the work of reclaiming the fertile soil and of maintaining a system of embankments and ditches, which no doubt made continuous progress, demanded capital and favoured the division of the land into large estates (...). The importance attached to raising 'famine' crops suggests that the land as a whole was not so productive in the conditions of the Republic and early Principate as to permit a vast growth of population, and the most noted exports, wool and pork, were those of a pastoral economy, which could not support dense settlement.'* (Brunt 1987, 184). Can rank-size and locational analysis offer additional insights into the settlement hierarchy and spatial patterning that go beyond Brunt's description? At the basis of the analysis will be the publication by De Ligt (De Ligt 2008) and the Barrington Atlas of the Greek and Roman World (Talbert 2000).

De Ligt size-segmented the 78 civic centres, in a juridical and administrative sense, and created a three tier urban hierarchy of very important, important, and unimportant towns, based on size (table 5.1). For two important and fifteen unimportant settlements, archaeological evidence on the size is lacking. The smallest centre, Forum Novum, covers a humble 2 ha. Using civic status and size as criteria for classifying its population as urban offers the highest level of data integrity, but assumes that large non-civic settlements would not significantly affect the cumulative area of the civic centres. From a demographic view this is a fair assumption. *Coloniae* and *municipia* are prominently mentioned in Roman legal texts and the settlements that existed at the sub-municipal level, the *pagi* (districts) and *vici* (villages) are generally ignored (Bispham 2007, 12). The civic centres are part of a colonial landscape and the process in which the gaps in the landscape between these civic centres could have been filled with lower order rural market centres, required from a functional perspective (Brown 1995), was not overlooked by De Ligt (De Ligt 2008, 144, ft 18).

The use of analogies
De Ligt uses an Early Modern European population threshold for urban status of 3,000 to facilitate a comparison with the datasets published by Bairoch and De Vries (Bairoch *et al.* 1988; De Vries 1984). The presupposition is that the urbanisation ratio during the Early Principate could not have exceeded that of the more advanced economy of North Italy in 1600 AD, which is in-line with Brunt's view. This line of reasoning simplifies the estimate of the rural population, which otherwise needs to be determined based on absent field survey data.

The total population of Italy in 1600 AD is estimated at 13.3 million (Bairoch *et al.* 1988, 297), and ca. 5.4 million by Beloch for Northern Italy (De Vries 1984, 36-7). The degree of urbanisation is 21.7% for a population threshold of 3,000 and 18.4% for a threshold of 5,000 (De Ligt 2008, 154, ft 57). The challenges in determining an accurate population size of towns for the period 800-1850 AD, as collected in a database by Bairoch, should not be underestimated. For those towns for which census data exist he estimates the probable margin of error below 10%. If the size of the population is established based on the number of households, as counted by the number of hearths or by the number of marriages, then the margin of error can exceed 10%. Bairoch considers the highest level of uncertainty, with an error of at least 30%, associated with those towns for which the population is estimated on the built surface area. The error for the size of the urban population for Southern Europe in 1600 AD is ca. 15-17% (Bairoch *et al.* 1988, 298). It is likely that population reconstructions, which are based on archaeologically determined sizes for nucleated settlements and estimated population densities, would also be subject to an error of at least 30%.

De Vries has highlighted the weaknesses in total population estimates for Early Modern Europe and feels more confident analysing larger territorial aggregates and

Table 5.1: Size-segmentation of the towns of Cisalpine Gaul (De Ligt 2008, 141-4).

Segment	Size [ha]	Towns [Pliny]	Known [Archaeology]	Missing
I – very important	> 40	15	15	0
II - important	20 – 40	31	29	2
III - unimportant	< 20	32	17	15

looking for directional changes in the level of urbanisation than on adherence to absolute numbers. The first reliable censuses in most countries are dated to the Napoleonic period and are referring to contemporary country borders. Total population numbers predating 1800 should be viewed as best estimates, and become fuzzier when a subset of a larger territory is taken (De Vries 1984, 23, 38). The absence of a reliable list of settlements with a population below 3,000 for Early Modern Italy hinders further analysis of the settlement system of 1600 AD. Assuming that the populations of the large settlements are reliably known, the question of the accuracy of the size of the rural population, relative to a chosen urban population threshold, becomes relevant. Bairoch estimates the margin of error for the urbanisation ratio at ca. 3-4%, which means that the degree of urbanisation for Northern Italy in 1600 AD for a population threshold of 3,000 persons is in the range of 14.4-22.4% (Bairoch *et al.* 1988, 299). The challenges for establishing the urbanisation ratio during the Late Medieval and Early Modern period might, depending on the quality of the literary sources, not be so much different from estimating the size of the rural population in Early Imperial Roman times.

Musgrave made a study of the small towns of Northern Italy (Musgrave 1995). He argues that the historiographical tradition for describing the Medieval and Early Modern period is intimately connected to the rise of the Italian nation-state, with a strong focus on the top of the settlement hierarchy (Genoa, Milan, Turin, Bologna and Venice) and regional centres (examples are Padua, Vicenza, Verona, Brescia, Mantua, Modena and Parma). Remarkably little is known of the small urban centres of this period, and the archives that once existed rarely survive to the present day. The next layer of the settlement hierarchy then consisted of smaller centres with urban functions, such as retailing, administration and professional groups like notaries, doctors and pharmacists. The regional centre of Verona, for example, was encircled by small towns within a 15-25 km radius. Most of these small towns, of which Musgrave identifies eight, had a population between 2,000 and 5,000 around 1630 AD; which equates to a town size of ca. 13-33 ha at a hypothetical population density of 150 persons/ha. He envisions 150-200 of these small towns in Northern Italy, and perhaps two to three times that number of settlements with a population below 2,000 people. Musgrave does not provide references to primary or secondary sources, making this number speculative. Conceivably, he was reconstructing these layers on the model of central place numerical relationship. Could a similar settlement hierarchy have existed for Early Imperial Cisalpine Gaul? Before trying to formulate an answer to this question a closer look needs to be taken at the political and socio-economic forces that shaped the settlement pattern and the distribution of the population of 1600 AD. Rivalry between the second order towns and the major centres resulted in the centralization of political and administrative functions in regional cities. The ruling elite dominated these dominant cities, in which patronage and clientele networks were very important for building status. Little patronage happened in the small towns. The commercial sector ended up being monopolised by traders and merchants from the regional centres, to the exclusion of the smaller towns. Moreover, guilds established a monopoly of urban functions. Musgrave explains the gravitation of power and resources to the regional centres by the mechanism in which citizenship is obtained and the associated privileges in terms of access to markets, law courts and taxation. Citizenship in the regional centres was open to migrants that could afford it and resulted in an influx of land under the control and taxation of the regional centre. The conservative local elite, with strong kinship ties, restricted citizenship in the small towns, which provided access to the popular assembly and to the communally owned pastures (Musgrave 1995, 250-9).

Returning to Roman Northern Italy: individual cases for which the number of first settlers sent out to newly founded *coloniae* are known from literary sources and can be used for estimating the urbanisation ratio for Cisalpine Gaul. Examples are offered by Placentia, Cremona, Comum and Augusta Praetoria. These examples demonstrate that a wide range in the degree of urbanisation could have existed, in the range of 17-27% for Placentia, Cremona and Comum, up to 50-63% for Augusta Praetoria. De Ligt suggests an urbanisation ratio of 10% for the official civic centres under 20 ha, and 15% for those civic centres above 20 ha. This assumes that the Early Modern urbanisation ratio provides a cap-value (De Ligt 2008, 156-8).

For determining the population of a civic centre a population density needs to be established, which can be based on a contemporary analogy, like the Latin *colonia* of Cosa (Fentress 2003), or a historical one. This estimated 'typical' population density, which is in the range of 100-120 persons/ha for Cosa, can then be used as a multiplier for estimating the population size of other settlements. Reference can also be made to Late Medieval and Early Modern Italy, which demonstrates wide ranges in population densities that changed over time and as a function of geographical considerations (De Ligt 2008, 148-9, 159). Two segments of towns have been identified for this period. The first segment contains towns with a population density between 100 and 175 persons/ha; among these cities are Milan, Padua, Bologna, Verona, Arezzo, Florence and Pistoia and a second segment of cities has population densities above 300 persons/ha, like Siena and Genoa. The deciding factor seems to be the architectural make-up of the towns, especially the occurrence of high buildings. The type of multi-storey apartment *insulae* for Roman times and occupied by multiple families has been found in Rome and Ostia, but not in other large centres of Roman Italy. De Ligt suggests a population density for the civic centres of Cisalpine Gaul in the range of 120-150 persons/ha (De Ligt 2008, 153). Wallace-Hadrill suggested that this method incorporates assumptions that undermine the whole interest of the enquiry (Wallace-Hadrill 1994, 95). He thinks that by reducing the figures to an average, enquiry into the circumstances that made one city more crowded than another is ruled out. In the cases of Pompeii and Herculaneum, not only a wide variation in size of houses has been observed, but also upper floors, even for

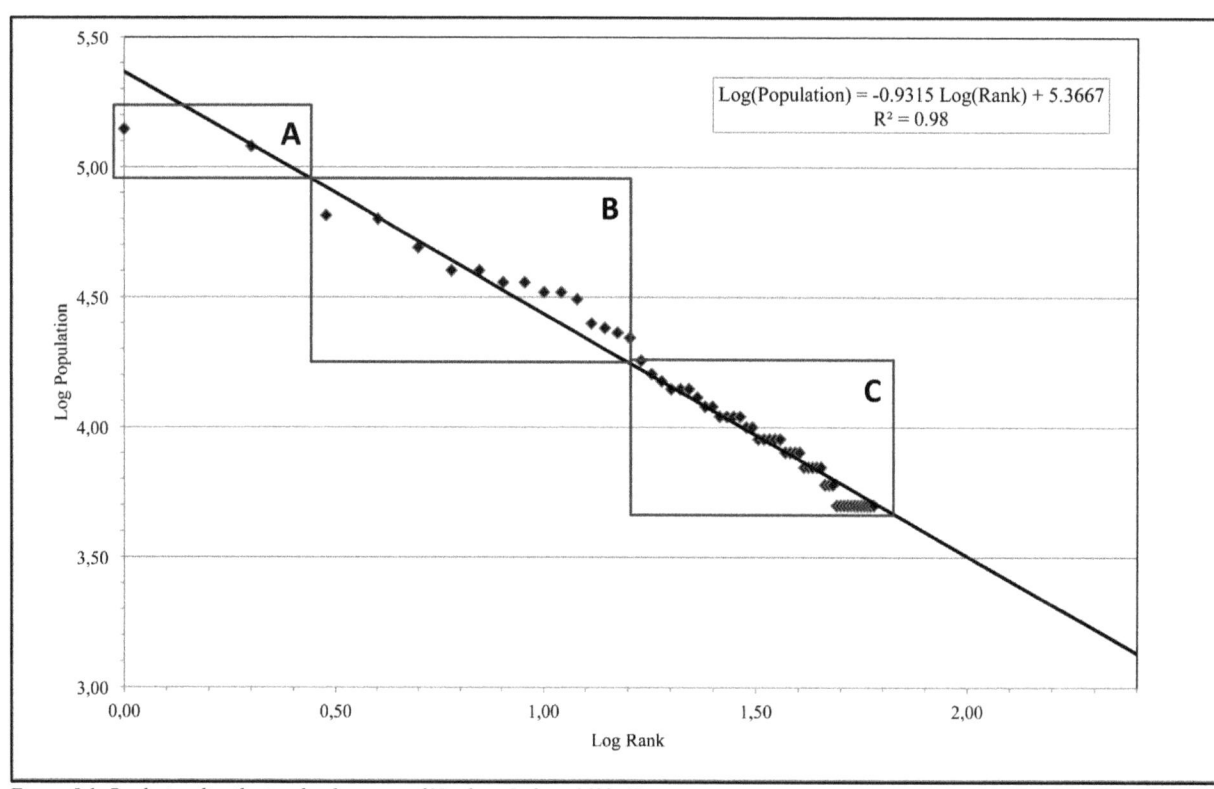

Figure 5.1: Rank-size distribution for the towns of Northern Italy in 1600 AD.

small shops and houses below 100 m² (Wallace-Hadrill 1994, 80). These upper floors were not present in the few large settlements of Cisalpine Gaul, like Aquileia for which excavation reports exist, but can also not be completely excluded as most large centres were overbuilt during later periods. Normally the upper floor of private houses belonged to the ground floor and do not represent multiple ownership. In Ostia and a few other towns of the Empire, separate floors represented individual families in apartment blocks.

Would it be possible to take De Ligt's arguments a step further by introducing rank-size and locational analysis, and develop a hypothesis on how a functional settlement pattern could look like?

Rank-size analysis

Rank-size analysis provides a method for comparing the level of economic and political integration of society and the distribution of population across the settlements. An empirical log-linear rank-size correlation exists for the 60 cities of North Italy in 1600 AD with at least 5,000 inhabitants (figure 5.1). At the top of the hierarchy is Venice, with a population of 140,000 people. This town is significantly smaller than the rank-size predicted population size of 232,650 people suggesting that this town did not occupy a primate position for the whole of Northern Italy. The second ranked town, Milan, had a population of ca. 120,000 people, followed by Genoa with half the population size of the former. Of special interest is that during the fourteenth century AD the territory of Venice was sea based, whereas Milan was land based, suggesting that they were servicing divergent landscapes and that two primates could be hidden within the data. Venice began to expand control over its immediate hinterland from the the fifteenth century AD onwards, when its overseas trade was disrupted due to Ottoman expansion (Clark 2009, 112-3).

De Vries suggests a concave distribution of the Italian urban system in the fifteenth century AD, with the distribution below rank five close to the rank-size rule. This could be indicative for the existence of subsystems, centred on large settlements. He expected that merchant capitalism would have resulted in a more primate distribution, with the port settlements of Genoa and Venice competing for primacy (De Vries 1984, 101-12). It is plausible that from the Late Medieval period the settlement hierarchy changed from convex to log-normal (figure 5.1), suggesting a higher level of economic and political integration of the society of Northern Italy towards centralisation, for which Venice and Milan were competing for primacy. The rank-size rule predicts 151 small towns with a population between 2,000 and 5,000 in 1600 AD, which is not in conflict with the estimate of 150-200 small towns by Musgrave. This observation suggests that a log-linear correlation could have existed down to a population size of ca. 2,000 people (ca. 13.3 ha). A list of known small towns in this population range is not however provided in his publication.

Another way to read the rank-size graph (figure 5.1) is to use a banding-servicing perspective and to give separate interpretation of the groups. Box A represents two primates in their own political sphere. A large number of regional centres that function semi-autonomous can be identified in box B. The tertiary centres (box C) are more strictly interdependent on the primate and large regional centres (box A and B) in a rank-size relationship.

Table 5.2: Settlement hierarchy according to rank-size correlation based on the very important town segment.

Segment	Size [ha]	Towns [Pliny]	Hypothetical Towns	Missing
I	> 40	15	15	0
II	20 – 40	31	70	39
III	10 – 20	(16)	389	373

Table 5.3: Settlement hierarchy according to rank-size correlation based on the 20-50 ha segment.

Segment	Size [ha]	Towns [Pliny]	Hypothetical Towns	Missing
I	> 40	15	15	0
II	20 – 40	31	30	(-1)
III	10 – 20	(16)	88	72

A similar assessment can be made of the civic centres of Cisalpine Gaul in the time of Augustus. If the assumption is made that all the very important settlements above 40 ha were also civic centres then a rank-size analysis can be made. The size of only two civic settlements in the 20-40 ha range are missing, but are there 20-40 ha settlements missing in the archaeological and historical record that lacked civic status? The same question can be asked for the unimportant settlements with civic status, of which for 15 settlements the size is not known. For comparison purposes the same threshold with respect to settlement size has been used. A population of 5,000 in 1600 AD equates to a settlement size of ca. 33 ha. A good log-linear correlation exists for the settlements above 33 ha, but as expected, the data below this size depart from the log-linear line (figure 5.2). This departure from log-linearity could be indicative for incomplete settlement recovery, a concave distribution or a combination of the aforementioned. If the assumption is accepted that log-linearity could have extended to towns in the 20-40 ha range than an estimate can be made of the maximum number of missing settlements. The second size-segmentation of very important towns has a calculated number of 70 settlements, of which 31 are part of Pliny's list of civic centres. However, a hypothetical 39 large villages of 20-40 ha in size are potentially missing. If the assumption is accepted that half of Pliny's list of 32 unimportant civic centres is in the 10-20 ha range, then a hypothetical 389 sites in this range are missing (table 5.2). How realistic is a scenario in which 39 large nucleations in the 20–40 ha range and an even larger number in the 10-20 ha range are missing?

An alternative correlation is obtained when the first nine settlements are excluded from the linear regression analysis, assuming a concave distribution, which can be expected for a more decentralised organisation of the landscape. The resulting log-linear regression on the settlements in the 20-50 ha range provides a significantly different slope and consequent prediction of the number of missing settlements in the 20-40 and the 10-20 ha ranges (figure 5.3). In this alternative scenario a hypothetical 72 villages are missing in the 10-20 ha range

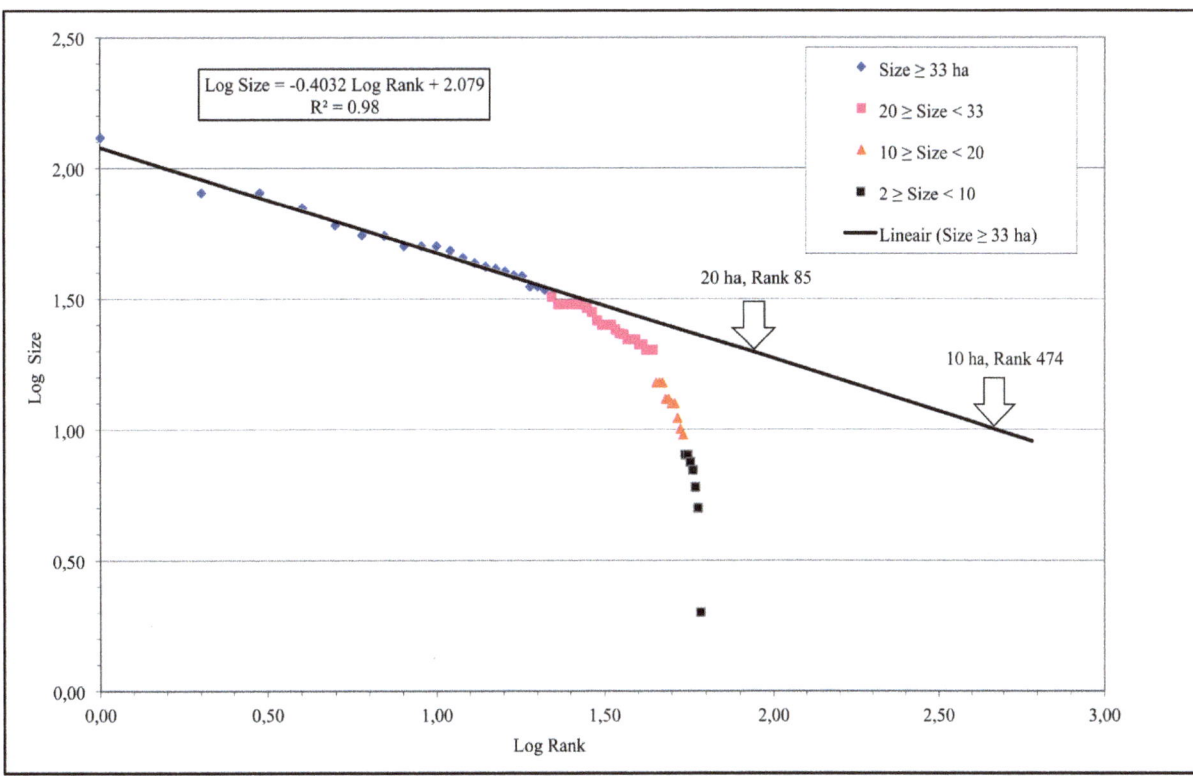

Figure 5.2: Rank-size distribution of the civic centres of Cisalpine Gaul in the time of Augustus, based on the very important town segment.

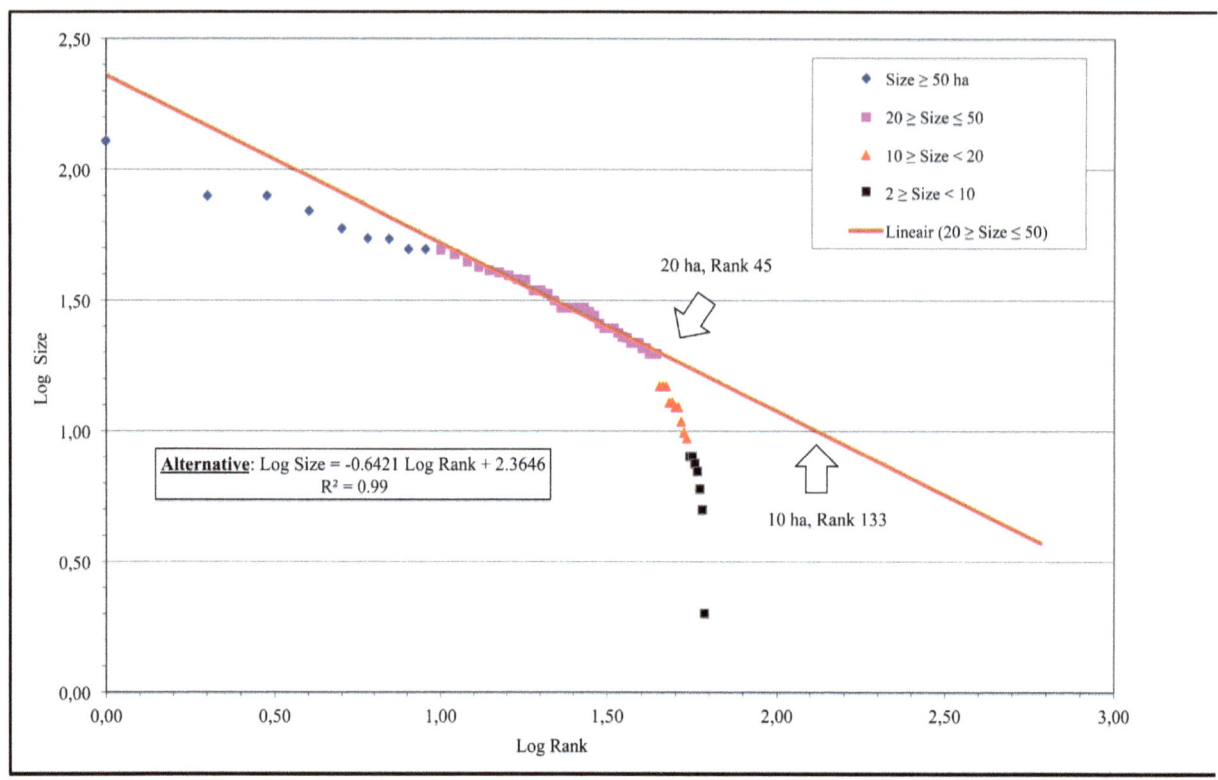

Figure 5.3: Rank-size distribution of the civic centres of Cisalpine Gaul in the time of Augustus, based on the 20-50 ha segment.

(table 5.3). The divergence of the tail away from the rank-size prediction might prompt speculation on a different form of relationship based on central place theory in which these smaller centres can be viewed more profitably on two-dimensional maps.

The differences in slope between the urban system of Cisalpine Gaul and Northern Italy around 1600 AD suggest a lower level of political and economic integration for the Roman civic centres during the Early Imperial period (table 5.4). The Early Modern settlement system is more hierarchical, which can be interpreted as the result of a more advanced economy and political centralisation. The more convex rank-size distribution of Cisalpine Gaul during the Early Imperial period could point to the existence of several independently from each other operating, and probably competing, emerging regional systems of which little size differentiation existed between the main centres. The moderate hierarchical system of Cisalpine Gaul could indicate that the consumption of rural surplus was not only limited to local towns, but that a network might have developed for the accumulation of surplus for export out of the region, or even the district of each small town (Bintliff 2002a, 234-5). The large settlements on the *Via Aemilia* that could function as economic nodes in a trade network would favour such a trajectory.

The main argument by Brunt for the limited role of Cisalpine Gaul in supplying food to the masses of Rome focuses on the cost of land transport, thus a commercially unfavourable geographical location versus Sardinia, Sicily and Africa. Brunt assumed that the transport cost, with reference to Diocletian's tariff, would have been prohibitive for the transport of bulk goods (Brunt 1987, 180-1). Laurence suggested that Diocletian's edict is often misinterpreted and that land transport complemented transport by river and sea, where actually delivered cost of goods should be compared (Laurence 1998, 130-5, 143). Navigation of the rivers was, according to ancient writers, at least possible to Augusta Turinorum, modern-day Turin (Brunt 1987: 179). Genoa, located at the Tyrrhenian coast, could have served as a port, but was relatively small (25 ha) as well as several medium-sized civic centres that were located at the coast of the stormy Adriatic Sea. Under the *Pax Romana*, special circumstances that would favour the export of surplus from Cisalpine Gaul are not obvious.

The estimation of the number of missing centres

Locational analysis provides a methodology for assessing the number of missing nucleated settlements. An estimate for the size of the hinterland, for which the civic centres formed the administrative and juridical heart, can be determined via the construction of Thiessen polygons. From a food sustainability perspective, these territorial areas could have supported second and third order settlements, and potentially the production of agricultural surplus for trade. Moreover, the spatial pattern might have been constrained to a traditional peasant market radius of 15-20 km from a central market place. Bintliff made a comparative study of Bronze to Iron Age Mediterranean urbanism to determine what sort of

Table 5.4: Slope of log-linear correlations.

	Slope
Northern Italy – 1600 AD	-0.93
Cisalpine Gaul : Civic centres > 33 ha	-0.40
Cisalpine Gaul : Civic Centres 20-50 ha	-0.64

geographical area is required to support urbanism at a certain scale, under the assumption that towns are self-sustaining by their own hinterland agricultural and pastoral production against through trade in subsistence foods (Bintliff 2002b). In his idealised model, he differentiates between the core access zone in which food is produced for the main settlement exclusively and the area beyond this zone where residents of second order settlements produce food, partially for the centre (table 5.5). The assumption is made that one-third of the local production of second order centres is available for export to the main centre. To allow for territorial scale ca. 50% of the landscape is treated as cultivable. For the Bronze and Iron Age, estimates are provided on the scale of the geographical territory required for such urban centres once satellite settlements and their food requirements have been added. An urban population density range of 120-210 persons/ha, was used in creating these estimates (Bintliff 2002b, 158-9). Bintliff tested the applicability of the model, via case histories, such as the Etruscan settlement system during the Orientalising and Archaic period (ca. 700-450 BC) (Bintliff 2002b).

Cornell estimates the average size of a city-state of *Latium Vetus*, when they were part of the Latin League (seventh century BC – 338 BC), at around 200 km^2 with an average *polis* population of ca. 5,000 (Cornell 2000, 215-7). His analysis is based on Beloch's reconstruction of territorial boundaries and he highlights that the numbers are conjectural, but in the right order of magnitude (Cornell 1995, 205). These hinterlands are referring to an organically formed settlement pattern, whereas the landscape of Cisalpine Gaul in the Early Imperial period is dominated by *coloniae*. Estimations of the hinterlands of eighteen Latin *coloniae*, founded in the period 334-263 BC can provide a good estimate for what could be expected for Cisalpine Gaul (Afzelius 1942b, 190-1). The average size of the hinterlands of these *coloniae* is estimated at 390 km^2, which equals a radius of 11 km, which is within the 15 km peasant market radius. The spread in the size of hinterland varies from 100 km^2 for Cales in Campania to ca. 800 km^2 for Luceria and Venusia in Apulia (figure 5.4). However, these two are exceptions, but indicate that in Cisalpine Gaul certain *colonia* could have a similar size of hinterland. These

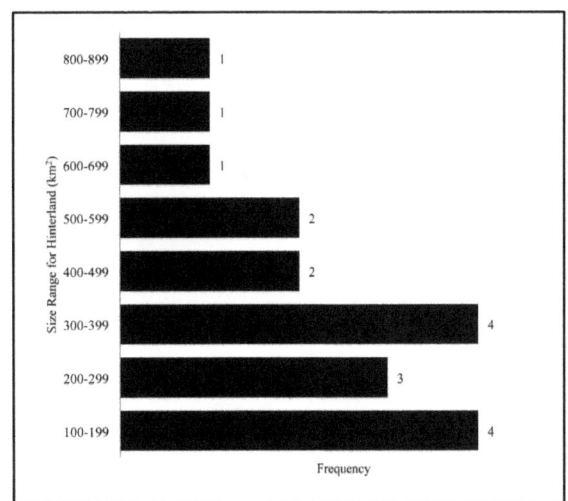

Figure 5.4: Frequency distribution for the size of the hinterland for Latin coloniae (334-263 BC).

hinterlands were, of course, not empty and would have contained *vici* and hamlets. Bekker-Nielsen classified the landscape of Cisalpine Gaul as 'Type B' colonial, in which the civic centres functioned as centres of exchange, administration and possibly religion. The rural population would not always have had the option to live in these towns. The civic centres had an average interdistance of 28.0 km (table 5.6) and a theoretical radius of the hinterland, following Bekker-Nielsen's methodology, of 17.5 km (Bekker-Nielsen 1989, 29-30), suggesting that not all civic centres were suitable for district marketing on a day-return basis in all directions, and gaps could have been filled with lower order market centres.

The average size of the civic centres of Cisalpine Gaul in the Early Imperial period is, based on the dataset collected by De Ligt, ca. 30 ha. In the Iron Age, a settlement area of 30 ha would have required a hinterland of ca. 52 km^2 in an isolated state scenario (absence of lower order settlements) and of ca. 117 km^2 when lower order settlements are included (table 5.5). The area representing Cisalpine Gaul covers 116,000 km^2 of which, according to Beloch, the Po-basin comprises less than a third (Brunt 1987, 172). De Ligt included the provinces of *Alpes Cottiae* and *Alpes Maritimae* in his

Table 5.5: Estimated actual size of Iron Age large settlement hinterlands (after Bintliff 2002b, 160, fig 1).

Settlement Area (ha)	Population (120 p/ha)	Cultivable Land (3.6 ha/family)	Hinterland (50% Cultivable)		Actual Scale of Territory	
			Radius (km)	Area (km^2)	Radius (km)	Area (km^2)
4	480	346	1.5	6.9	< 5	< 79
12	1,440	1,037	2.6	20.7	< 5	< 79
20	2,400	1,728	3.3	34.6	< 5	< 79
30	3,600	2,592	4.1	51.8	6.1	117
80	9,600	6,912	6.6	138.2	14.0	616
150	18,000	12,960	9.1	259.2	20.0	1,257

Table 5.6: Inter-urban distances per Augustan region of Cisalpine Gaul (after Bekker-Nielsen 1989, 25, tab 25).

Regione		Number of Towns	Avg. Distance (km)	Range (km)
VIIIa	*Via Aemilia* corridor	14	15.3	6 - 20
VIIIb	Aemilia (remainder)	8	24.9	19 - 39
IX	Liguria, Cispadana	16	26	14 - 56
X	Venetia	19	35.7	20 - 60
XI	Transpadana	12	35.6	24 - 55
	Total	69	28.0	

analysis with the civic centres of Segusio, Pedo and Cemenelum. Together with *regiones* VIII-XI, this area, including an expanded hinterland of Tergeste is estimated at ca. 130,000 km².

The Barrington Atlas provides an overview of the known areas that have been centuriated. These centuriated areas are not restricted to the Po basin and the lowlands, but can also be found at an altitude of 1,000 metres, such as

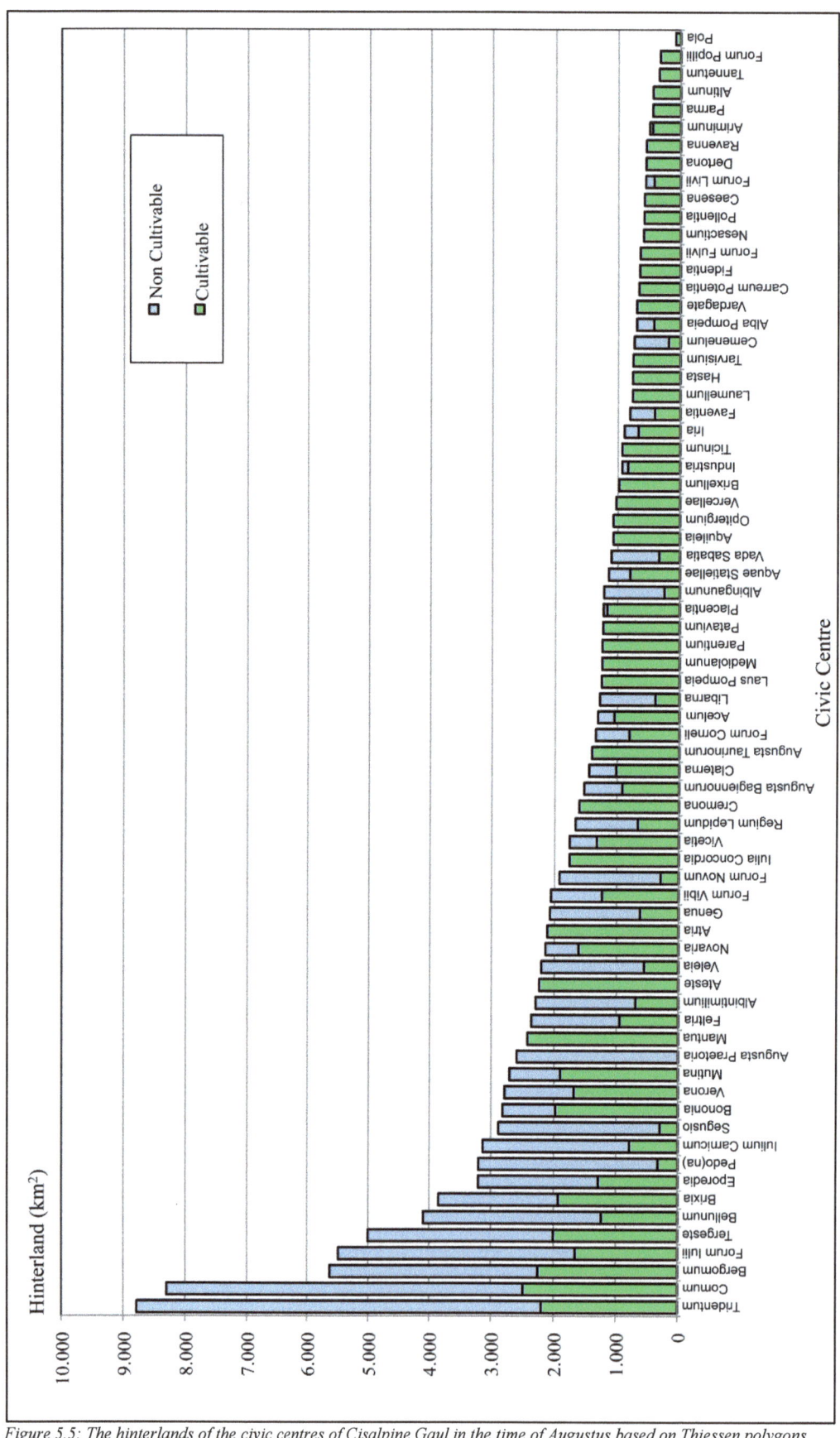

Figure 5.5: The hinterlands of the civic centres of Cisalpine Gaul in the time of Augustus based on Thiessen polygons.

Table 5.7: The unaccounted (hypothetical) villages of Cisalpine Gaul.

Hypothetical Centres	Civic Centres	Hypothetical Villages	Identified Villages	Missing Villages
333	78	255	84	170

in the cases of Pollentia, Augusta Bagiennorum, Eporedia, Pedo and Augusta Taurinorum, indicating that upland areas are not marginal. The Barrington Atlas does not differentiate between land between 1,000 and 1,500 metres, and when all land below an altitude of 1,500 metres is taken into consideration then ca. 50% of Cisalpine Gaul would potentially be cultivable. This is in-line with Bintliff's assumption when he determined the size of the hinterland during the Iron Age. The Barrington Atlas has also been at the basis of determining the hinterland of the civic centres by the construction of Thiessen polygons. For the hinterland of each civic centre, the potentially cultivable areas as well as the potentially non-cultivable, mountainous areas have been determined (figure 5.5). The average size of the hinterland of a civic centre in Cisalpine Gaul is ca. 1,815 km^2. This average size is significantly above the 390 km^2 average size that has been established for the hinterland of an average Latin *colonia*. For the hypothesis that *coloniae* and the villages of Cisalpine Gaul would have an average hinterland of 390 km^2, a hypothetical number of 333 large nucleations can be determined by dividing 130,000 km^2 by 390 km^2 of which 78 are official civic centres.

The Barrington Atlas also provides a count of 84 possible and certain villages, and a count of 111 road stations with limited chronological detail. The expected number of villages would be 255 of which potentially 84 have been identified, at least by name, and 170 are missing (table 5.7). Rank-size analysis predicted ca. 412 villages above 10 ha, based on an assumed log-linear correlation based on the civic centres above 33 ha. Based on locational analysis the number of villages, as determined via rank-size analysis of the very important towns is too high and 255 villages would be a better approximation. On average, the outcome of the locational analysis results in 3.3 villages and 1.4 road stations per civic centre. The number of villages predicted by the log-linear correlation, based on the 20-50 ha segment of civic centres is 72, which is below the number of identified villages. Further analysis, especially on the size of the population living in villages is hindered, because the sizes of these settlements are not archaeologically known. The population living in these villages could have been sizable, in the range of 300,000 people, which is speculative, but in-line with the estimate made by De Ligt (De Ligt 2008, 144-5, ft 18). Hundreds of hamlets scattered over the landscape probably existed, especially in the mountainous areas where mixed farming and herding could have sustained only a relatively small population. Significant differences exist between the civic centres of the Alps, with extended mountainous hinterlands, and the civic centres of the Po-plain, which approaches the 390 km^2 range hinterland.

The population of Cisalpine Gaul, assuming a degree of urbanisation of 10-15% and a population density that are in the same range as found for Medieval and Early

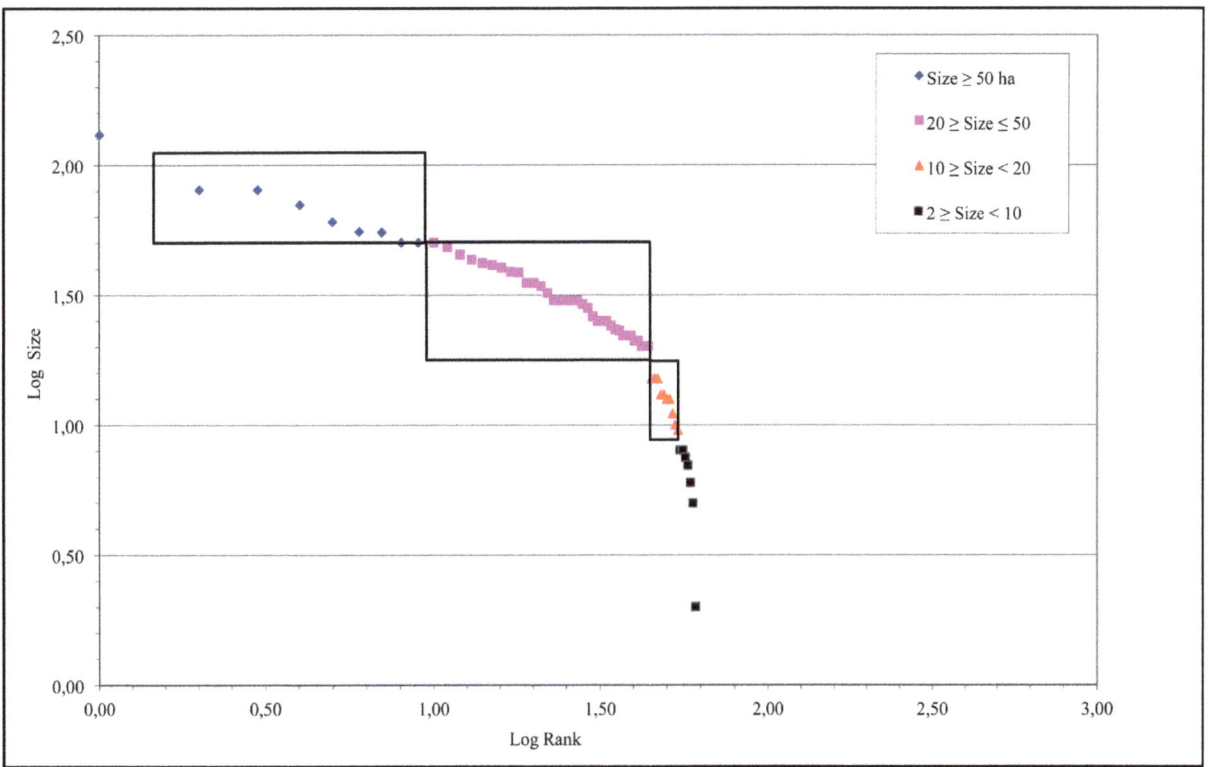

Figure 5.6: Rank-size distribution of the civic centres of Cisalpine Gaul in the time of Augustus and size bands for the different levels of servicing.

Modern North Italy, is estimated by De Ligt between 1.78 and 2.23 million people (De Ligt 2008, 159). Based on a combination of rank-size and locational analysis a hypothetical 4,500-4,750 ha of centres with a size of at least 10 ha could have existed. At a population density of 120 persons/ha, this would account for a population of ca. 550,000 people. The size of the population living outside of these centres in little villages, hamlets, *villae* estates and farms remains, in the absence of field survey data, the unknown determining factor. The use of historical analogy, which directs the estimation of the population size during the Early Imperial period, begs for field survey data that can confirm the suggested associated rural population density, such as available for the Potenza Valley, the *suburbium* of Rome, the Pontine region and the Biferno Valley.

Discussion

Rank-size and locational analysis provide a tool for estimating gaps in the settlement pattern of civic centres and large central places. As argued in the previous chapter, a banding-servicing view could be envisioned based on the civic centres that could reflect different levels of servicing. Interestingly, such a view does not conflict with the segmentation of *coloniae* and *municipia* by ancient authors and used by De Ligt (De Ligt 2008, 140-47). The very important, important and unimportant civic centres most likely provided different levels of services. Villages would have supplemented this system from a functional perspective with more basic services at a local level (figure 5.6). A more dendritic market system could have existed in mountainous areas resulting in large hinterlands. Locational analysis helped to estimate the number of hypothetical villages above 10 ha at ca. 257. Adding these to the segment of unimportant towns segment would provide a more balanced view of the central place system that can be expected for Cisalpine Gaul.

The analysis has resulted in three important observations. A tendency to hierarchy, as was identified by Morley for Capua and its associated major port of the *ager Campanus* Puteoli (Morley 1996, 173-4), can be multiple within the settlement system of Cisalpine Gaul, suggesting the bulk-up of local surplus to larger centres. For example, Patavium, Mediolanum, Aquileia, Ravenna, Cremona or Augusta Taurinorum can be envisioned as key centres in local hierarchies. Secondly, bands of centres fit better to central place theory. Finally, the underrepresentation of lowest settlement sites makes little sense in any rank-size graph, but can be improved by locational analysis and the logic of markets resulting in a functional landscape and potential locations for large nucleations.

6   Urban or Rural? The Potenza Valley Survey

A team from the University of Ghent has been active in the valley of the Potenza River, which is part of the Marche region, starting in 2000 (figure 1.1).[3] The natural boundaries of the valley are formed by the Apennine hills to the west, a wide and fertile foothill landscape, and a flat coastline zone that leads to the Adriatic shores south of Ancona. The area covers 400 km^2. In Roman times, the valley was a sub-region of the Augustan *regione* V (*Picenum*) and *regione* VI (*Umbria et Ager Gallicus*). The project work is in a final stage and preliminary reports have been published in *BaBesch*, *PBSR* (Papers of the British School at Rome) and the American Journal of Archaeology. The high level research objective is to "*measure the evolution of social complexity within the valley of the Potenza River*" and to "*examine how populous the region was, what the different types of settlements were and how the settlement patterns changed, in time as well as in space*' (Vermeulen and Boullart 2001, 1). A multi-millennium approach focussing on long-term processes and transformations is taken. However, the answer to the more narrow research question that intends to debate chronological demographic developments has not yet been published. The settlement pattern and hierarchy, as well as site typology and chronology, are well described in publications, allowing demographic estimates for the valley to be developed. The team from Ghent University used a wide array of methods and techniques that includes oblique aerial photography, intensive field walking, geophysical prospecting, small scale excavations, geomorphological investigations, the study of historical sources, and a restudy of excavated evidence. The team emphasises the micro-diversity of the landscape, expressed in the selection of the three areas (figure 6.1), which are shown together with the location of the Roman and *Piceni* (native) settlements, as well as the main Roman centres to the north and south of the valley (Vermeulen and Boullart 2001, 2). The landscape and climate conditions, especially the irregular rainfall, make the ca. 80 km long course of the Potenza River, *Flosis* in Roman times, difficult to navigate, although it has been suggested that the river was navigable up to Helvia Ricina (Vermeulen and Boullart 2001, 39). The valley functioned as an important corridor for the movement of people, goods as well as cultural contacts in all directions.

Nucleated settlements

The Roman conquest of *Picenum* was completed in 268 BC. A part of the population was deported, and the remaining indigenous population received full Roman citizen rights in the second half of the third century BC, when *Picenum* was under Carthaginian threat. This threat triggered the foundation of *coloniae* on the Adriatic coastline among which is the Roman citizen colony of Potentia in 184 BC (Vermeulen *et al.* 2006, 204-5). After the Social War, centres with *municipia* status developed with their own territory and administration (Verdonck and Vermeulen 2004, 182). During the Late Republican and Early Imperial period, Roman settlements (table 6.1) came to flourish in close proximity to the former *Piceni* centres of Monte Primo, Monte Pitino, Monte Franco and

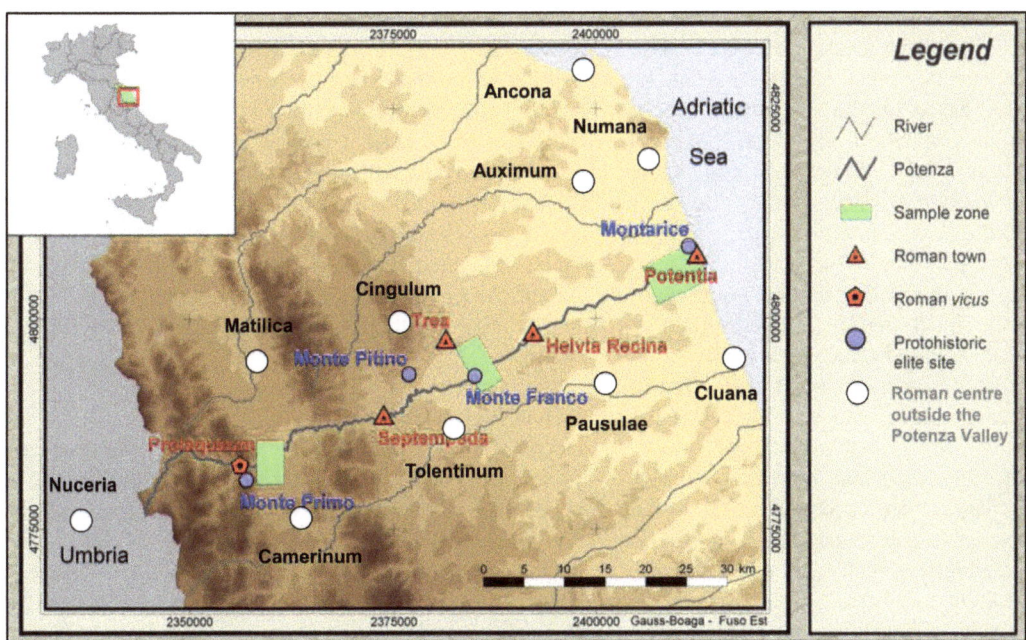

Figure 6.1: The main centres of the Potenza Valley and the large settlements in closest proximity (after Vermeulen et al. 2005: 34, fig 1).

[3] I want to thank Prof. dr. F. Vermeulen for sharing his thoughts on demographic developments and urbanisation in the Potenza Valley, and providing additional publications, which were of key importance for developing the demographic estimates in this chapter.

Table 6.1: Major Roman settlements in the Potenza Valley.

Roman Settlement	Dating	Status	Walled Area (ha)
Helvia Ricina	Mid first century BC	*Municipium*	22
Potentia	184 BC	*Colonia*	20.4
Septempeda	First century BC	*Municipium*	15
Trea	49 BC	*Municipium*	12
Prolaqueuem		*Statio*	?

Table 6.2: Interdistance between the civic centres of the Potenza Valley.

Civic Centre	Nearest Centre	Distance (km)	Second Nearest Centre	Distance (km)	Avg. Inter-Distance (km)	Avg. Radius (km)
Potentia	Numana	10	Cluana	15	12.5	7.8
Helvia Ricina	Pausulae	8	Trea	11	9.5	5.9
Trea	Cingulum	8.5	Helvia Ricina	11	9.8	6.1
Septempeda	Tolentium	7	Trea	12	9.5	5.9
			Average		10.3	6.4

Montarice, at the expense of the *Piceni* centres, which ceased to exist as important political and socio-economic foci. The road system was further developed, and a network of Roman roads connected the Potenza Valley with the other regions of Italy. The side-branch of the *Via Flaminia* led via Nuceria, through the Potenza Valley towards the port of Ancona and formed an important artery for the transport of people and goods (Vermeulen and Boullart 2001, 2). Besides Prolaqueuem, minor centres have not been identified. Are any nucleated settlements in the valley, such as large *vici*, missing? Without relevant literary or archaeological sources, this question remains hypothetical, but still valid within the framework defined in the theoretical justification. The likeliness of second and third order settlements depends on the spatial distribution of the large settlements and the opportunity for farmers to visit (periodic) markets in central places on a day-return basis. The empirically established spatial regularity, or catchment, for a regional market town, equalling to a travel time of 2-3 hours, equals a radius of ca. 15 km. The average distance between the civic centres of *Picenum*, reported by Bekker-Nielsen is 13.6 km, with a range of 7 to 25 km. Within his line of reasoning, these settlements can be classified as primitive, based on the city-state form of town with a radius of control of 5.5-8 km (Bekker-Nielsen 1989, 28, tab 6.5). Following the same methodology as Bekker-Nielsen, the average interdistance between the centres in the Potenza Valley is 10.3 km with an average radius of 6.4 km (table 6.2). These parameters suggest that the Potenza Valley could have been one of the most densely settled areas of *Picenum*. The established interdistances are well within the 15 km that facilitates farmers to make a day-return trip and nesting of central places can be observed when circles of 15 km radius are drawn around the known nucleated settlements, suggesting that all relatively large settlements in the valley are accounted for. The settlement hierarchy suggests a decentralized organisation of the centres and potentially a high level of autonomy, which is in-line with their civic status. The shape of the river valley conditioned the settlement pattern. The locations of the Roman settlements, with the exception of Potentia, are mirroring the organically formed *Piceni* settlement system, which had a different historical trajectory for the location of central places. The size of the immediate hinterland of the civic centres of the Potenza Valley, based on the construction of Thiessen polygons, was ca. 153 km^2.[4] The road station of Prolaqueum, located in the more mountainous upper valley, had a theoretical hinterland of 159 km^2. For comparison; the average size of the hinterland of the city-states of Latium Vetus, as highlighted in the previous chapter, was ca. 200 km^2 and for Latin *coloniae* from a later period (334-263 BC) ca. 390 km^2 (Cornell 2000, 215-7). The data suggest that the settlement pattern of the Potenza Valley was organically distributed with *Piceni* antecedents supplemented by the *colonia* of Potentia.

The size of the 'urban' population
Estimates for the size of the population that could have lived in these local centres require a good understanding of settlement archaeology, especially the area covered by *insulae* and the number of families that could have occupied an *insula*. Moreover, public space, and especially architectural features can hint towards the possible presence of an elite with accumulated wealth, which has been associated with an urban nature and also monumental burials outside towns. How can the function and nature of these civic centres be described; urban or rural? The presence of public buildings is indicative for the presence of certain urban functionality, but does not directly contribute to determining the size of the population engaged in non-agricultural occupations or social stratification. The civic centres of Helvia Ricina, Potentia, Septempeda and Trea will be discussed and the size of the population estimated, followed by an analysis of the size of the population outside of these main centres.

Helvia Ricina (figure 6.2)
Helvia Ricina, located on the left bank of the river at ca. 23 km from Potentia, was the largest settlement in the valley. The settlement was situated on the crossroads with the *Salaria Gallica* that connected Urbs Salvia with Aesis, and a side branch of the *Via Flaminia* leading to Potentia, where it joined the coastal road that led from Ancona to Aternum. The site occupation goes back to the late second century BC, but most information comes

---
[4] Potentia: 122 km^2, Helvini Ricini: 183 km^2, Trea: 140 km^2, Septempeda: 165 km^2.

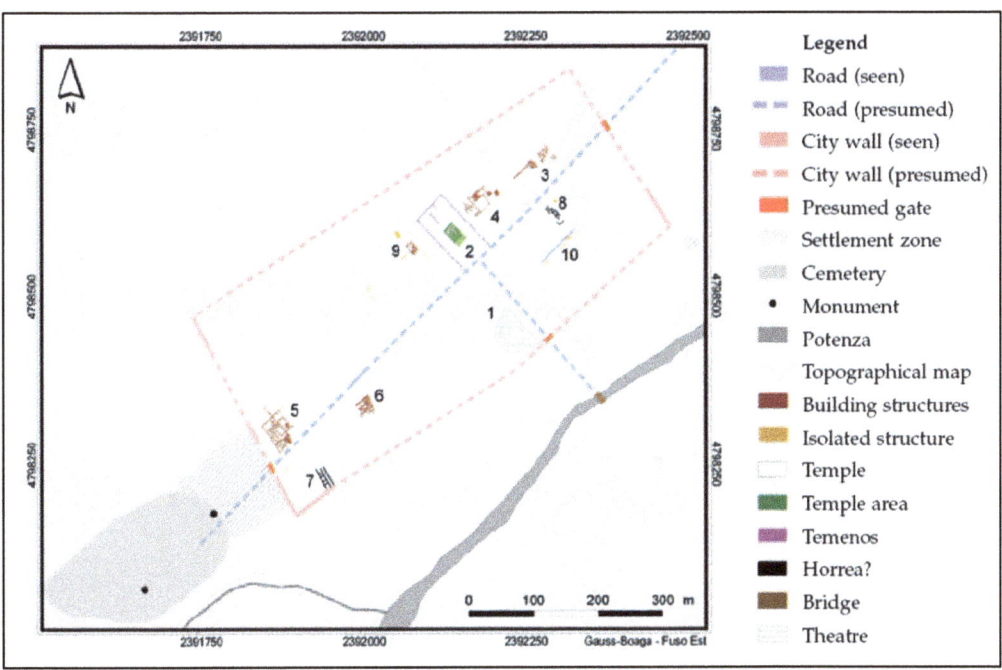

Figure 6.2: Plan of Helvia Ricina (Vermeulen et al. 2005: 40, fig 10).

from the first century BC, when the settlement received *municipium* status, and veterans of the civil wars settled as colonists (Vermeulen *et al.* 2005, 39-40). The city flourished during the Early Imperial period and the first tentative plan of the settlement (figure 6.2) includes a theatre (1), a temple (2), *domus* (3-6), possible *horrea* and *tabernae* (7, 8) and a monumental building with cistern (9). The city wall delimits an almost rectangular shaped area of ca. 22 ha. The town was centrally crossed by the road between Trea and Potentia that functioned as the *decumanus maximus*. Individual *insulae* could not be identified via oblique aerial photography, but short linear crop marks suggest the presence of a grid plan. One of the roads running from northwest to southeast could have been connected to a Roman bridge over the river Potenza, linking it with the *decumanus* and passing the theatre. The location of the *forum* has been envisioned near this intersection. A major part of the ancient settlement is currently built-over by houses and roads, hindering archaeological investigations. The presence of extra-mural activity zones cannot be ruled out; such as the area near the bridge. During the second century AD an extensive public building programme remodelled the squares and streets (Vermeulen *et al.* 2005, 40-3).

Potentia (figure 6.3)
In 184 BC the Romans founded the *colonia* of Potentia. Three phases in the development of the settlement defence works have been identified (Vermeulen 2008, 236-7). During the first phase, following the initial settling of the first colonists, the *colonia* was probably surrounded by a ca. 2 m wide ditch, flanked by an earthen bank, surrounding an area of 525 by 300 m. According to Livy, the circuit wall, which was erected in 174 BC, had three arched gates, a street network with a sewer system, an aqueduct, a temple for Jupiter and a *portico* with shops enclosing the *forum* square (Vermeulen *et al.* 2006, 205-

6). This event marks the second phase. The wall, enclosing the ca. 18.4 ha large rectangular town, has been identified in most areas as well as the position of the three gates (Vermeulen *et al.* 2009, 92). The settlement wall measures 525 by 343 m intra-murally. The survival of the regular layout of the Late Republican town into the Early Imperial period has been confirmed during excavations (Vermeulen *et al.* 2003, 82). A third phase, in which the east wall was moved 50 m, is still hypothetical and the chronology is not clear. A street replaced the initial eastern wall of Potentia (Vermeulen 2008, 237). If the expansion of the intra-mural area is accepted than Potentia would have measured 525 by 393 m, 20.6 ha. Some internal structures are visible on the aerial photographs and the excavations of the *forum* area revealed the presence of the Republican temple for Jupiter surrounded by a *portico*, both mentioned by Livy, and other buildings from the Republican and Imperial period, possibly a *macellum* located to the north of the temple. The *forum* measures 30 by 120 m (Vermeulen *et al.* 2006, 206, 227). It seems to have been bordered on both long sides by rows of shops fronted by a *portico*, some of which contained mosaic floors (Vermeulen 2008, 238). A magnetometer survey focussing on the western half of Potentia extended the knowledge of the layout of the settlement. The street layout in the eastern half of the town conforms to the grid system defined by aerial photographs and the magnetometer survey of the western half of the town. The *insulae* located between the streets lack clarity in floor plan, which is needed for assessing partitioning, however, the evidence does suggest the presence of houses, probably of the *domus* type, with central courtyards. Magnetic anomalies indicate several large buildings surrounding the *forum* and the presence of a temple with *macellum* located to the east. On the southern side of the *forum* the presence of a large building, possibly a *basilica* is considered and on the

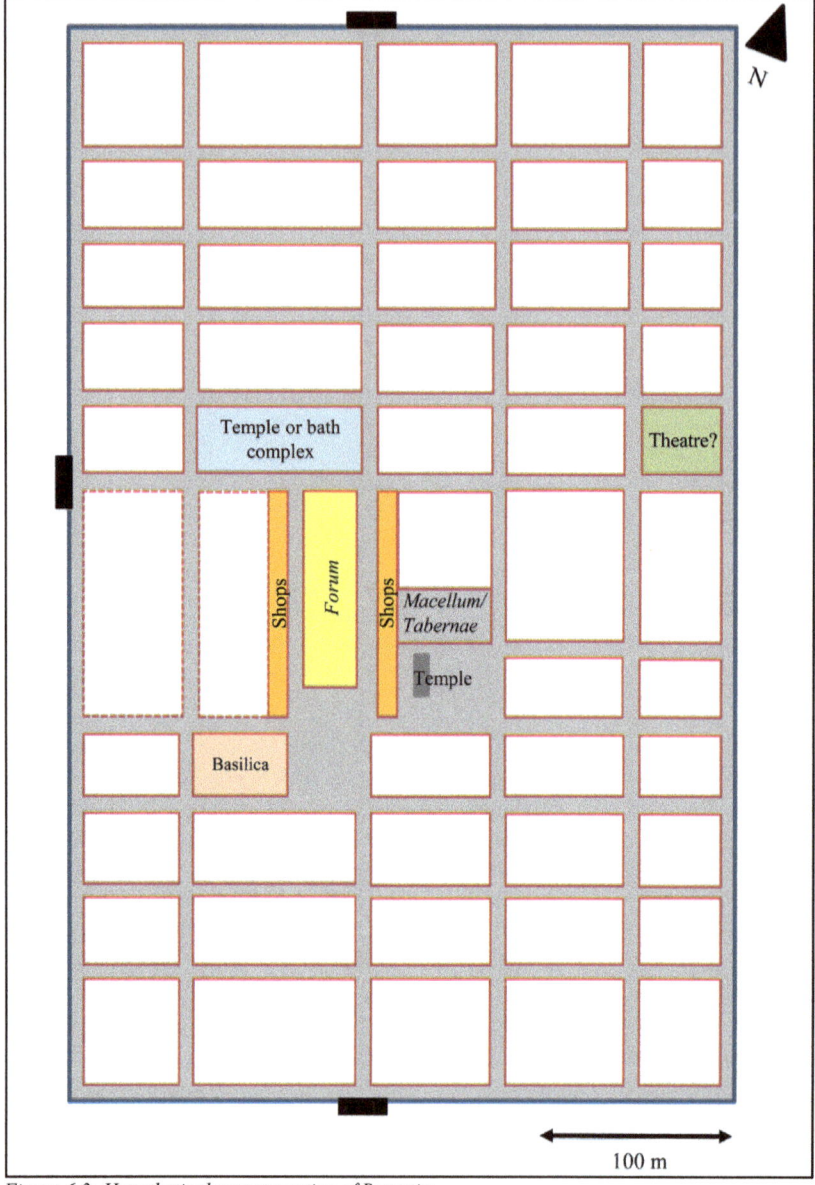

Figure 6.3: Hypothetical reconstruction of Potentia.

northern side maybe a temple or bath complex (Vermeulen *et al.* 2006, 233; Vermeulen 2008, 238). All three detected roads leaving the city gates are bordered by cemeteries with funeral monuments facing the road (Vermeulen *et al.* 2006, 232-3). The main road leading in a western direction has traces of possible *mausolea*, suggesting the presence of an elite. During the Principate the intra-mural area was intensely built-over and the results from the survey suggest the occupation of suburban *extra -mural* areas, southwest of the *colonia* (Vermeulen 2008, 237-9). Some indications on the 2007 aerial photographs point towards the presence of harbour facilities in this area, quite close to the southern gate of the town (Vermeulen *et al.* 2009, 93).

The team from Ghent University suggests that the urban space is divided into at least 50 *insulae* of different sizes. The northern zone had five and the southern zone four east-west oriented rows of five *insulae*. The central zone seems to have six larger *insulae*. A small road that follows the wall on its inner side is suggested on the north-side of the built area (Vermeulen *et al.* 2006, 221, 232). A reconstruction of a detailed settlement plan is absent from current publications. A preliminary reconstruction will be suggested in this study, based on the published street grid and the description of the public and private areas of the *colonia*. From this hypothetical settlement plan (figure 6.3), an estimated population density can be established. This density can be used, assuming the population densities of the four major centres in the Potenza Valley are of the same order of magnitude, for calculating the size of the population in these settlements. In the absence of excavated residential quarters, which reveal complete floor plans of the houses that made up an *insula*, an assumption needs to be made on the size and the number of houses for a certain size of *insula*.

The often cited point of reference for determining population density is the Latin *colonia* of Cosa. The best estimate for the number and size of the houses in Cosa comes from the beginning of the second century BC and

Table 6.3: Attested functional public features.

	Helvia Ricini	Potentia	Trea	Septempeda
Forum		X	X	
Temple	X	X	X	
Basilica		X	X	
Aquaduct		X		
Theatre	X	?		
Macellum		X	X	
Tabernae	X	X	X	
Horrea	X			

is 24 large houses and 224 smaller ones, the latter being half the size of the larger ones. It is very likely that the local elite occupied the larger houses. The ratio between the larger and the smaller houses is approximately 10. There is no evidence of an upper storey to any of the houses, but stairs suggest that they were equipped at least with a loft, probably for storage and sleeping (Fentress 2003, 24-5). The dimensions of the houses can be obtained from the detailed excavation of one of the elite houses on the side of the forum, the House of Diana, an *atrium* house with *hortus*. The plot covers an area of ca. 660 m^2, including the garden (161 m^2) and two small shops at the entrance of the house. If the assumption is accepted that the typical size of the houses in Potentia mirrors the situation at Cosa, than an estimate can be made of the number of families that occupied Potentia. This approach feels like circular reasoning as it models the size of the population density based on Cosa (ca. 100 persons/ha). It is assumed that the size and ratio of large to regular houses excavated at Cosa is representative for the Late Republican and Early Imperial periods, where the key variables that influence a deviation from the estimated population density of Cosa are the area within the defensive walls and the area of private space. Moreover, Cosa was not a thriving *colonia* at the beginning of the Early Imperial periods when the occupied space merely covered 5 ha and contained potentially 500 people (Fentress 2009, 142). Nevertheless, if the assumption is made that in Potentia a similar ratio between small and large houses can be expected, and that the size of the houses would equal the situation at Cosa then 350 houses, of which 34 large and 316 regular sized, can be fitted into the reconstructed *insulae*. The private space covers ca. 61% of the intra-mural area and the public space accounts for ca. 5%. The latter also includes an *insula* of public space, which could have been the location of a theatre, which was commonly found in Late Republican and Early Imperial contexts, such as in Helvia Ricina, Fanum Fortunae, Pisaurum, Ostra, Aesis, Ancona, Urbs Salvia, Falerio, Firmum and Asculum (Sisani 2006). The street network of Potentia makes up ca. 34% of the *intra-mural* area. Conventi assessed the distribution of space by function for 40 towns and the data suggest that *insulae* made up ca. 69% of the intra-mural area of 10 towns that had enough data to make an assessment (Conventi 2004, 168). The

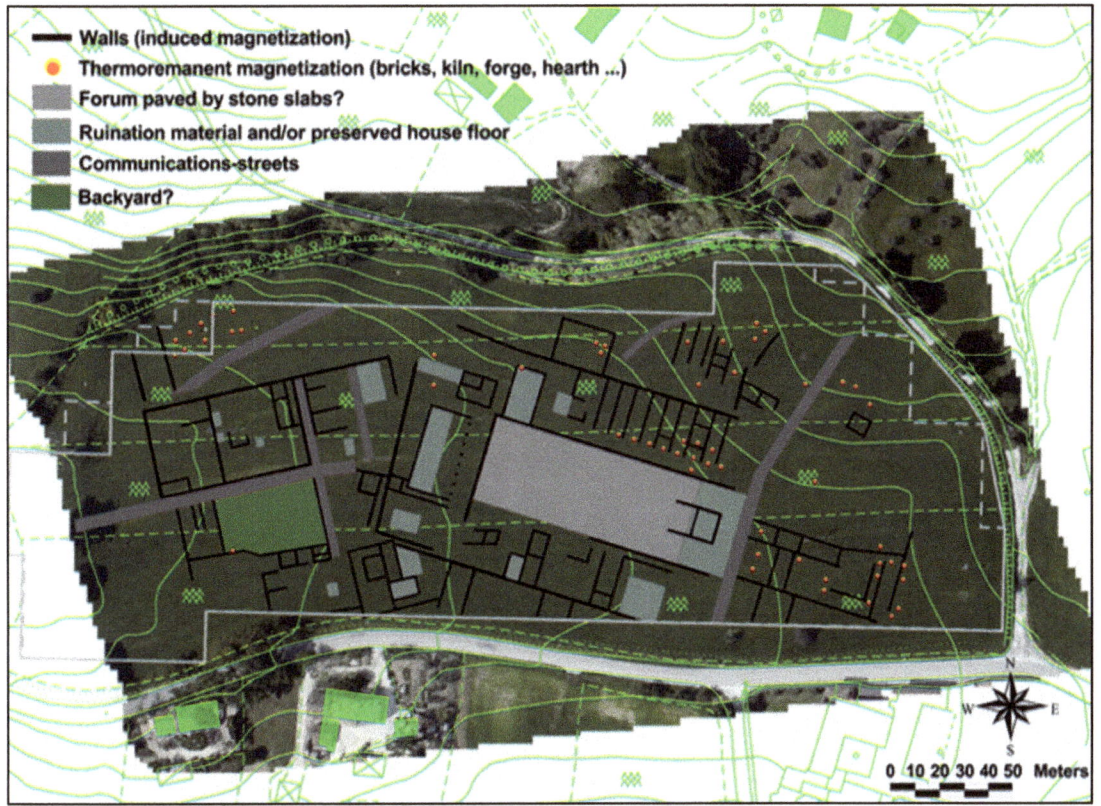

Figure 6.4: Results of geophysical prospection for Trea (Vermeulen et al. 2009, 106, fig 23).

Table 6.4: Surveyed area (Verreyke and Vermeulen 2009, 104-5).

Valley Zone	Extensive Survey (km^2)	Intensive Survey (km^2)
Upper	17.5	3.15
Middle	18.8	3.69
Lower	32.7	3.88
Sum	69.0	10.72

magnitude of the area covered by *insulae* at Potentia does not differ significantly from this average. If a population of 5-6 persons is assumed for the regular houses and 10-12 persons for the large houses than the population of Potentia was in the range of 1,920-2,304 persons living on 20.6 ha intra-mural space. An unknown number of people lived extra-murally, possibly in hamlets located in close proximity to Potentia. The population density of Potentia could have been in the range of 93-112 persons/ha.

A competing reconstruction can be suggested based on the data presented by Wallace-Hadrill for Pompeii. The weighted average size of the houses in Pompeii was 271 m^2 (Wallace-Hadrill 1994, 81, tab 5.2). The acceptance of this dimension as being representative for the size of a typical house in Potentia leads to a slightly higher population range of 2,332 to 2,799 people and a density of 113-136 persons/ha. Based on the movement of the eastern wall and the presence of *suburban* population, significant population pressure was very likely, suggesting that the size of the population of Potentia was more likely to be in the 113-136 persons/ha range.

Septempeda

The third settlement in rank is Septempeda, located in the middle Potenza Valley, on a river terrace bordering the stream, at some 40 km inland from the coastline. It has been suggested that the settlement developed from a road station along the side branch of the *Via Flaminia*, on the crossroads with the *Via Salaria*. The settlement is almost pentagonal in shape and is estimated to have measured 15 ha. Parts of the first century BC walls and two gates were excavated, and along the central *decumanus* several rooms of two imperial *domus* and large thermal installations were found. In the south-eastern part of town, a new gate was discovered connected to a road leading out of town in the direction of Tolentinum (Vermeulen *et al.* 2009, 110-1).

Trea (figure 6.4)

Trea was, according to the *Itinerarium Antonini*, located on the *Via Flaminia* that led past Septempeda, Trea and Auximun to Ancona. It has been suggested that the settlement origins are *Piceni*. Trea became a Roman *municipium* shortly after 49 BC. The city-wall was probably built just after this event, and the territory was, according to the *Liber Coloniarum*, centuriated during the second triumvirate (Vermeulen *et al.* 2009, 102). Geophysics revealed the presence of a rectangular *forum* square, with a temple on the eastern short side, while the presence of a *basilica* with the bases of a colonnade on the short western side of the *forum* is suspected (fig 6.4). A public building, possibly a *macellum* is located at the south side of the *forum*. Along its northern and partly southern sides, the *forum* is flanked by a series of buildings, possibly *tabernae*. The street plan forms a complex and probably partly diachronic pattern. Many building structures, e.g. houses and shops, are located

Type	Description	Size (m²)	Building Material	Pottery Finds	Associated Structures
1	small house unit	200–1,200; <700 avg.	simple (e.g., roof tiles, uncut stones)	very small amount (no fine wares)	–
2	farm	1,200–2,500	slightly more, mostly simple (e.g., roof tiles, [un]cut stones, brick)	normal variety (fine and common wares)	compact regular building
3	large farm or simple villa	2,500–4,000 (max.)	diverse (e.g., roof tiles, [un]cut stones, brick, concrete)	large variety (fine and common wares)	several functional units with living quarters, simple outhouses, and activity zones
4	*villa rustica*	3,000–6,000 (avg.)	great diversity e.g., *crustae*, *tesserae*, column fragments, *tubuli*)	larger variety (more fine and/or imported products); several cores of finds	one main building; one or more outhouses and activity zones (dominant position)
5	roadside settlement	3,000–6,000 (avg.)	large diversity	good variety (higher number of tablewares, amphoras, lamps)	longitudinal building aligned with a Roman road or bridge
6	small *vicus* or village	very large area (ca. 12,000 m²) with several concentrations	great diversity	great variety (more fine and/or imported products)	none (but connected with a Roman road)
7	town	–	–	–	–

Table 6.5: Site typology for classifying Roman settlements (Verreyke and Vermeulen 2009, 108, tab 1).

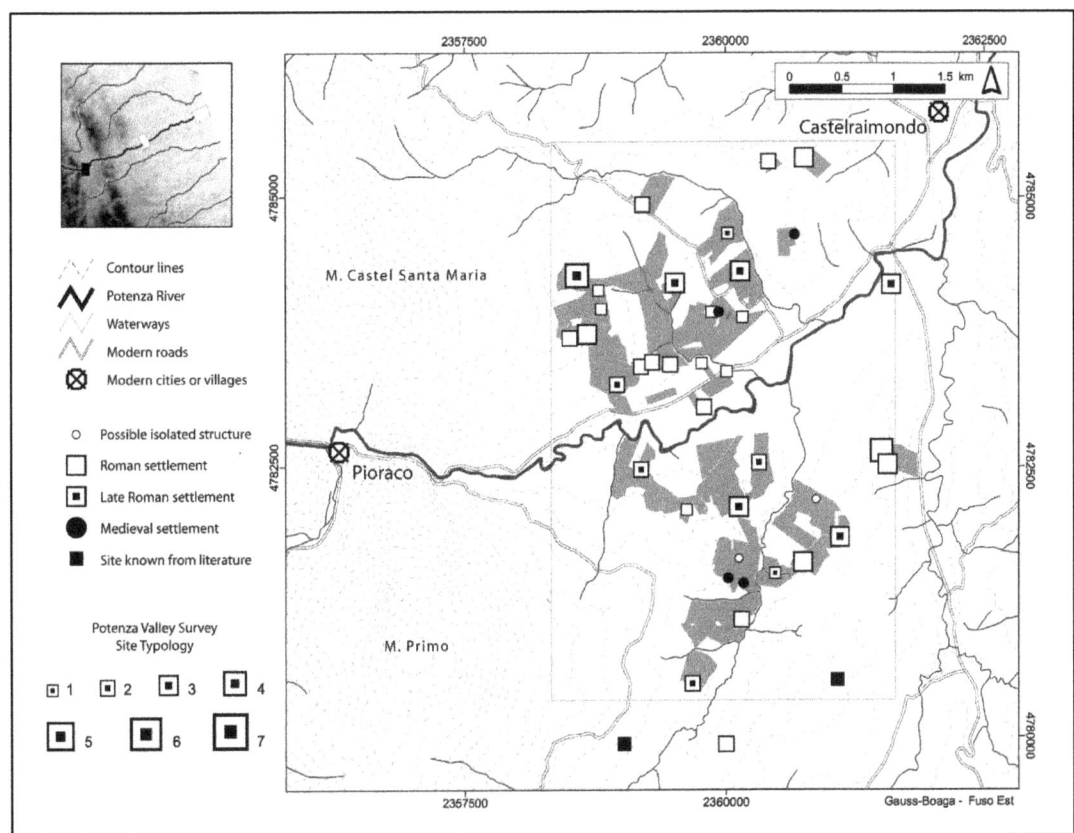

Figure 6.5: Upper Potenza Valley – Zone 1 (Verreyke and Vermeulen 2009, 111, fig. 4).

outside the *forum* area. Magnetograms indicate the possible presence of workshops (Vermeulen *et al.* 2009, 106-7). The *forum* area contained a wide range of fine and coarse wares, dating from the first century BC to the fifth century AD. The survey team suggests an intramural area of 12 ha. A gate is suggested in the northeast corner of the site, probably leading in the direction of Ancona. A new and detailed plan of the topography of ancient Trea has not yet been published (Vermeulen *et* al. 2009, 110).

The last important settlement is Prolaquaeum, which has been completely overbuilt, and considered a road station (Vermeulen *et al.* 2003, 73-4, 100).

The size of the population living in the five civic centres of the Potenza Valley can be estimated at ca. 8,630 people. The urban-rural dichotomy, for instance by the use of a population threshold, has consequences for calculations of the size of the urban and rural population, and how urbanisation in the Potenza Valley can be described. It is obvious that the Romans themselves, by granting *municipium* or *colonia* status had a different, more functional view, and the presence of public buildings (table 6.3), can be indicative for the presence of an elite.

Intensive rural field surveys
Three survey zones (table 6.4) have been selected based on geography and landscape features, and spaced at regular intervals, covering the upper, middle and lower valley (Vermeulen and Boullart 2001, 4). The intensive field survey consisted of line-walking at 5-15 meter intervals of ploughed fields in these zones. All potential chronologically diagnostic artefacts, feature sherds (rims, bases, handles) and lithics have been systematically collected and classified. A detailed pottery reference collection, for determining site chronology, was created based on pottery from secured stratified contexts during the excavations at Potentia (Verreyke and Vermeulen 2009, 104-6). A site typology, based on the quantity and quality of the artefact scatter, topographical position and the presence of structures and building materials, was developed (table 6.5). The site typology explicitly takes the character and quality of the finds into account (Verdonck and Vermeulen 2004, 208-14).

A lot of attention has been paid to site visibility, where the use of oblique aerial photography aided in the recovery of sites; however no indication of the site recovery ratio has been suggested. Site occupation, abandonment and reoccupation have been well established, resulting in detailed maps for each sample area. The site density reached a maximum during the Early Imperial period. The location of Late Roman settlements does not differ much from the Early Imperial period. The maps show the latest occupation period of the sites. A concentration of rural sites was noted near contact zones of different landscape types, such as between the valley bottom and the hill slopes (Verreyke and Vermeulen 2009, 110).

The first sample area (figure 6.5) is located in the upper part of the valley, east of Prolaqueum, modern day Piocaro (Vermeulen *et al.* 2003, 95-6). The Roman settlements have been mainly located around the 375-405

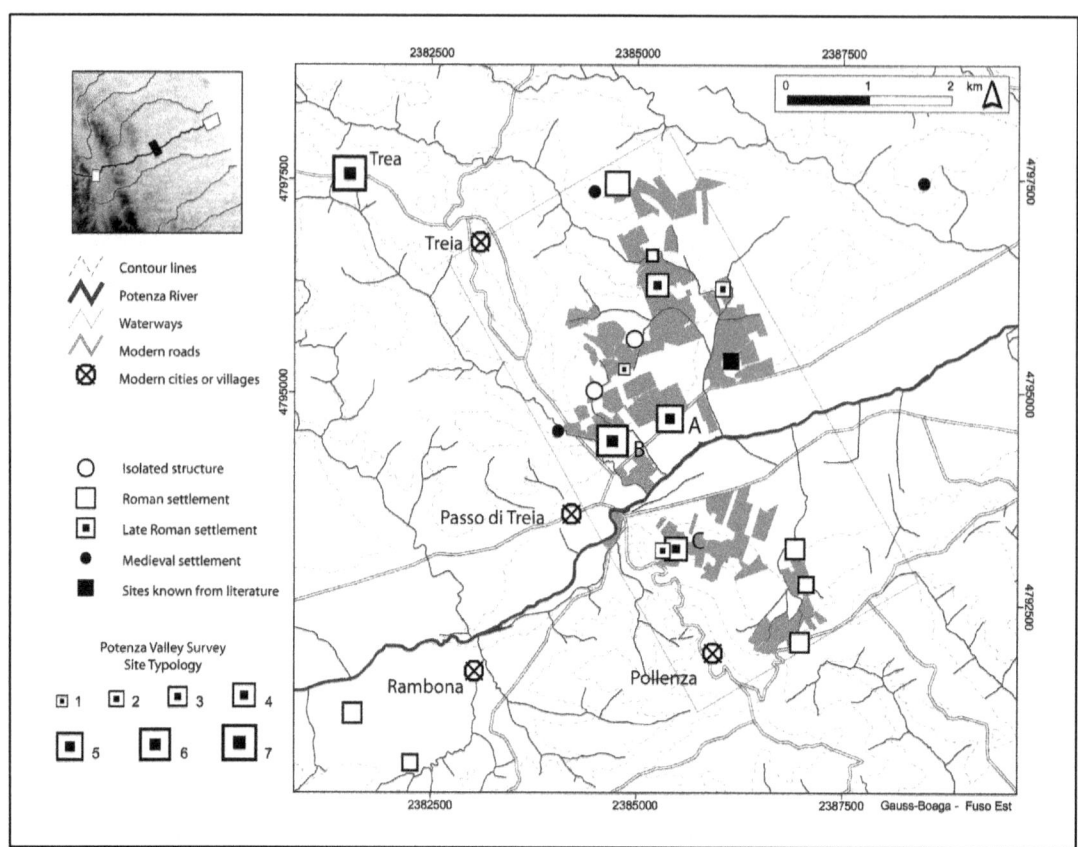

Figure 6.6: Middle Potenza Valley – Zone 2 (Verreyke and Vermeulen 2009, 113, fig 6).

m altitude contours, where a lot of natural springs could be found (Verreyke and Vermeulen 2009, 110). The sample area of the middle valley (zone 2) is located at ca. 30 km from the Adriatic coast shore (figure 6.6). The Roman *municipium* Trea was strategically located on a plateau. An earlier survey, which does not overlap with zone 2, has been reported by Moscatelli in the *Forma Italiae* series (Moscatelli 1988). In contrast to the results of the upper Potenza Valley, where most sites should be interpreted as fairly simple farms, this region of the Potenza Valley shows a dispersed and varied Roman settlement pattern. The majority of the sites are small and simple, but larger complexes have also been identified. These sites display a more extensive surface scatter, the presence of building materials and more imported pottery and glass, coins and lead artefacts (Vermeulen and Boullart 2001, 57-8).

The importance of the road network is best seen in the middle valley, where the *Flaminia Prolaquense* turned towards Trea. Another road continued along the northern side of the Potenza River, connecting Septempeda with Potentia via Helvia Ricina. Along this road a series of roadside settlements, possible hamlets could be identified. Aerial photography, supported by rescue excavations in 2007, helped in the identification of a village, possibly a *vicus* along the Roman road near modern-day Passo di Trea. The aerial photography also showed the presence of a side-road of the Septempeda to Ricina road towards Trea. The presence of these nucleated settlements and the location of a large *villa*, suggest that this region was an important north-south passage. Important *Piceni* settlements were also located along this line, suggested continuity from the pre-Roman to Roman period (Verreyke and Vermeulen 2009, 110-3). The sample area of the lower valley is bordered by the medieval hilltop town of Potenza Picena and Recanati and includes the *Piceni* hilltop site of Montarice, and the *colonia* of Potentia (figure 6.7). Some *villae* and larger rural settlements are located on the foot slopes of the hills, just outside the centuriated area (Vermeulen et al. 2003, 79, 84). Several sites with *villa*-like features, all located near the Roman town of Potenza, not far from the Adriatic shoreline and a major *Piceni* site north of the river mouth have been identified (Vermeulen and Boullart 2001, 7). The valley floor poses a challenge in terms of visibility due to later flooding and clay deposition. In the lower Potenza Valley a dense pattern of rural sites along the adjacent hill ridges, aligned with the centuriated valley plane has been found in the immediate hinterland of Potentia. The centuriation occurred during the Late Republican period. The sites that have been located on the crests of the hills that border the plain on the north and the south were very suitable for viticulture. This activity seems to have been connected with the amphora production along the coast. Viticulture and amphora production suggest that wine was exported from this region. During the Roman period, it seems that intensive agriculture is conducted from a dense network of farms, *villae* and small hamlets. The main rural produce of the valley was grain, fruit, olives and wine (Verdonck and Vermeulen 2004, 162). The maximum

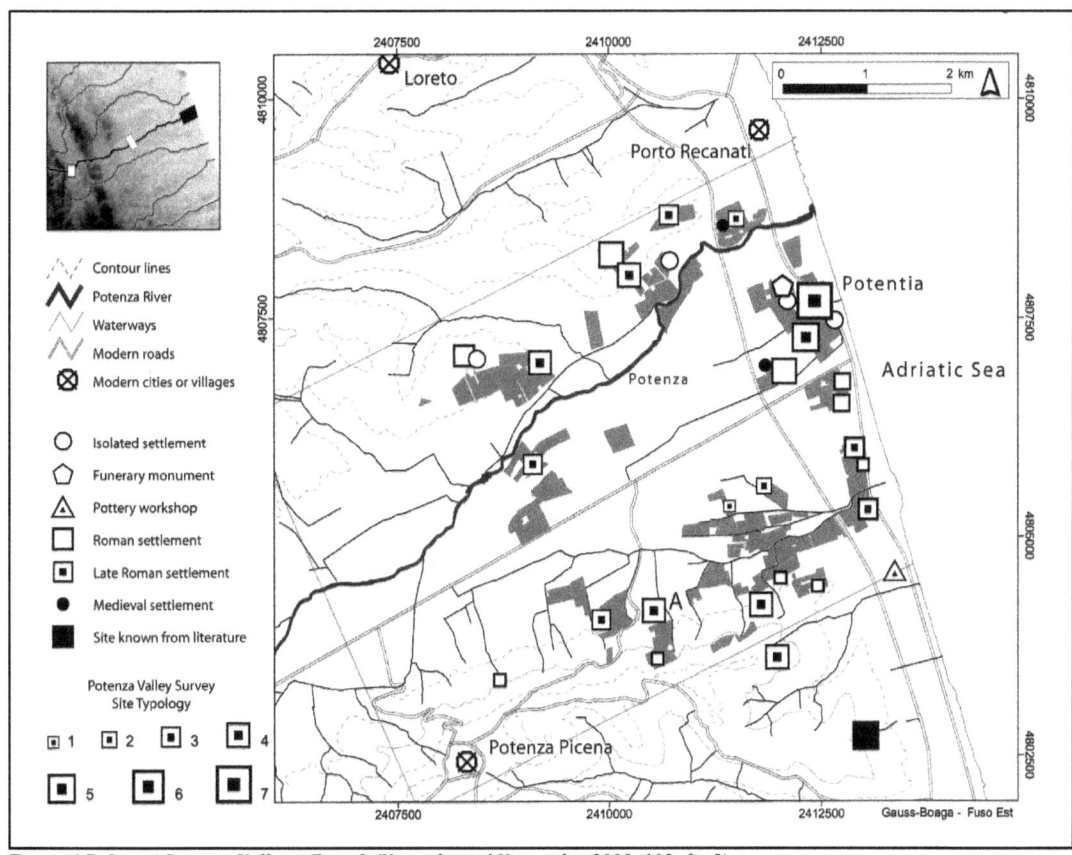

Figure 6.7: Lower Potenza Valley – Zone 3 (Verreyke and Vermeulen 2009, 112, fig 5).

settlement density arose in the Late Republican period but peaked in the first century AD.

Separate analysis of the rural demography for these two periods has been done because of the strong contrast in numbers. This is however not a realistic option for the major settlements, as these are all accounted for, and a constant population of these settlements will be assumed. The site count by type, the number of sites/km², and an estimate can be extrapolated to total valley area (400 km²) (table 6.6). The upper valley, roughly west of Septempeda, is at an altitude between 500-1,000 meters, at which small scale mixed farming and pastoralism seems to have been an appropriate economic strategy. The next challenge would be to assign ranges for the number of inhabitants for each site type, resulting in a set of data that can be compared versus the other case histories. For this purpose, site types need to be grouped logically, resulting in two scenarios that will be used in the remainder of this chapter. In the first scenario the small farms and farms are grouped and the large farms/small *villae* and *villae rusticae* (table 6.7). In the second scenario the small farms, large farms and small *villae* are grouped and the *villae rusticae* are counted separately (table 6.8). Finally, the roadside settlements and *vici* can be grouped in the category of villages; however, hamlet might be a more appropriate term, as it often refers to a group of farms, located either by a road or in the countryside. To what extent these site patterns can be extrapolated over the full area is highly debatable. The first scenario suggests 1 farm and 2 *villae*/km² for the

Table 6.6: Potenza Valley Survey – Site densities for the Late Republican and Early Imperial periods.

Site Type	Late Republic					
	Upper	Middle	Lower	Total	Sites/km²	Potenza Valley
Small Farm	1	0	0	1	0.09	37
Farm	5	2	3	10	0.93	373
Large Farm/Small *Villa*	4	2	6	12	1.12	448
Villa Rustica	2	1	6	9	0.84	336
Roadside Settlement	0	1	1	2	0.19	75
Vicus	0	0	0	0	0.00	0

Site Type	First century AD					
	Upper	Middle	Lower	Total	Sites/km²	Potenza Valley
Small Farm	9	2	5	16	1.49	597
Farm	13	4	4	21	1.96	784
Large Farm/Small *Villa*	10	3	6	19	1.77	709
Villa Rustica	2	3	6	11	1.03	410
Roadside Settlement	0	1	1	2	0.19	75
Vicus	0	1	0	1	0.09	37

Table 6.7: Small sites - first scenario.

Site Type	Late Republic					
	Upper	Middle	Lower	Total	Site/km²	Potenza Valley
Small Farm + Farm	6	2	3	11	1.0	410
Large Farm + *Villa*	6	3	12	21	2.0	784
Ratio					0.5	

Site Type	First century AD					
	Upper	Middle	Lower	Total	Site/km²	Potenza Valley
Small Farm + Farm	22	6	9	37	3.5	1,381
Large Farm + *Villa*	12	6	12	30	2.8	1,119
Ratio					1.2	

Table 6.8: Small sites – second scenario.

Site Type	Late Republic					
	Upper	Middle	Lower	Total	Site/km²	Potenza Valley
Farm + Small *Villa*	10	4	9	23	2.1	858
Villa Rustica	2	1	6	9	0.8	336
Ratio					2.6	

Site Type	First century AD					
	Upper	Middle	Lower	Total	Site/km²	Potenza Valley
Farm + Small *Villa*	32	9	15	56	5.2	2,090
Villa Rustica	2	3	6	11	1.0	410
Ratio					5.2	

Late Republican period and 3.5 farms and 2.8 *villae*/km² for the Early Imperial period. The ratios of farm to *villa* are respectively 0.5 and 1.2. The high ratio of farm to *villa* could be indicative for a low site visibility of farms relative to *villae*, or that an alternate grouping, such as the second scenario is more appropriate. It needs to be stressed that both scenarios are artificial constructions that can be revisited in future research. The second scenario suggests 2.1 farms and 0.8 *villae*/km² for the Late Republican period, and 5.2 farms and 1.0 *villa*/km² for the Early Imperial period. The ratios of farms to *villa* are respectively 2.6 and 5.2 and are more in line with the expectation that there would be more farms than *villae* in the landscape.

The size of the total population

The outcome of the intensive field survey should provide useful ranges for the size of the rural population outside of civic centres for the two scenarios. The next step involves an estimate of the population per site. Based on Roman census figures for Roman Egypt a typical household size of 5.31 was established (Bagnall and Frier 1994, 66-8, 138-9) and for the Potenza Valley a population of 5.5 people per farm will be assumed. There is no direct equivalent evidence for establishing a typical population of a *villa*. Estimates do exist for large complex *villae*, such as Settefinestre, but these are exceptions and the typical *villa* is more modest in size. Witcher used a minimum size of 15 people, a maximum of 50 and an informed population of 25 people/*villa* based on Perkins (Perkins 1999, 166-8). The high end would apply to large

Table 6.9: Potenza Valley Survey - population reconstruction - first scenario.

Parameter	Late Republic				
	Farm	Villa	Hamlet	Road Station	Town
No of Sites	410	784	75	1	4
Population per Site	5.5	20	50	150	
Estimated Population	2,255	15,680	3,750	150	8,630
% of Total Population	7.4%	51.5%	12.3%	0.5%	28.3%

Parameter	First century AD				
	Farm	Villa	Hamlet	Road Station	Town
No of Sites	1,381	1,119	112	1	4
Population per Site	5.5	20	50	150	
Estimated Population	7,596	22,380	5,600	150	8,630
% of Total Population	17.1%	50.5%	12.6%	0.3%	19.5%

Table 6.10: Potenza Valley Survey - Population reconstruction - second scenario.

Parameter	Late Republic				
	Farm	Villa	Hamlet	Road Station	Town
No of Sites	858	336	75	1	4
Population per Site	5.5	20	50	150	
Estimated Population	4,719	6,720	3,750	150	8,630
% of Total Population	19.7%	28.0%	15.6%	0.6%	36.0%

Parameter	First century AD				
	Farm	Villa	Hamlet	Road Station	Town
No of Sites	2,030	410	112	1	4
Population per Site	5.5	20	50	150	
Estimated Population	11,165	8,200	5,600	150	8,630
% of Total Population	33.1%	24.3%	16.6%	0.4%	25.6%

Table 6.11: Estimates for the size of the rural and total population and population densities for the Potenza Valley.

Period	Scenario	Rural Population	Rural Population Density (p/km^2)	Total Population	Total Population Density (p/km^2)	% Urbanisation
Late Republic	1	21,835	55	30,465	76	28%
First Century AD	1	35,726	89	44,356	111	19%
Late Republic	2	15,339	38	23,969	60	36%
First Century AD	2	25,115	63	33,745	84	26%

estates in regions with a low population density and it can be questioned if such estates existed in the Potenza Valley. An arbitrary number of 20 people/*villa* will be used for the Potenza Valley. Perkins suggests 50 people for a hamlet (Perkins 1999, 166-8), which equates to 9-10 farms. An estimated population of a road station is not available, however road stations can be below one ha in size as work in the Tiber Valley at Baccanae, Forum Cassii and Castellum Amerinum has demonstrated (Johnson *et al.* 2004). It is very likely that the size of the population at a road station may have been in the range of 100-200 persons. A guestimated 150 persons will be assumed for Prolaqueum.

The summary of small sites from table 6.7 and table 6.8 can be used for estimating the size of the total population by extrapolating the small site count from the surveyed area to the total valley. The population reconstruction for the Potenza Valley that follows from the first scenario (table 6.9) is dominated by the high count of *villae*. The second scenario is thought to be more realistic in terms of the ratio of farms to *villae*. The outcome of the population reconstruction that follows from the second scenario (table 6.10) provides a more balanced distribution of the population, but with a relatively high percentage living within the civic centres. During the Early Imperial period the rural population expanded rapidly with a noticeable increase of 2.4 times in the number of farms. In both scenarios hamlets can be considered an important part of the rural landscape. A high-level reconstruction of the rural and urban population and population densities is possible for the two scenarios and two periods under study (table 6.11). The total population of the Potenza Valley is estimated to have ranged from 24,000 to 30,000 people during the Late Republican period and from 33,000 to 44,000 people in the Early Imperial period. The corresponding rural population densities show a spread of 38 to 55 persons/km^2 for the Late Republican period and 63 to 89 persons/km^2 for the first century AD. This means that the Potenza Valley belonged to one of the most densely rural populated areas of Roman Italy. The four regional administrative and juridical centres most likely housed the wealthy elite. Relative to the size of these large settlements, they offer the typical urban architecture expected also for larger towns of similar status, and the question can be asked if these settlements are urban or rural? In the calculations, the population in the four centres was kept constant, which means that the urbanisation ratios ranged from 28-36% for the Late Republican period and dropped to 19-26% during the Early Republican period. The premise then of course is that the four centres would be seen as urban, otherwise the total of the Potenza Valley is considered rural.

Discussion

Three variables can be envisioned that could compromise these reconstructions. The first one is the introduction of a recovery ratio primarily of farms. Putting a multiplier of 2 or 3 (50% and 33% site recovery) could create a potentially over-populated rural landscape, however this could be compensated for by areas of the valley that were less suitable for farming, thus having a much lower density of farms and *villae*. Correction of the number of rural sites would also result in lower urbanisation ratios. The next chapters will take a deep dive into the issues and demographic implications of the establishment and use of recovery ratios. The second observation deals with the mathematical implications of hamlets and the *vicus*. Although only two hamlets and one *vicus* have been identified in the surveyed areas, once extrapolated over the 400 km^2 (0.19 hamlet/km^2 and 0.09 vicus/km^2) of the Potenza Valley, these sites would house 14-17% of the population. The transects are located in close proximity to the major centres, so the question is justified if they are representing suburban areas or that the landscape really contains a significant number of hamlets/*vici*. Finally, the question can be asked, how representative are the three transects for estimating the size of the rural population of the Potenza Valley? The transects are in close proximity to the major centres and if it is assumed that the rural density decreases with increased distance then the implications can be significant. Additional field survey work needed for getting a better feel for these variables is not foreseen.

The overall picture that emerges for the Potenza Valley is a densely populated valley that relied on four, relatively small, civic centres for services. Each of these centres was situated within a day-return trip for farmers. The population density for the civic centres of the Potenza Valley, although excavations of residential quarters have not been conducted nor published suggest a layout with a relatively low population density and low population per centre. The occupational structure of the population remains obscure, although signs of elite euergetism are present. A very limited part of the population of these centres could be envisioned to be associated with the provision of services. The region flourished from the Republican to the Early Imperial period, with an increase in population as well as in trade.

7 Demographic Modelling: The *Suburbium* of Rome

Rome and its *suburbium* is considered the most densely populated area on the Italian peninsula in antiquity, and has attracted the attention of historians and archaeologists who took a Rome-centric view on urbanisation, demography and the nature of the ancient economy. In today's modern society a suburb is an outer district lying within the commuting zone of an urban (metropolitan) area and generally consists of houses and its own shopping areas (Johnston *et al.* 2000, 805-6). In the context of this study, it refers to the town and country relationship between Rome and its immediate hinterland; the settlement pattern, land use and demography. Discussions of the relationship between Rome and its immediate territory have been dominated by the topic of food supply. Rome obtained its goods, and especially grain, not exclusively from its own hinterland, and relied on a network of dispersed hinterlands, stimulating inter-regional connectivity (Morley 1996, 4-11, 55-7; Finley 1985, 191-201). Access to the agricultural surplus of the wider Mediterranean would have reduced pressure on the *suburbium* to produce grain and offered room for specialisation, such as stockbreeding for meat, dairy products and perishable goods, such as fruits, but also demographic growth. Morley envisions zones of farming systems and different intensity of cultivation around Rome, expanding on the isolated state model, while analysing the effect of transport costs, climate, soil fertility, and referencing ancient sources (Morley 1996, 83-107). This appears to resemble the concept of the consumer city, developed by Sombard, and applied to the ancient city by Weber, which is based on the dichotomy of town and country, and contrasts the ancient city from the producer medieval town, and downplays urban production and rural consumption (Hansen 2004, 910).

Witcher has intensively researched the demographic dimension for Rome's *suburbium* that would demonstrate the integration of urban and rural supply and demand (Witcher 2005, 123-4). He estimated the size of the population during the Early Imperial period via a rigid mathematical approach, based on the analyses of site typology and applying crude demographic estimators for each settlement type. The model has been based on the outcome of selected field surveys and excavations in the *suburbium* area around Rome, and relies heavily on the fieldwork of the British School at Rome in the Tiber Valley and the older South Etruria Survey. The research considers the urban and especially the rural population as a sizeable and integral part of the population of Rome, potentially functioning as one single unit, an extended *metropolis* (Witcher 2005, 120). The region that Witcher arbitrarily has selected for more detailed analysis to demonstrate how the population density increased with proximity to Rome, equates to a 50 (figure 1.1) and 100 km radius from Rome. Within both concentric radii, a large variety of landscapes, micro-ecologies, and settlement patterns existed; coastal and inland regions, as well as river valleys, mountainous terrain and marginal areas are present.

The '*suburbium* model' will be deconstructed to develop a better understanding of the value of such mathematical demographic modelling and the trade-offs that were made. By using wide ranges for site population, any methodological weaknesses are within wide margins of error that are intrinsically part of such an approach. Information that can be challenged needs to be separated from the researcher's own (rational) belief, not only for

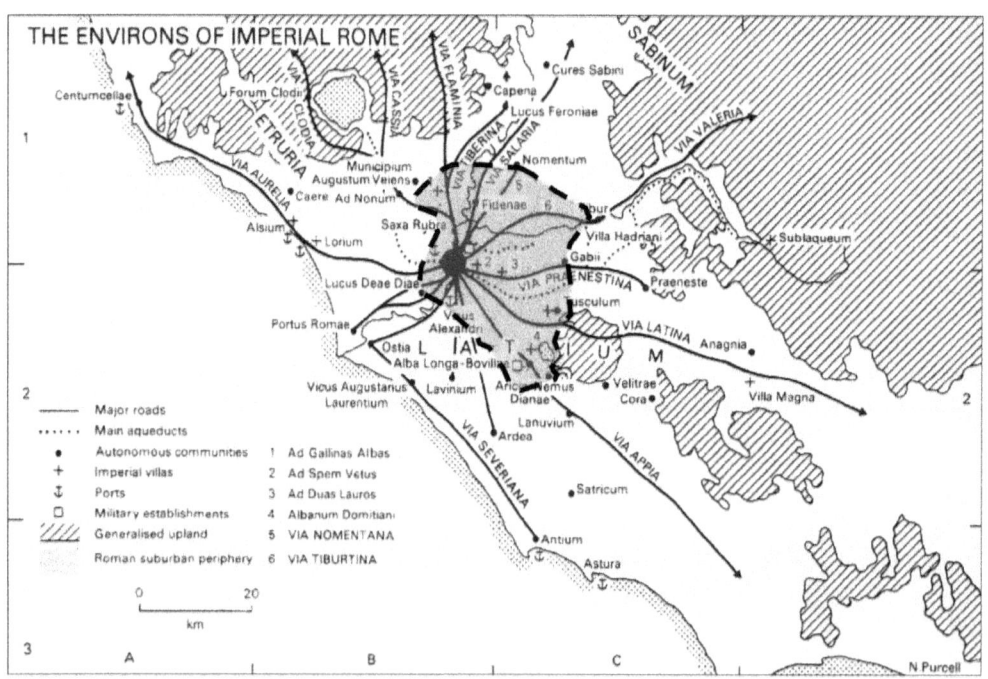

Figure 7.1: The Roman suburban periphery (after Talbert 1985, 122). Area accentuated by the author.

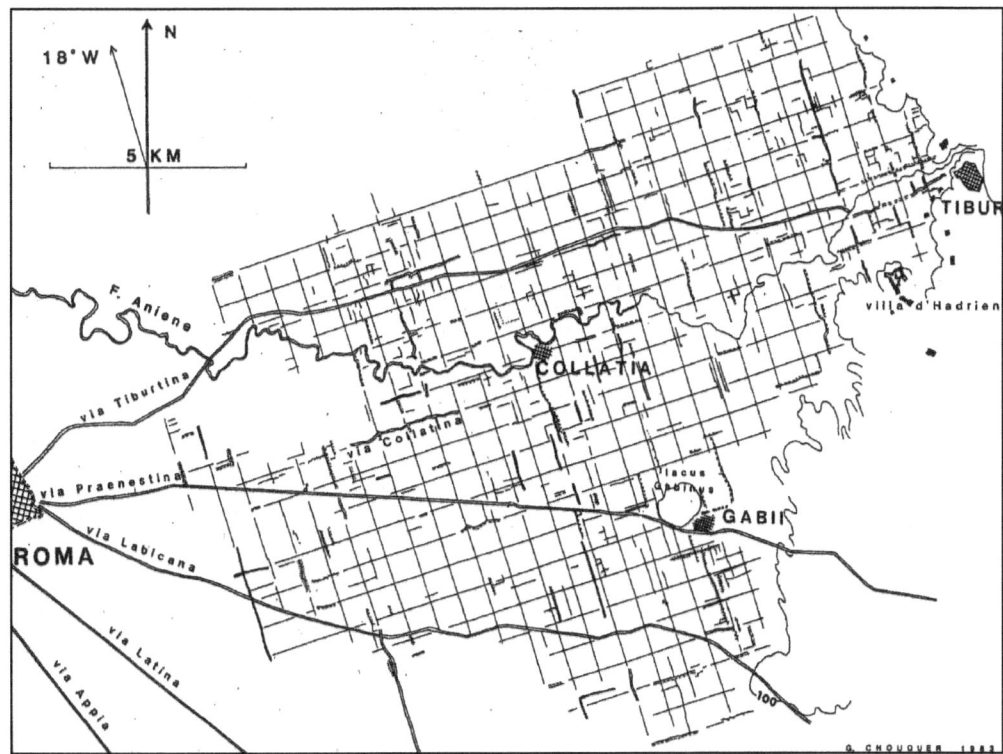

Figure 7.2: The Collatia Survey. Reconstruction of the centuriation grid (Mari 2008, 145-6, 326, fig 79).

the nucleated settlements, but also for the densities of farms and *villae*.

The suburbium of Rome

The Greek Historian Dionysius of Halicarnassus lived in Rome at the end of the first century BC. He described a dense built-up area and occupation, *suburbs*, outside of the Servian walls, and noted the absence of a clear boundary between Rome and its surroundings (Spelman 1758, 167-9). The area within the Servian wall measures 1,373 ha and the fourteen Augustan districts, which expanded also outside of these walls, covered ca. 1,783 ha. Estimates for the uninhabited area for public buildings and gardens vary between 28 and 50% of this extended area. The population of Rome during the reign of Augustus has been estimated in the range of 850,000 to a million people (Morley 1996, 34). However, a case for half a million inhabitants has a good empirical basis too (Storey 1997).

The Atlas of Classical History provides a view of the extent of the Roman *suburbium* according to Purcell (Talbert 1985, 122). The grey area, which has been highlighted by a dotted line, measures ca. 770 km^2 and could represent the Roman *suburban* periphery. The distance from Rome varies between 5 and 25 km. In this reconstruction, the *suburbium* could have reached as far as Gabii and Tibur to the north-east and Bovillae to the south (figure 7.1). An imaginary journey, based on literary sources, starting at the *Forum Romanum*, leaving the walled *metropolis* on the *Via Tiburtina* has been described by Purcell to visualise the integration of town and country (Purcell 1987). The ancient sources primarily relate to the presence of elite *villae* and their function, especially in terms of horticulture. The display of elite wealth in close proximity in the Roman *suburbium* would have put land prices under pressure, which can be of importance for the densities of farms and *villae*. A triangular area, starting at ca. 4 km from Rome was centuriated during the reign of Tiberius. This area stretched up to Tibur and Gabii (figure 7.2). Centuriation suggests that the land was used for agriculture and for the assignment of allotments to farmers. How this fits with views on the nature of the *suburbium* can be debated. For the Collatia Survey a density of 1-2 farms and 3-4 *villae*/km^2 was established (Witcher 2005, 127, table 1).

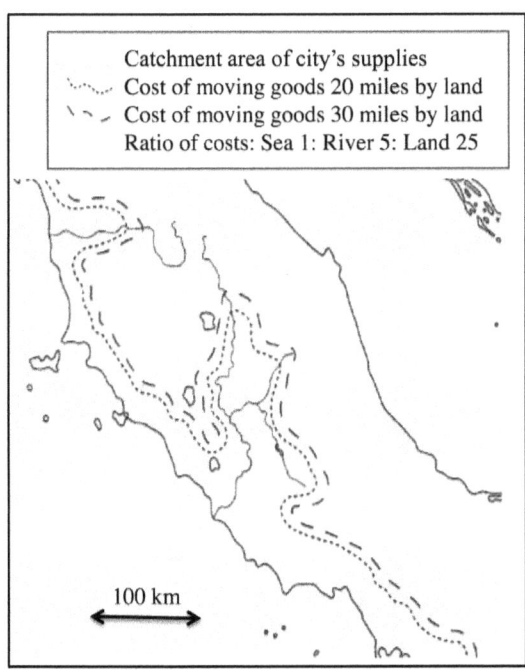

Figure 7.3: The effect of tranport cost on the catchment area of Rome's supplies (after Morley 1996, 64, map 1).

Morley has suggested that Rome was not surrounded by concentric zones of production and that the economic hinterland, with good access to Rome, would have extended along the coast of Italy, and the Tiber Valley, in part due to favourable costs of transport (Morley 1996, 68). He also made a contour plot of the effect of transport cost on the catchment area of the immediate hinterland of a settlement (figure 7.3). Focussing on the hinterland of Rome, the cost of moving goods ca. 38 km (30 miles) inland does not conflict with Purcell's map (figure 7.1), and emphasises the importance of the navigable Tiber and Anio rivers. The high density and regular distribution of civic centres to the south is in line with Purcell's map. The Roman lowlands that are demarcated by the Monti Sabatini, Sabini, Tiburtini, and the Alban hills have been considered as a territorial unit by Morley, of which most of this area lies within a 30 km radius from Rome, forming the immediate hinterland of the *metropolis* (Morley 1996, 83).

A narrow definition of the Roman *suburbium* can be based on the Early Iron Age *ager Romanus*. The precise boundaries are subject to debate and Coarelli suggests, based on literary and archaeological sources, that sanctuaries could have demarcated this area (figure 7.4 and 7.5). The *ager Romanus* would have measured ca. 400 km^2, with a radius between 5 and 13 km from Rome, which is within the 15 km market radius for farmers making a day-return trip. The Early Imperial Roman periphery, using Purcell's reconstruction, would have been double this area. If the population size of Rome during the Early Imperial period is taken into consideration, then this extended area could be realistic. This Roman periphery would have absorbed large settlements, like Gabii, Fidenae, Ficulae, Bovilae, and

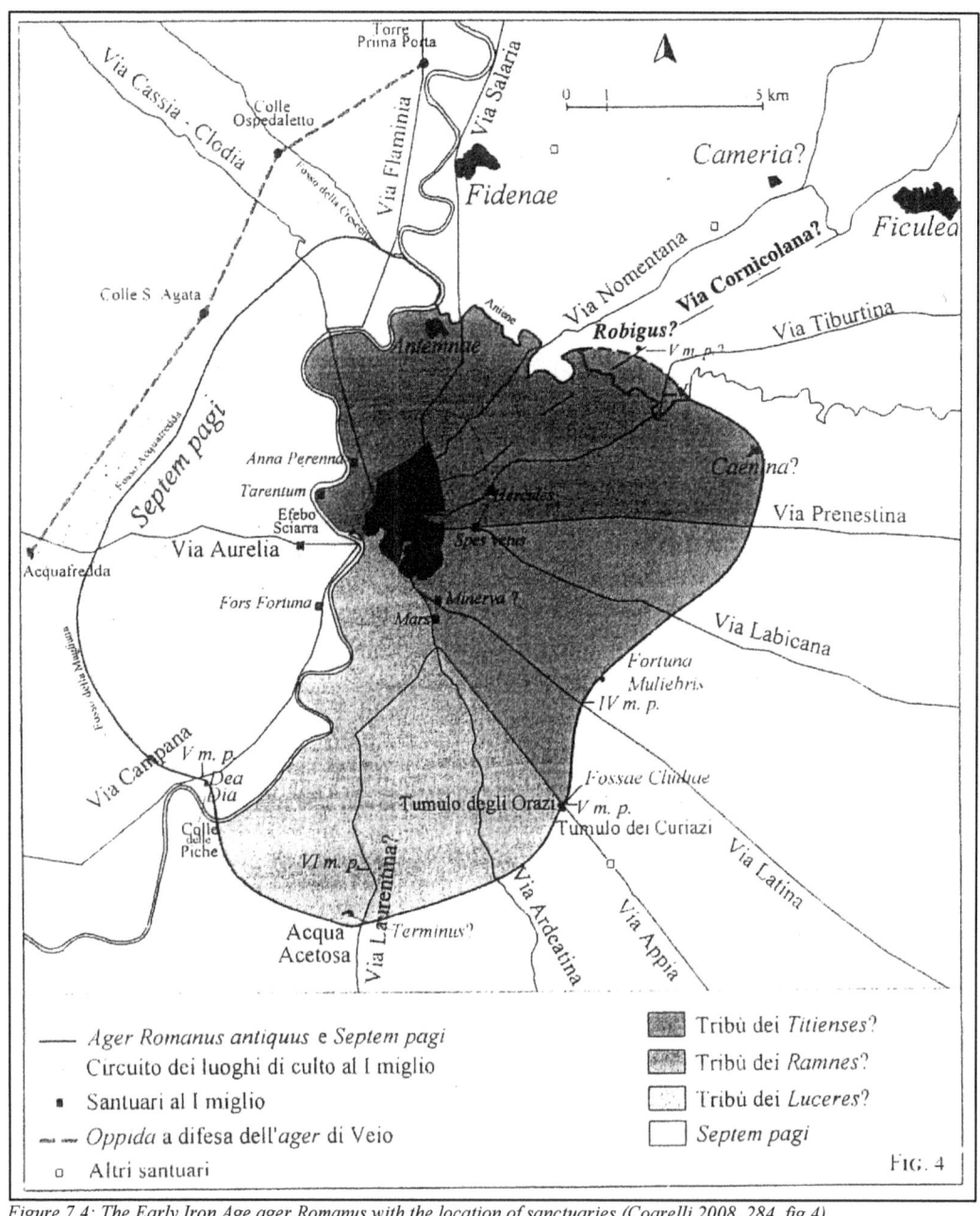

Figure 7.4: The Early Iron Age ager Romanus with the location of sanctuaries (Coarelli 2008, 284, fig 4).

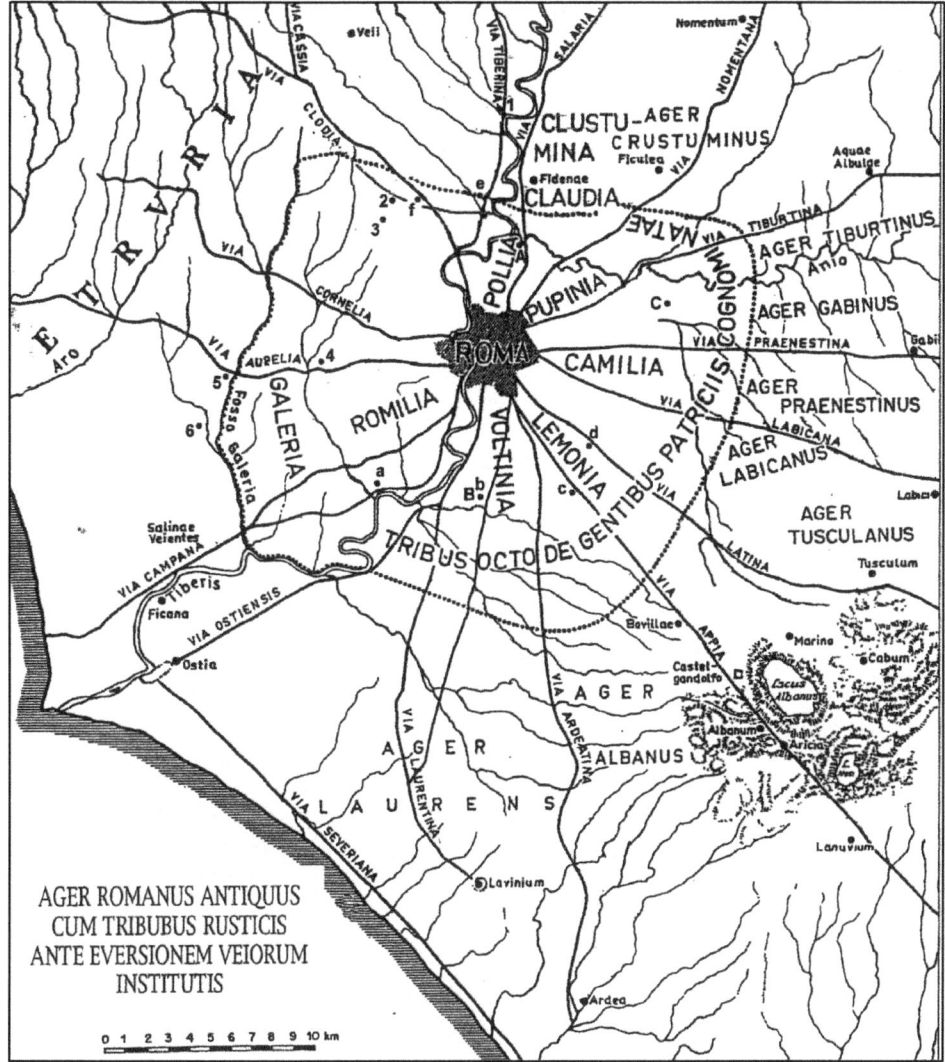

Figure 7.5: The Early Iron Age ager Romanus and surrounding landscape (Coarelli 2008, 285, fig 5).

possibly Tibur and Nomentum into its area with a zone of intense rural population density and market gardening with nested hierarchies and each centre with surplus movements. The *Lexicon Topographicum Urbis Romae: Suburbium* is a multi-volume set that has high quality entries on the topography and sites within the presumed Roman *suburbium*. The lexicon unfortunately does not provide a synthesis that can be used for determining settlement pattern for a certain chronological period, which needs to be constructed from individual entries and scholarly contributions. Developing this synthesis could be part of future research.

Nucleated settlements

Witcher introduces a settlement typology based on the size of the population that comprises the classificatory types road station, small town, town, and the special case of Ostia. Villages are not considered urban, and the informed estimate of 100 people per village that he uses, qualifies his villages as more like hamlets! The minimum and maximum population numbers are based on previous publications and Witcher used informed estimates, which are consensus numbers that take the middle ground between published extremes. The estimated sizes of nucleated settlements, established via archaeological enquiry or by deduction in combination with an estimated population density, are at the basis of these population numbers and an integral part of the synthesis. Establishing workable population densities are highly problematic as it requires excavated settlement plans, and even when these are available, as for Ostia and Pompeii, the estimates vary significantly (Morley 2008, 123).

In the 50 km radius from Rome Witcher identified seven towns,[5] Ostia and Rome excluded, and twenty small towns.[6] The count of towns in the 50-100 km range from Rome is thirteen,[7] but a listing of the small towns used in the model has not been part of the publication. *Municipia* and *coloniae* are the most likely candidates of being of type 'town' or 'small town'. Additional enquiry is needed

---

[5] Towns: Praeneste, Tibur, Caere, Lucus Feroniae, Veii, Falerii Novi and Tusculum.

[6] Small Towns: Pyrgi, Fregenae, Lavinium, Forum Clodii, Sutrium, Nepet, Capena, Forum Novum, Cures Sabini, Trebula Mutesca, Nomentum, Gabii, Ardea, Lanuvium, Aricia, Cora, Velitrae, Signia, Antium and Alsium.

[7] Towns: Tarquinii, Volsinii Novi, Ocriculum, Ameria, Tuder, Carsulae, Interamna Nahars, Narnia, Spoletium, Alba Fucens, Fabrateria Nova, Tarracina and Centumcellae.

Table 7.1: Revised demographic model for the nucleated settlements of the suburbium within a 50 km distance from Rome.

Parameter	Road Station	Small Town	Town	Ostia	Total
No of sites	22	22	10	1	
Min. Population/site	200	500	3,000	20,000	
Max. Pop./site	500	3,000	10,000	60,000	
Informed Estimated Pop./site	200	1,500	5,000	30,000	
Min. Pop.	4,400	11,000	30,000	20,000	65,400
Max. Pop.	11,000	66,000	100,000	60,000	237,000
Informed Estimated Pop.	4,400	33,000	50,000	30,000	117,400

Table 7.2: Revised demographic model for the nucleated settlements of the suburbium at 50-100 km from Rome.

Parameter	Village	Road Station	Small Town	Town	Total
No of sites	50	10	25	14	
Min. Population/site	50	200	500	3,000	
Max. Pop. per site	200	500	3,000	10,000	
Informed Estimated Pop./site	100	200	1,500	5,000	
Min. Pop.	2,500	2,000	12,500	42,000	59,000
Max. Pop.	10,000	5,000	75,000	140,000	230,000
Informed Estimated Pop.	5,000	2,000	37,500	70,000	114,500

to complete the list. The first source is Pliny and his list of civic centres (Afzelius 1942a); the second is a list of Roman Republican *municipia* (Bispham 2007, app. 3, 462-70), and finally the list of *coloniae* published by Salmon (Salmon 1969, 110-11, 161-3). Salmon highlighted that certainty about a civic centre's status is not always possible, which means that personal judgement might also come into play for specific cases, such as Lucus Angitiae, Forum Clodii, Fescennium, Castra Albana and Cliternia.

For each (small) town, the question can be asked if they are in the right category. The smallest settlement that Witcher considers type 'town' is Veii, with an estimated size of 20 hectares. In the 50 km radius, the author identified six small towns that are missing from Witcher's list: Bovillae, Fidenae, Trebula Suffenas, Afilae, Carsioli and Castrimoenium. An indication for their size could not be established from literature. Although chronology and the extent of the built area are always a concern, three 'small towns' should be considered as type 'town'; Cora (20 ha), Ardea (46 ha) and Antium (Cornell 1995, 204-8). In the 50-100 km outer shell, 25 potential small towns have been identified and one additional town Ferentinum (27 ha) (Cornell 1995, 204-8).[8]

Witcher assigned an informed number of 10,000 people to each of the 13 towns in the 50-100 km ring, referring to the estimated population of Spoletium of 23,000 (Witcher 2005, 130, ft 65). This arbitrary population number was derived from beneficiary gifts provided to the *municipes* in the form of a banquet, and population estimates derived from this benefit vary between 18,000-23,000 people (Duncan-Jones 1982, 267-8, 275). A point of debate has evolved around the question on who counts as a member of the *municipium*. With great certainty, this would have included the rural population, which could have accounted for a significant number of the beneficiaries. Interamna Nahars (35 ha) and Alba Fuscens (34 ha) are the only two civic centres that can function as anchor points for a more realistic population number (Conventi 2004, 134). Witcher's supposed ideal Roman town of 10,000 people might be imaged to be 50 ha in size, at a high population density, or much larger with a lower population density. For example, at a moderate 100 persons/ha, the typical town would be 100 ha. However, he does not make any calculation, making the size uncertain, outside of the population. The preliminary conclusion is that the assumption that a typical town at 50-100 km distance from Rome would contain a population of 10,000 people is exaggerated. If a population density of 150 persons/ha is assumed, then the size of the population of Interamna Nahars and Alba Fuscens would be ca. 5,200 people. A similar problem occurs for the estimates of the size of the population of small towns, road stations and villages. Witcher estimated the size of the population in these settlements at 100,000 people (Witcher 2005, 130). Several scenarios could lead to this number. Realistically, the 22 small towns that are below 20 ha, with an unknown average size, would probably account for not more than 50,000 people. Witcher accounted for 22 road stations and 50 villages within the 50 km radius from Rome. With the help of the Barrington Atlas, at least 50 potential villages and at least 10 road stations can, on first inspection, be identified.

The size of the urban population

The number of people living in nucleated settlements living within 50 km of Rome reaches an informed total of ca. 129,400 people in Witcher's publication (Witcher 2005, 128, tab 2). He used, as mentioned earlier, published population ranges per nucleated settlements and informed estimates. The exception is Ostia for which he assumes a population of 60,000 people, which is mentioned as the maximum population size in his table. Rome is not considered in his analysis of the settlement pattern in the 50 km radius. This creates a distorted picture on how this area would have functioned, especially as the population dynamics of the study area would be linked to the increasing prosperity of the town, the emergence of a huge market in Rome, and the attraction it would have had on the population living in the settlements of the *suburbium*. As most of the walls of the towns and small towns surrounding Rome are pre-

---

[8] Small Towns: Castrum Novum, Graviscae, Verulae, Arpinum, Cereatae Marianae, Aletrium, Horta, Circeii, Anagnia, Frusino, Statonia, Tuscana, Treba, Visentium, Fundi, Privernum, Antinum, Ferentium, Sora, Marruvium, Blera, Setia, Vulci, Reate and Amiternum.

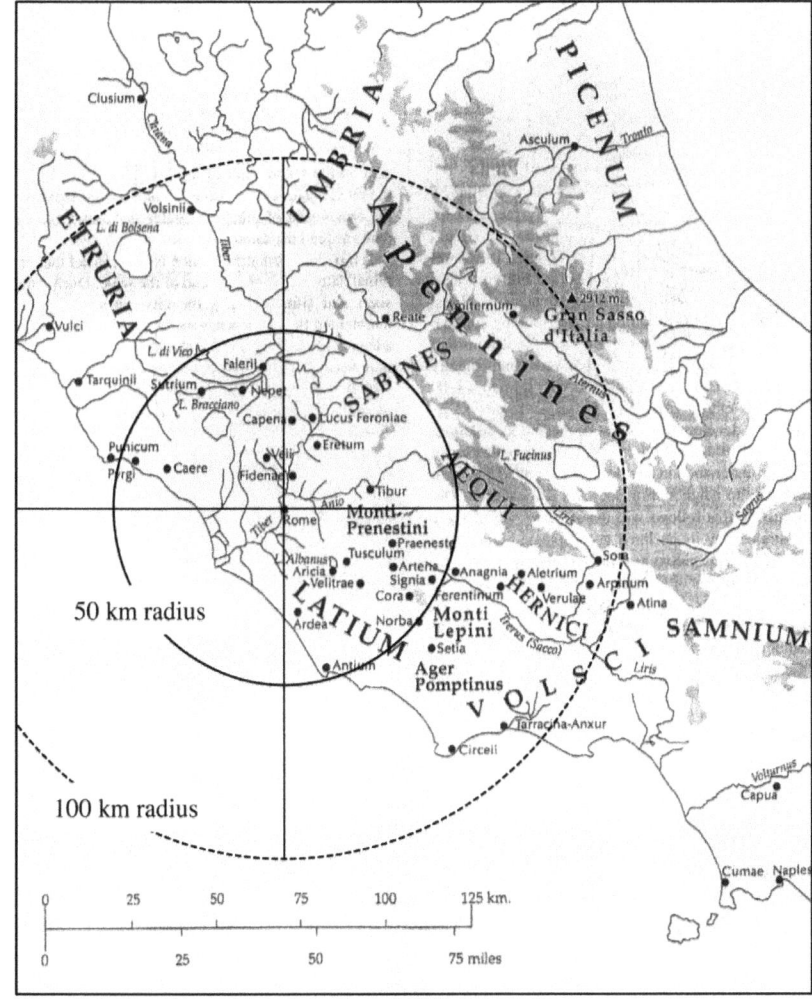

Figure 7.6: Map of central Italy (after Cornell 2000, 210, fig 1).

Roman, the possibility exists that migration could have led to 'empty towns', resulting in overestimates for the residing population. Recent geophysics and core sampling at Gabii confirmed that the use of archaic walls (60$^+$ ha) can be misleading. The urban area within the town walls was densely populated during the Archaic, Early and Middle Republican period, but contracted to ca. 15 ha from the Late Republican to the Imperial period (Becker *et al.* 2009, 633).[9] The area within the walls of Etruscan Veio covers 190 ha (Patterson 2004, 5), but the main occupation for the Roman town of Veii was only 20 ha (Potter 1979, 60-1).

Starting from Witcher's population numbers per site, a revised population size can be suggested for the nucleated settlements of the *suburbium* within a 50 km radius from Rome (table 7.1). The revision results in a small adjustment of the population size by of the population by -9% to 117,400 people. A revised population size can be established for the nucleated settlements of the outer *suburbium*. Witcher's account suggests a population of ca. 230,000 people, including those living in villages (Witcher 2005, 130). The reassessment indicates a significantly lower number of 114,500 people, a reduction of 50% (table 7.2). What do these population estimates for nucleated settlements mean in terms of population densities? Witcher calculated the population densities using a surface area that excludes coastal changes, sea, lakes, marshes, and land over 650 metres elevation for the inner and above 750 metres for the outer *suburbium*, 5,415 resp. 9,051 km^2 (Witcher 2005, 127, ft 46, 129, ft 64). This construction limits the distribution of the population, ignoring the (small) towns that were

Table 7.3: Urban population density estimates for the inner and outer suburbium.

	Area	km^2	Population	Inner *Suburbium* (p/km^2)	Outer *Suburbium* (p/km^2)
Inner *Suburbium*	Model Witcher	5,415	129,400	24	
	Revision	6,116	117,400	19	
Outer *Suburbium*	Model Witcher	9,051	230,000		25
	Revision	14,137	114,500		8

---

[9] Reference to a 15 ha urban area was conveyed during a guest lecture of Prof. dr. N. Terrenato at Leiden University.

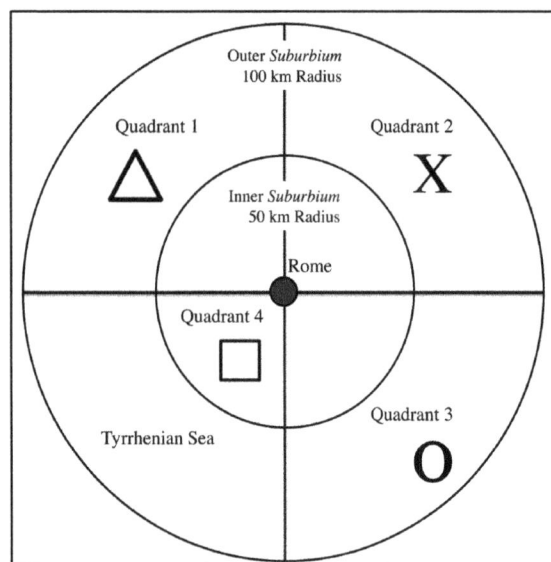

Figure 7.7: The division of the inner and outer suburbium of Rome into four quadrants with symbols used in further analyses.

located in mountainous areas at an elevation of at least 1,000 m as well as the presence of a potentially noticeable rural population. If only sea and coastal changes are taken into consideration the area of the inner *suburbium* covers 6,116 km^2 and 14,137 km^2 for the outer *suburbium*. The revisions result in a modest adjustment of the population density attributed to nucleated settlements for the inner *suburbium* (from 24 to 19 persons/km^2). The impact is more significant for the outer *suburbium* where the population density has been reduced from 25 to 8 persons/km^2 for the nucleations (table 7.3).

Locational analysis

The size of the immediate hinterland of each civic centre has been determined by drawing Thiessen polygons on the maps in the Barrington Atlas. The mean size of the immediate hinterland of the towns and small towns, based on these polygons, is ca. 222 km^2 for the inner *suburbium*, and ca. 320 km^2 for the outer area, so a higher density of towns and small towns for the inner *suburbium*.[10] The former area, however, contains ca. 9% of mountainous surface and the latter ca. 32% of area above an altitude of 750 m. Many centres in the more mountainous areas have a relatively large hinterland, required for food production on more marginal terrain. The average interdistance has been determined at 11.2 km for the inner and 14.7 km for the outer *suburbium*, with radii, following Bekker-Nielsen's methodology, of 7.0 respectively 9.2 km, suggesting that centres had good accessibility for farmers making a day-return trip. Moreover, the region was very well connected via an intensive system of Roman roads (Morley 1996, 84, map 2, 173). Farmers that had their fields within a 5 km radius could have chosen to live in the civic centres. The size of the hinterland within a 50 km radius from Rome is of the same order of magnitude as the hinterland of Classical Greek *poleis*, for which Hansen estimated that 80% had a territory of maximum 200 km^2 (Hansen 2006, 29).

The use of concentric circles by Witcher ignores regional differences in landscape, the size of the immediate hinterland and the presence of a pre-Roman settlement pattern. He admits that there are variations within the inner and outer areas, where the areas closest to Rome were more densely populated compared to the more mountainous and forested areas (Witcher 2005, 127-9). In a 2006 publication, he differentiated between the *suburbium*, the coastal, and the inland region of Etruria. His analysis does not cover the extended *suburbium* of Rome completely (Witcher 2006b). The originally Etruscan, Faliscan, Sabine, Latin and Volscian settlement pattern might have followed a different historical trajectory, based more on differences in landscape and social organisation (figure 7.6).

A bivariate analysis of the data can help to make regional and landscape differences visible. The resulting ellipsoids are a function of the means and standard deviations of the distance from Rome and the size of the hinterland for a given subset of data, and show where a given percentage of the data are expected to lie. A value of 0.66 (66%) has been used as a basis for analyses. A standard deviation can be established for distance and size of hinterland and is a measure of the spread of the distribution around the mean. The ellipsoid collapses diagonally as the correlation between the two variables approaches either 1 or -1, and the shape is more circular if the two variables are uncorrelated. The inner and outer *suburbium* can be divided in four quadrants that can roughly be associated with historical population groups (figure 7.6 and 7.7). The next step involves a subjective assessment of the landscape into three categories. The first landscape type is mixed, consisting of the potential fertile coastal and alluvial areas, as well as hill slopes and the slopes of mountainous areas. These areas would have potentially favoured high agricultural production and could have supported a large population density. The second category consists of upland areas, roughly in the range of

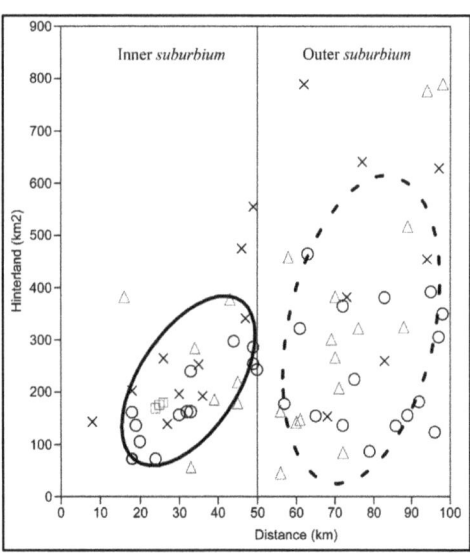

Figure 7.8: Bivariate analysis of the size of the hinterland for the inner and outer suburbium.

---

[10] Amiternum, at a distance of 77 km from Rome, and a hinterland of ca. 1,363 km^2, is considered an outlier, and has been excluded from analysis.

500-1,000 m altitude, and finally the mountainous area above 1,000 m. Additionally, the distance from Rome and the size of the hinterland, based on the construction of Thiessen polygons, was determined. The hinterlands of the civic centres located in hilly and mountainous areas are via this method underestimated due to two-dimensional distortion, but this is within an acceptable margin of error for the method.

The size of the civic centres has been excluded from the analysis, because this information exist for only 25% of the dataset. When the distance from Rome and the size of the hinterland are plotted then it can be confirmed that it is very plausible that the inner and outer *suburbium* had a different settlement density of towns and small towns. The size of the hinterland increases with distance from Rome. This effect is more profound for the outer *suburbium* (figure 7.8). A significant difference in the standard deviation for the hinterlands of the two datasets exists (110 versus 201 km^2), suggesting the possible presence of important dimensions, other than distance. One of these dimensions can be further analysed. The interpretation focuses on the first three quadrants, as the fourth quadrant covers a small area of land and just includes the settlements of Ostia, Fregenae and Lavinium. Although debatable in detail, quadrant one can be associated with Faliscan and Etruscan, the second with Sabine and potentially Umbrian, and the third quadrant with Latin and Volscian tribes.

The outcome of the bivariate analysis suggests that quadrant three has different properties from quadrant one and two. There is limited correlation between distance from Rome and the size of the hinterland for quadrant three, an area historically populated by Latins and Volscans. This region contains all different landscapes; mixed, upland and mountainous. This lack of correlation with distance from Rome, at least for the towns and large towns, undermines a demographic model based on a concentric *suburbium* zone to the south of Rome. This quadrant also has the lowest standard deviation in the size of the hinterland (105 km^2) compared to the two northern quadrants (200 km^2). This dense network pre-dates the Roman conquest of Latium (Cornell 2000), and the observed density cannot be explained by the impact of Rome only.

A better correlation between distance and size of hinterland exist for the quadrants north of Rome (figure 7.9), an area on which the extended *metropolis* model relies heavily. It can be debated if this increase in the size of the hinterland with increased distance to Rome can be attributed to the size and function of Rome during the Late Republican and Early Imperial periods. Moreover, the average interdistance for civic centres located north of Rome was 14.1 km with a radius of 8.8 km whereas the area south of Rome was more densely packed with civic centres at an average interdistance of 11.8 km and a radius of 7.3 km. A difference in settlement pattern between the more northern and southern regions of Etruria already existed in the Archaic

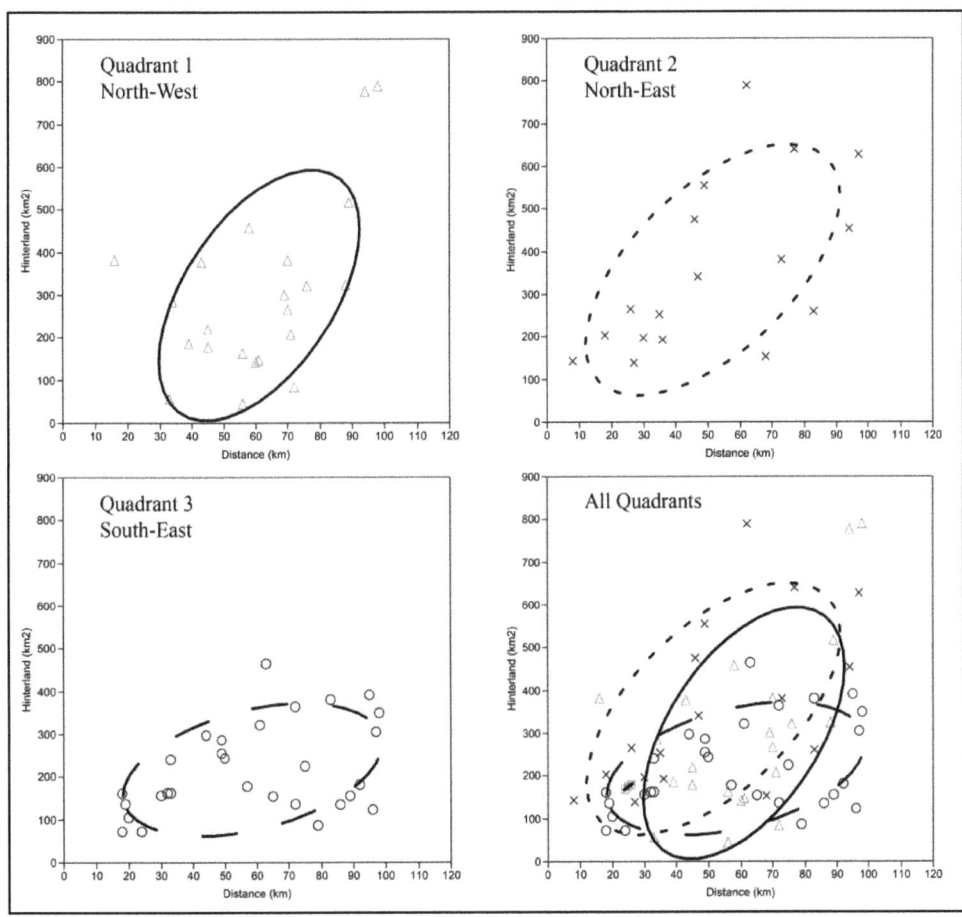

Figure 7.9: Bivariate analysis of regional variations based on a quadrant analysis of the suburbium.

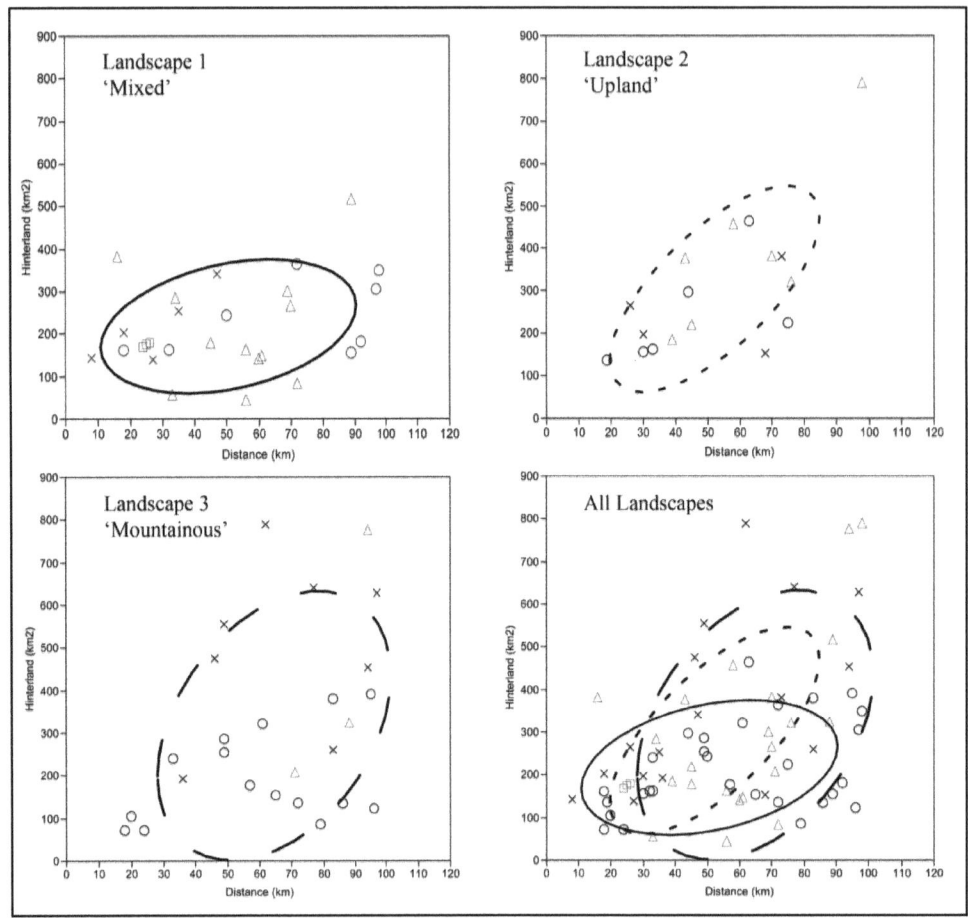

Figure 7.10: Bivariate analysis of regional variations by landscape type.

period (580-400 BC). The landscape of the northern region was more marginal resulting in a much less centralised settlement organisation focussed on subsistence farming, whereas the settlements in closer proximity to Rome were located on more fertile soil, and followed a different trajectory with a higher level of economic development (Spivey and Stoddart 1990, 56-61; Barker and Rasmussen 1998, 174-8).

A key dimension in the assessment of the *suburbium* model could be landscape. Although a crude classification has been applied, high level generalizations can potentially be formulated based on the bivariate analysis (figure 7.10). An interpretation of the results suggests that for the mixed landscape below ca. 500

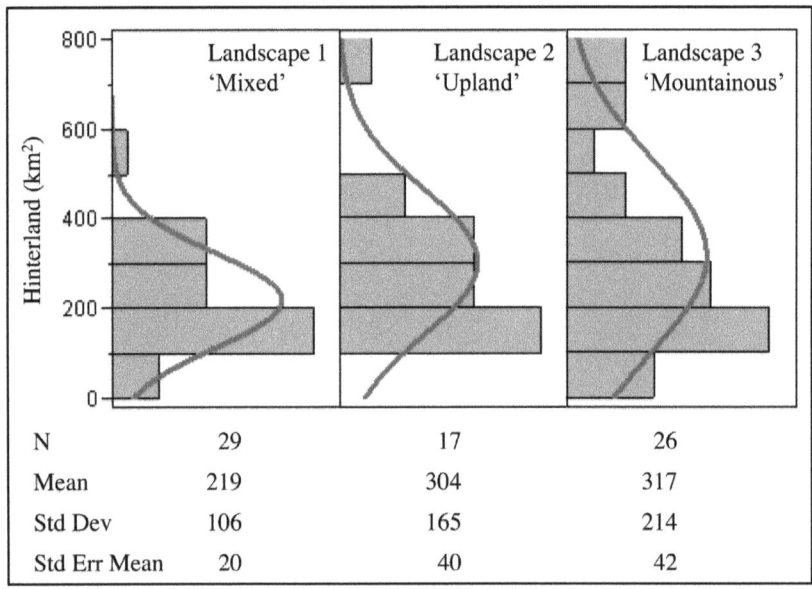

Figure 7.11: Distribution of size of hinterland per landscape type.

metres, a weak relationship between the distance from Rome and the size of the hinterland exists. The northern quadrants show more traits that can be associated with Witcher's expectation for the *suburbium* of Rome, with towns and small towns more densely patterned with proximity to Rome. For the upland located settlements the size of the hinterland increases with distance from Rome and, although this observation can also be made for the mountainous area, the difference in spread (width of the ellipse) is noteworthy. This could suggest that the locations of these towns are more driven by availability of resources, such as springs and marginal agricultural lands. The size-frequency distribution per landscape type confirms this observation. The mean and standard deviation values increase from mixed landscape to mountainous (figure 7.11). The difference would have been more noticeable if the hinterland of the civic centres located in hilly and mountainous areas, which are with the current method underestimated, was corrected.

The reassessment of the settlement pattern of towns and small towns reveals that the size of the hinterland increases with distance from Rome for the area to the north, but not significantly for the region to the south. Both observations can be explained by studying the Archaic Etruscan and Latin settlement patterns. By using a simple landscape classification it becomes clear that the mixed landscape with hill slopes, coastal areas and river flood plains was more densely settled with civic centres than the upland and mountainous areas, regardless of distance from Rome. Could the landscape have been an essential prerequisite for the early development of the region and later imprint of the settlement pattern and not the result of the presence of Rome?

Rural field surveys
The field survey summaries from the extended *metropolis* publication have been augmented with data from a later publication in which Witcher studied the settlement pattern and society in Early Imperial Etruria (Witcher 2006b), and the PhD dissertation of Goodchild in which Roman agricultural production in the Middle Tiber Valley has been modelled (Goodchild 2007). Several observations can be made based on this summary (table 7.4). Not all quadrants are represented equally and the extended *suburbium* model relies heavily on field survey data from the region north of Rome, especially the Tiber Valley. The area south of Rome is only represented by the Tusculum Survey, located within the 50 km radius from Rome, and the Liri Valley Survey, located on the outer *suburbium*. The introduced quadrant approach can also be applied for analysing the rural landscape. A plot of distance from Rome and site density suggests that site density is the highest for the inner *suburbium* and decreases with distance (figure 7.12). The civic centres that Purcell considers part of the suburban periphery are mentioned and have relatively high rural site densities. Witcher has suggested informed estimates for the densities of farms and *villae* for the Early Imperial period, based on published intensive field surveys. He assumed, based on a subset of table 7.4, an average rural density of two farms and one *villa* per km^2 for the inner (dotted line A), and 1.5 farms and 0.2 *villae* per km^2 for the outer *suburbium* (dotted line B) (Witcher 2005, 127-9). When viewed as the sum of farms and *villae*, used for the *suburbium* model, these numbers could represent a mean of the individual data points (figure 7.12). Although Witcher argues that his data shows declining site densities in the outer *suburbium*, the use of an average

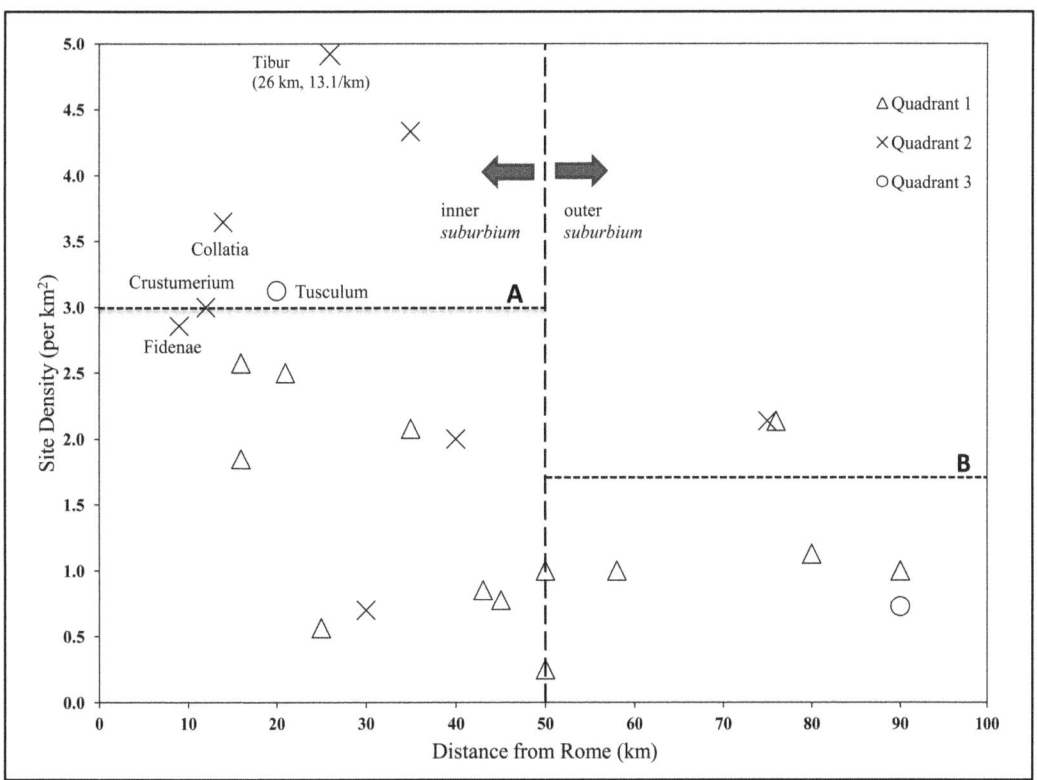

Figure 7.12: Distance from Rome versus site density during the Imperial period.

Table 7.4: Field surveys in the inner and outer suburbium (after Goodchild 2007; Witcher 2005; Witcher 2006b).

Distance from Rome	Suburbium Model	Quadrant	Field Survey	Survey Area (km²)	Density (sites/km²)	% Villae	Farms (per km²)	Villae (per km²)
35	X (Coast)	Inner 1	Caere	90	2.1	c. 30%		
16		Inner 1	Veii	118.5	2.6		1.2	1.3
16		Inner 1	East of Veii	57.4	1.8		1.0	0.8
45		Inner 1	*Ager Faliscus*	210.3	0.8	20-30%	0.5	0.3
43		Inner 1	Sutri	90.4	0.9		0.5	0.3
25		Inner 1	*Via Cassia & Via Clodia*	140.2	0.6		0.2	0.4
21		Inner 1	Torrimpietra	96	2.5	c. 20%		
50		Inner 1	Vicus Matrini	192	0.3	c. 15%		
50		Inner 1	Civitella Cesi	96	1	c. 15%		
35	X (North)	Inner 2	Cures Sabini	3	4.3		2.0	2.0
9	X (North)	Inner 2	Fidenae	31.5	2.9	c. 20%		
30		Inner 2	*Ager Capenas*	247.7	0.7		0.3	0.4
26	X (East)	Inner 2	Tibur	6.5	13.1			
14	X (South)	Inner 2	Collatia	96	3.6		1.5	2.5
12		Inner 2	Crustumerium	33	3	Significant		
40		Inner 2	Farfa	35	2	c. 33%+		
20	X (East)	Inner 3	Tusculum	96	3.1			
80	X (Coast)	Outer 1	Tarquinii/Vulci	55	1.1	c. 33%		
76	X (North)	Outer 1	Tuscania	96	2.1			
58		Outer 1	Blera	96	1	Few		
90		Outer 1	Vulci/Bolsena	100	1	Significant		
75	X (North)	Outer 2	Rieti basin	22	2.1			
90	X (South)	Outer 3	Liri Valley	125	0.7			

site density or the construction of a trend line for the inner and outer *suburbium* inadequately represents the very broad scatter of points on the graph. Moreover, site densities should be interpreted with great care because they have not been corrected for differences in survey intensity, visibility and site typology.

Wilson explored if the Von Thünen model of agricultural location would apply to Rome by studying the distribution of large rural cisterns (200-700 m³) and *villae*, and associating them with irrigated horticulture (Wilson 2008). Wilson his study focussed on 96 cisterns in *Latium Vetus* and South Etruria. The density of these large cisterns increases with proximity to Rome and along the Tiber where favourable transport costs can be expected. This pattern is in agreement with the rural settlement pattern that Potter described for the Imperial period in South Etruria and the Tiber Valley. Wilson recognises that it is not possible to present precise figures for the density of such large cisterns, but mentions that the number is abnormally high compared to the rest of Italy. He sees this as an archaeological indicator of intensive market gardening focussed on Rome (Wilson 2008, 732-3, 746-9). In 1994, Bintliff suggested a zone of market market gardening around Classical Athens based on the increased village *deme* density (Bintliff 1994, 237).

The survey data can also be viewed differently by taking the size of the survey area into consideration via the calculation of a weighted site density for the Early Imperial period. Witcher suggested a rural population reconstruction with a denser rural inner *suburbium* versus a less densely rural populated outer *suburbium*. This hypothesis can be considered possible based on the plot of distance from Rome against total site density (figure 7.12), but not evident from the perspective of weighted site densities per quadrant (figure 7.13). In addition, as already shown on figure 7.12, only two points in quadrant three physically conformed to this trend.

The quadrants north of Rome have a lower weighted site density for the inner zone than for the outer zones. However, the site density of the outer quadrant two has been based on the outcome of only the Rieti Survey, which covered an area of 22 km². The weighted site density for quadrant three represents the only quadrant that explicitly meets the logic of Witcher. The data for this quadrant have also been based on limited survey data, and are contradictory to the observation made on the densities of towns and small towns for quadrant three. Based on this weighted site density analysis per quadrant, a rationale that uses a site density of 3 sites/km² for the inner, and 1.7 sites/km² for the outer *suburbium* is hard to sustain, unless different site recovery ratios per survey are

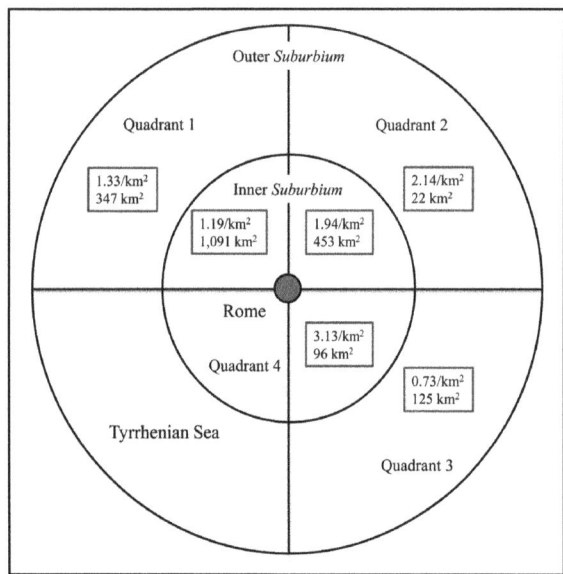

Figure 7.13: Weighted site densities and total survey area per quadrant for the inner and outer suburbium.

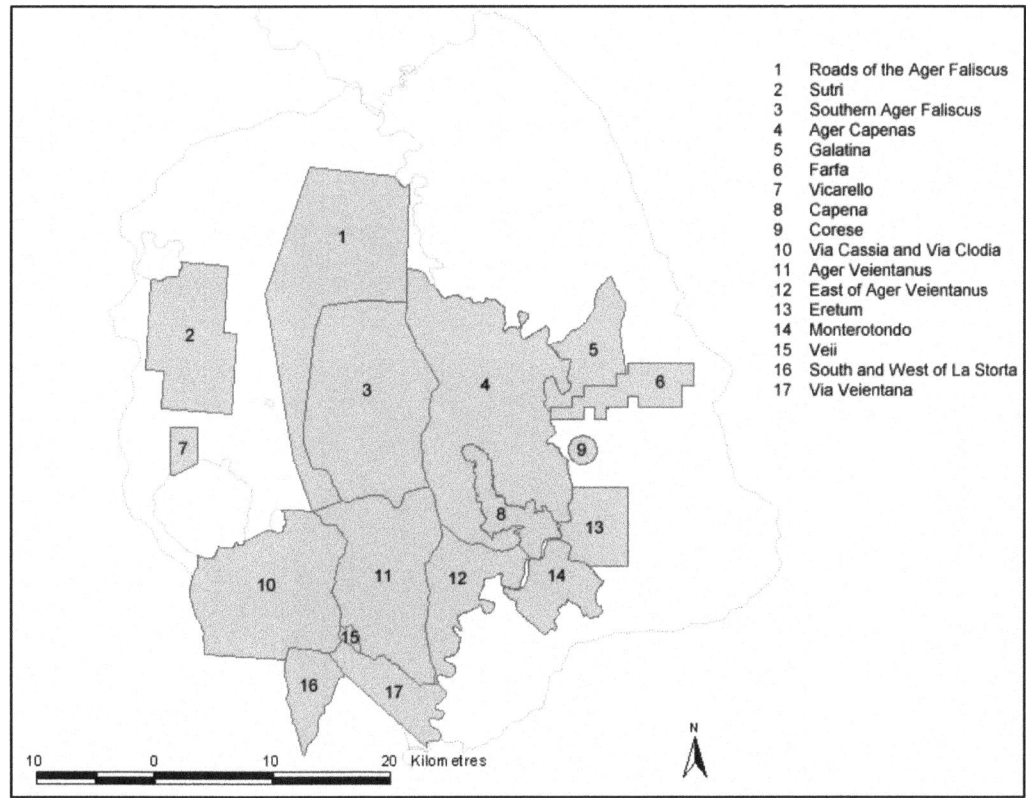

Figure 7.14: Location of the South Etruria Surveys within the study area (Goodchild 2007, 68, fig 2.12).

hypothesized and more surveys are taken into consideration, especially the survey data from the Pontine Region Project. Witcher refrained from making an estimate of the recovery ratio for the *suburbium*, but it is unlikely that all sites have been recovered. He also recognizes that introducing site recovery into the argumentation could push the population density above 100 persons/km^2. Such a density, which is based on ca. one hectare per person per annum in a biennial fallowing system, would approach the limits of self-sufficiency, based on early modern, pre-industrial dry-farming (Witcher 2008b, 290). Jongman has suggested that dry-farming in a two-fold system differentiated the Mediterranean from Northern Europe. However, he indicates that a system of short-fallow, so a higher intensity, would allow for higher population densities, such as for Campania, which he considered an exception. A key issue that he highlights is that biennial fallowing would allow the land to retain more water than possible when more (labour) intensive cultivation is pursued (Jongman 1988, 78-83). It is not fully clear why agricultural intensification could not have happened in the Roman *suburbium*?

Goodchild suggest that the most likely agricultural practice for the Middle Tiber Valley was quarter-fallowed intercropping at a reasonably high rate of production; a yield of 8-15:1 (Goodchild 2007, 390). Her study area measures 2,600 km^2 (Goodchild 2007, 4), of which the South Etruria Surveys cover ca. 920 km^2 (figure 7.14). She used available survey data for locational analysis and combined the outcome of this analysis with a study of literary sources, information on nineteenth-twentieth century AD smallholders in Italy, and productivity estimates to decide on the hypothetical average size of the land under cultivation by a *villa* or farm. A 12 *iugera* plot (ca. 3,1 ha) represents a veteran allotment at 200 metre interdistance. At a four-fold yield, this plot would only suffice for subsistence farming. Without access to other food sources a larger plot would be required (Goodchild 2007, 100-20, 328). A 100 *iugera* plot for a *villae* (25 ha), would support 14-26 people at a four-fold yield (Goodchild 2007, 326-7). The carrying capacity and the potential agricultural production at higher yields and heavy sowing rates would have supported a more dense settlement pattern of farms and medium sized *villae* and provide surplus for the non-agricultural population living towns and small towns (Goodchild 2007, 375, 383-4)

Rural population densities

The *suburbium* model has been based on site densities per km^2 of 2 farms and 1*villa* for the inner, and 1.5 farms and 0.2 *villae* for the outer *suburbium*. These densities equate, when using Witcher's informed estimated individuals per site (8 for a farm and 25 for a *villae*) and definition of cultivatable land, to a rural population density of 41 persons/km^2 for the 50 km radius and 17 persons/km^2 for the outer ring. Although these estimated numbers of individuals per site take the middle ground between what other scholars have published, a scenario with higher site densities and lower individuals per site could also be envisioned, especially in view of Egyptian census numbers (Bagnall and Frier 1994). Such a reconstruction would consider survey intensity, site-specific recovery ratios, fuzzy site classifications and alternate population estimates per farm and *villae*. In her study, Goodchild provides a summary of the proportion

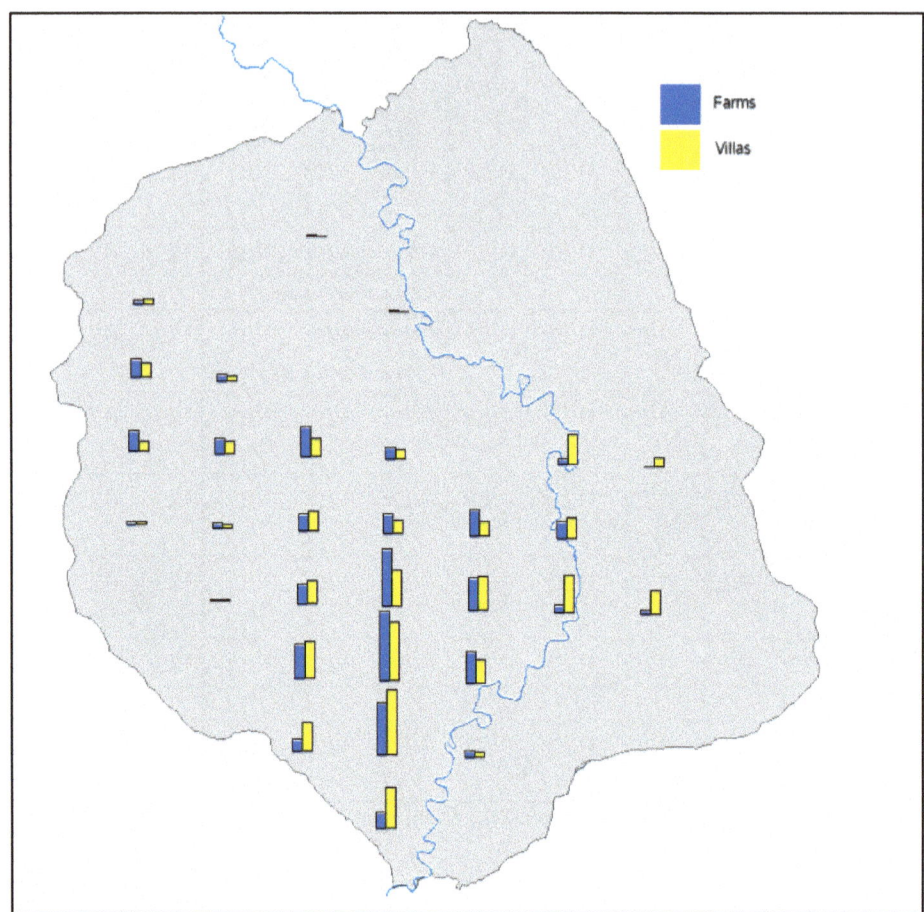
Figure 7.15: The proportion of farms to villae in the Early Imperial period (Goodchild 2007, 107, fig 3.7).

of farms to *villae* for the Middle Tiber Valley in the Early Imperial period (figure 7.15). This graphic representation suggests a ratio of farms to *villae* very close to one. The ratio between farms and *villae* that Witcher used suggests that differentiated recovery ratios were hypothesized, which can also be seen in table 7.4, which contains conflicting data for the percentage *villae* versus the reported site density of farms and *villae*. Besides overlapping and/or incomplete site classification and recovery ratios, also functional aspects can be debated. A *villa* probably had outbuildings that are currently counted as individual farms, and individual farms could actually be part of a villa/farm estate.

If the assumption is made that the typical nucleated family on a farm consisted of 5.5 people, a typical *villa* was populated by 15 people, and a hypothetical site recovery ratio of 50% for farms and 80% for *villae* are assumed, then the rural population density for the inner *suburbium* would result in the same number, 41 persons/km^2. The landscape of the area around Rome would then be more densely built-up and the perception of contemporary travellers could be guided towards a perceived higher population density.

The suburbium of Classical Athens

The Greek world offers an interesting opportunity to compare the *suburbium* of the *megalopolis* of Rome with its Greek counterpart, the *suburbium* of the *megalopolis* of Athens during the Late Archaic and Early Classical period. The walls of Classical Athens enclosed an area of 211 ha (Bintliff 1994, 234) and the territory of Attica is estimated at ca. 2,500 km^2. Traill reconstructed the 139 deme-villages on late sixth century BC Kleisthenic reforms. The number of representatives per deme in the council has been used as a proxy for population size, suggesting that town like settlements were hidden in the settlement hierarchy (Traill 1986). The deme system (figure 7.16) shows a complete coverage of all the cultivable land by modular village territories with a significant smaller radius of 1.72 km (ca. 9 km^2) for the villages in the immediate hinterland of Athens versus the average radius of a deme territory of 2.53 km (ca. 20 km^2) (Bintliff 1994, 234). The deme-villages in the immediate hinterland form a cluster, running east and west from Athens on the plain around the *megalopolis*, suggesting a *suburbium* area with a radius of ca. 8 km from the town wall, covering ca. 200 km^2. Bintliff suggested a different land use for this area, most probably market gardening (Bintliff 1994, 237). The Early Iron Age *ager Romanus* was double this area and the settlement pattern and agricultural practices can also be described by building on the Von Thünen model of agricultural location.

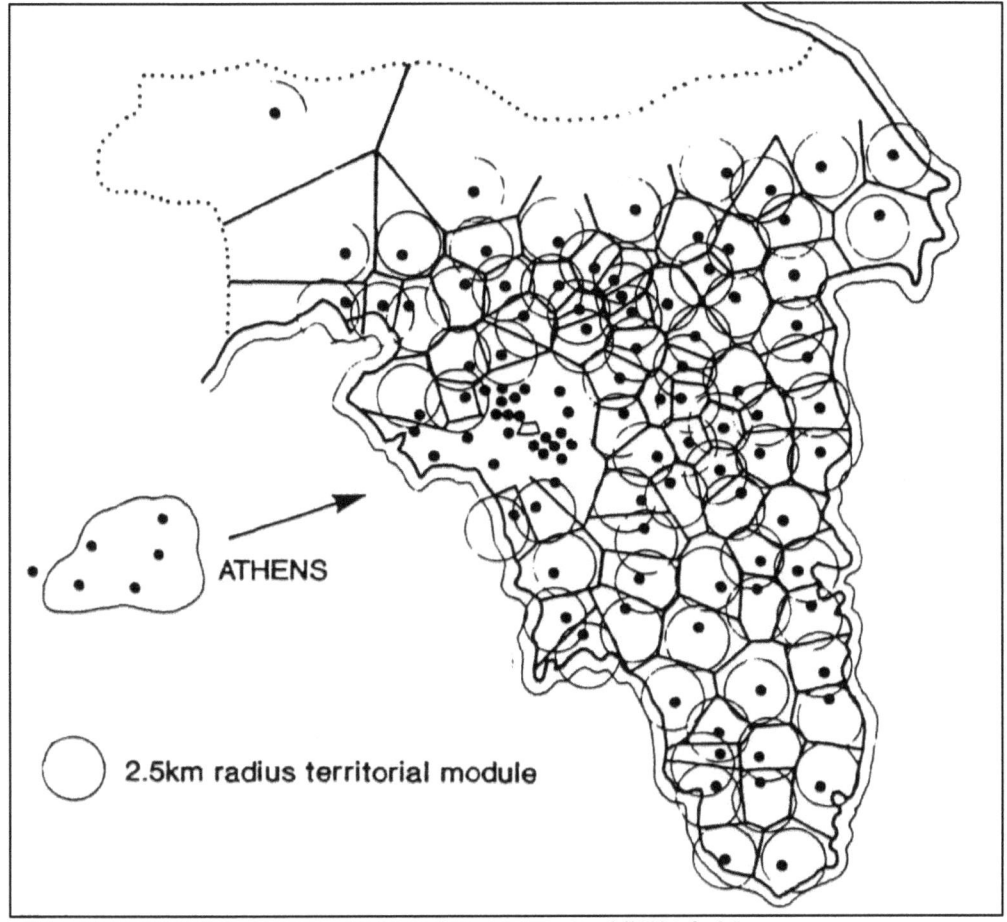

Figure 7.16: Thiessen analysis of the rural deme-villages in Attica (Bintliff 1994, fig 36).

In an area the size of Attica (2,500 km²), which equals to a ca. 30 km radius from the centre of Rome, fifteen civic centres[11] are located and an additional six civic centres[12] are located in the 30 to 35 km radius. With the help of the Barrington Atlas, at least 34 villages and 15 road stations can, on first inspection, be identified within this 30 km radius. As mentioned earlier; Attica contained 139 attested villages with a hinterland of 9 km² for the inner zone and 20 km² for the outer zone. Each of the 64 Roman nucleated settlements within a 30 km from the centre of Rome had a hinterland of ca. 38 km² (a radius of ca. 3.5 km). This means that the density of nucleated settlements surrounding Rome was less dense compared to Athens, but Rome had a significantly larger population. Although the absolute population of Athens and Attica is still debated, a population in the range of 120-200,000 has been suggested; a population density of 48 to 80 persons/km² for the Classical period, including the *polis* of Athens. An upper range of 110 to 130,000 people has been established based on the carrying capacity of Attica, resulting in grain imports to sustain the high estimated population density (Cavanagh 2009, 405, 406 ft 1). Excluding Athens, the density at an estimated total population of 200,000 is in the same ballpark range as envisioned by Witcher for the Roman *suburbium*, but the carrying capacity of the latter could have supported a higher population density.

Discussion

In the introduction to this chapter, a general belief of historians and archaeologists with respect to the uniqueness of the (inner) *suburbium* of Rome in terms of settlement and population densities was highlighted. The demographic model that Witcher developed has been challenged and further refined in this chapter. Locational analysis and a bivariate analysis that uses a quadrant approach of the inner and outer *suburbium* suggest that the settlement pattern around Rome is structured and organised around landscape and the carrying capacity of the immediate hinterland. Moreover, most of the later Roman civic centres have pre-Roman archaic antecedents. The area north from Rome seems to conform to the model that Witcher developed, but also landscape plays a dominant role in the settlement pattern for this region. Limited correlation was found between distance from Rome and the size of the hinterland for the areas originally populated by Latins and Volscans. The increase in density of farms and villae, as well as large cisterns when approaching Rome could indicate a zone of intensive market gardening that is in agreement with the Von Thünen model of agricultural location.

---

[11] Veii, Lucus Feroniae, Fidenae, Capena, Nomentum, Tibur, Aricia, Castrimoenium, Tusculum, Bovillae, Lanuvium, Gabii, Ostia, Fregenae and Lavinium.

[12] Alsium, Caere, Cures, Ardea, Velitrae and Praeneste.

How sustainable is the view on the uniqueness of the (inner) *suburbium* of Rome compared to for instance the Potenza Valley, a region discussed in previous chapter? The average size of the immediate hinterland of the towns and small towns within the 50 km radius from Rome, based on the construction of Thiessen polygons, is ca. 223 km^2. The size of the hinterland of towns and small towns of the Potenza Valley is 153 km^2 for the centres with civic status. The road station of Prolaqueum, located in the mountainous upper valley, has a theoretical hinterland of 159 km^2. The landscapes of both regions are very comparable. When Rome and Ostia are considered special cases, the average size of the towns with known size is ca. 23 ha for the *suburbium* compared to 17 ha for the centres of the Potenza Valley. This puts the centres of the Potenza Valley in the same size and potential population as Nepet, Sutrium, Roman Veii and Cora. Although there are indications for hamlets, the Potenza Valley seems to lack villages. The *suburbium* has a complete settlement hierarchy as well as an elaborate road system leading to Rome. The limited area of the Potenza Valley compared to the Roman *suburbium* could potentially mask the presence of a settlement hierarchy for the wider region of Picenum.

The rural density of the *suburbium*, represented by two farms and one *villa*/km^2 for the Early Imperial period, can also be compared with the densities of these types of sites in the Potenza Valley. The high intensity survey in the lower, middle and upper Potenza Valley revealed a site density of 5.2 farms and 1 *villa*/km^2 for the Earlier Imperial period based on a site typology in which the farms are grouped with small *villae*, and *villae rusticae* are counted as *villae*. Although can argue about the relative small survey area and the proximity of the three survey areas to the civic centres, a picture emerges in which the Potenza Valley, with an estimated rural population density, including hamlets, of ca. 68 persons/km^2 is at least as populated as the inner Roman *surburbium* for which the rural population was modelled at 41 persons/km^2. Both densities contain uncorrected numbers. Would survey intensity be the dominant bias in comparing intensive field surveys? Could the suburbium have been (at least) as densely populated as the Potenza Valley?

The area that can provide additional insights in the organisation, functioning and spread of the population in the surroundings of Rome, which takes a landscape approach, is the Pontine region.

8   The Land Systems of the Pontine Region

The Pontine Region (figure 1.1) falls within the 50 to 100 km radii from Rome that Witcher studied for building his extended *metropolis* and *suburbium* demographic model (Witcher 2005). He did not consider the fieldwork by the Groningen Institute of Archaeology (GIA) and recent publications offer the opportunity to study and refine regional population differences. The outcome of this study can also be discussed in a broader context, especially the growth of the population of Rome and the demographic impact on this sub-region of Latium. In the previous chapter, it has been argued that landscape was a key driver to variations in micro-region demography. The quality of the GIA publications puts an ecological approach based on land systems within reach. A land system is an area or group of areas with a recurring pattern of landforms, soils and vegetation important to its agricultural potential (Attema and Van Leusen 2004, 163).

The Pontine region is located in modern-day Lazio, ca. 60 km south of Rome, and comprises the formerly marshy Pontine plain bordered to the northwest by the volcanic area of the Alban hills and a part of the Sacco Valley, and to the northeast by the Monti Lepini and the Monti Ausoni. The boundaries of the region vary in the numerous publications, resulting in the in- or exclusion of major settlements. The area that has been arbitrarily demarcated on Map 44 of the Barrington Atlas covers ca. 1,850 km^2 (figure 8.1).

Nucleated settlements
Roman expansion and domination of *Latium Vetus* was achieved through the foundation of *coloniae* on strategic locations, and the outcome of the Latin War (340-338 BC), resulting in Rome granting *municipia* status to several of the large Latin centres (Attema and Van Leusen 2004, 158; Cornell 2000, 209-11). The construction of the *Via Appia*, at the end of the fourth century BC, is considered important for agricultural and commercial developments in the central part of the plain (Attema and De Haas 2004, 2).

Pliny has listed the following settlements: Antium, Circeii, Aricia, Alba Longa, Cora, Forum Appii, Norba, Setia, Signia, and Velitrae. An obvious omission is the *municipium* of Lanuvium (Afzelius 1942a, 51-3). Of special notice is the absence of the Latin towns Artena, Satricum (ca. 40 ha) and Pometia from this list. Livy

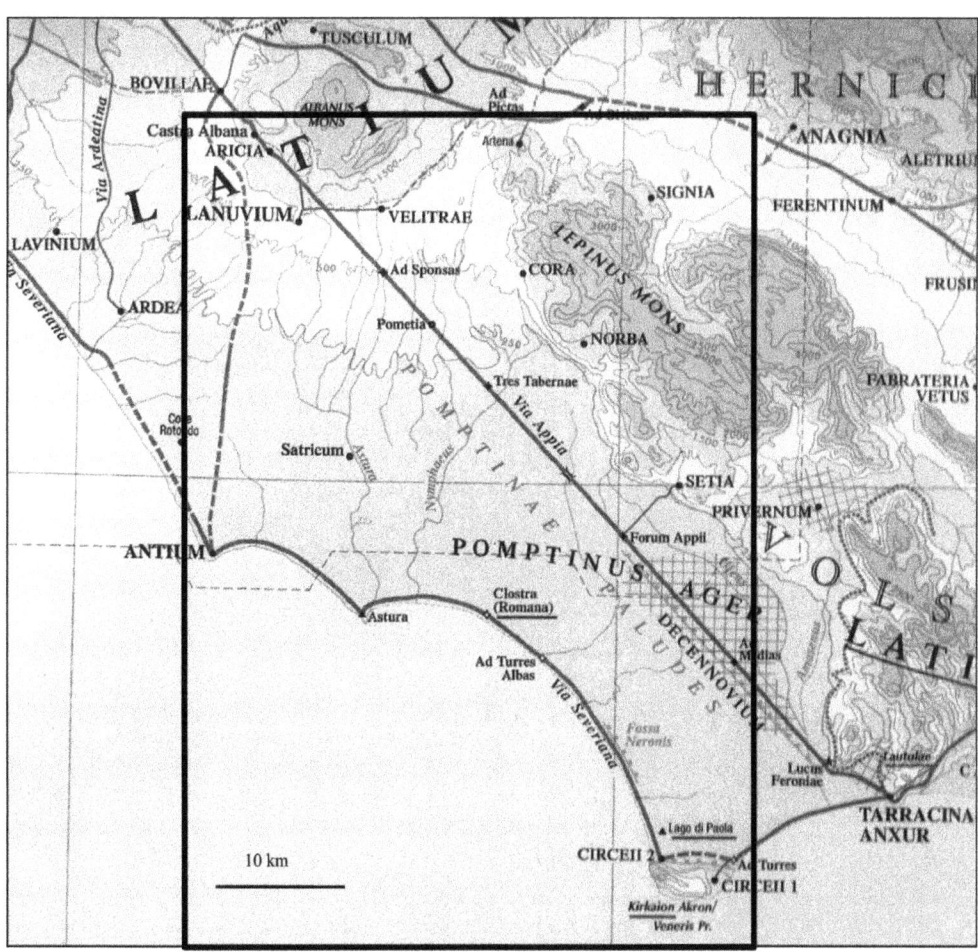

Figure 8.1: Approximate geography covered by the Pontine region (after Talbert 2000, map 44).

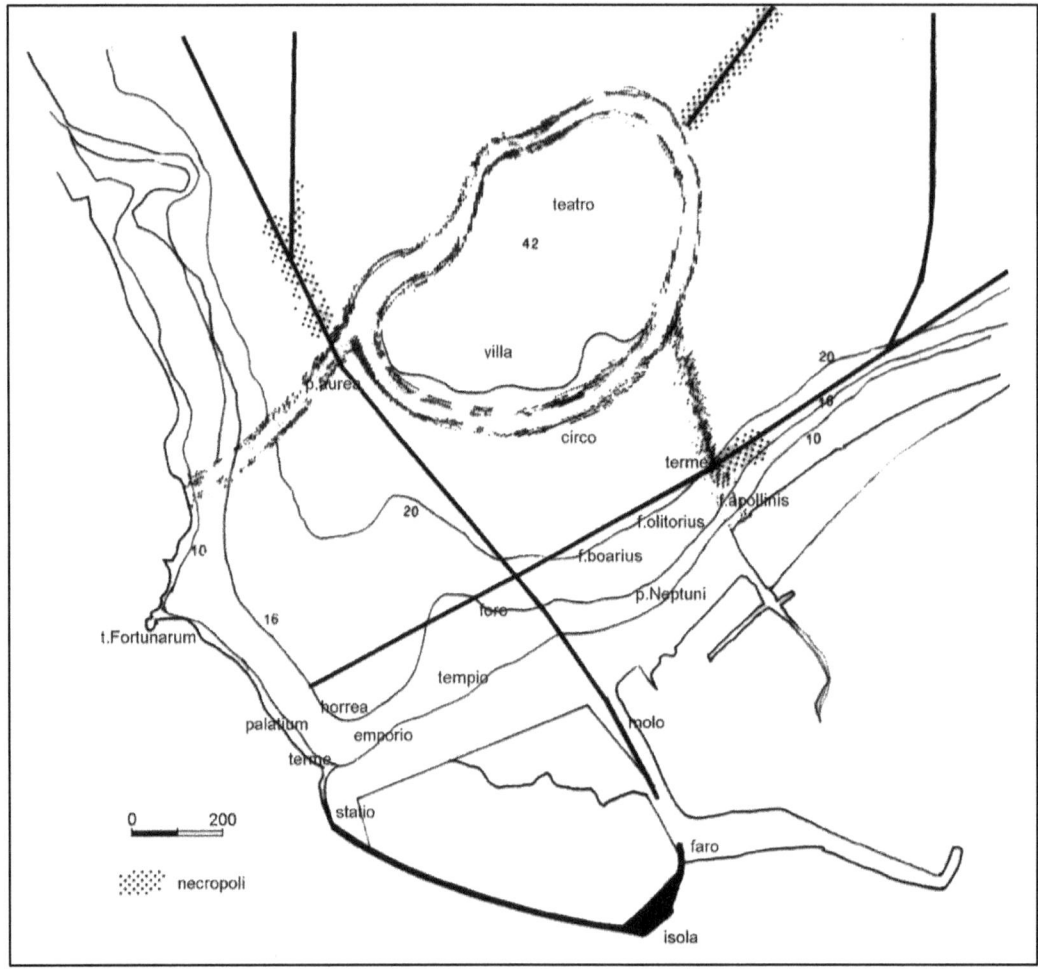

Figure 8.2: Antonine period urban features of Antium (Brandizzi Vittucci 2000, 119, fig 56).

wrote that the last two had ceased to exist (Livy N.H. 3.9; Cornell 1995, 204). Excavations at Artena (ca. 20 ha) indicate that this town was abandoned in the course of the third century BC (Coarelli 1993, 172). The walled area of the *coloniae* of Signia (15.5 ha), Cora (20 ha), Setia (12) and Norba (40 ha) can be determined based on the town plans collected and published by Coarelli (Coarelli 1993, 173-8, 254-78). Norba was abandoned in 81 BC after its devastation by Sulla (Van Leusen *et al.* 2005, 321-2). On the map in the Barrington Atlas the above-mentioned chronological refinements are absent for Artena, Norba, Satricum and Pometia. Citing ancient sources, Brunt painted a picture of thriving Latin towns that disappeared or were faced with declining populations in the Republican period, and of large areas of uncultivated land. In his personal view, the region was not so desolate and dominated by estates (Brunt 1987, 347-50). A settlement size of 70 to 120 ha has been proposed for Roman Antium, based on the location of *necropoleis*, tombs, *villae* and public buildings (Attema and De Haas forthcoming; Attema *et al.* 2009, 27-30). Roman Antium consisted of an upper town and a harbour area that was established during the reign of Nero (figure 8.2). The ancient town lies unfortunately under modern-day Anzio, and the urban make-up of the Roman town remains obscure. Latin Antium has an estimated urban area of 25 ha (Cornell 1995, 204). It is not unlikely that there was a concentration of people living near the harbour, but it is debatable if the area between the upper town and the harbour was densely populated resulting in a population of 10,000 people during the Early Imperial period, as postulated by Attema (Attema and De Haas forthcoming). For population calculations, an area of 25 ha will be used for the Late Republican period and a guesstimated 45 ha for the first century AD based on figure 8.2. The size of Circeii, Lanuvium, Velitrae and Aricia are not known and require an educated estimate. The assumption is made that the urban area would be in the same range as Signia, Cora and Setia, which is ca. 16 ha. It is not unlikely that Forum Appii only covered a few hectares. However, there are several large *Fora* (market-centres), especially in Cisalpine Gaul that exceeded their original function and their sizes are significant, with Forum Corneli and Forum Livii being in the 30 ha range (De Ligt 2008, 170). The Barrington Atlas also shows several road stations. Three are located on the *Via Appia* (Ad Sponsas, Tres Tabernae and Ad Medias) and three, dating to a later chronology on the *Via Severiana*.

The area covered by the large nucleated settlements shows a decrease from the period before the Latin War (ca. 242 ha), through the Late Republican (ca. 177 ha) and up to the Early Imperial (ca. 157 ha) periods. This decline can be attributed to the abandonment of Latin towns, such as Artena, Satricum and Pometia, as well as

Table 8.1: Intercentre distance for the Pontine region in the Late Republican period.

Civic Centre	Nearest Centre	Distance (km)	2nd Nearest Centre	Distance (km)	Avg. Distance (km)	Avg. Radius (km)
Antium	Ardea	19.5	Lanuvium	25.5	22.5	14,1
Cora	Norba	7.0	Signia	11.5	9.3	5,8
Norba	Cora	7.0	Signia	12.0	9.5	5,9
Signia	Norba	11.5	Cora	7.0	9.3	5,8
Setia	Privernum	11.0	Norba	13.0	12.0	7,5
Velitrae	Lanuvium	6.5	Aricia	9.5	8.0	5,0
Circeii	Terracina	16.5	Setia	28.0	22.3	13,9
Lanuvium	Aricia	6.0	Velitae	6.5	6.3	3,9
Aricia	Bovillae	5.8	Lanuvium	5.8	5.8	3,6
			Average		11.6	7,3

the *colonia* Norba, suggesting a population decline of people living in the major centres. One possible explanation could be that a shift in the distribution of the population occurred from the Latin towns to the countryside and to Rome. The former would suggest a different level of urbanisation after the Latin War and the latter a general decline in the population of the region.

The size of the urban population
An educated guess of the size of the population that lived within the major centres can be made by multiplying the total area of the major centres by an estimated population density. The obvious point of reference would be Roman Pompeii. The population estimates for Pompeii (ca. 64.7 ha) are between 10,000 and 30,000 people resulting in a density between 154 to 462 persons/ha (Morley 2008, 123). Wallace-Hadrill narrowed this wide range, after a detailed study of the urban make-up, to 120-300 persons/ha (Wallace-Hadrill 1994, 96). Additional information comes from the size of the theatre, which could hold up to 5,000, and the amphitheatre, which could seat up to 20,000 spectators in the Augustan period (Zanker 1998, 45-6, 70). This could suggest that many people from the countryside and neighbouring towns visited the games or that the amphitheatre primarily would welcome spectators from Pompeii. The latter would mean a population density that was closer to the upper limit of 300 persons/ha. Important considerations for the high estimates are the frequent occurrences of multi-storey buildings, and for the more humble estimates the area that was not built on. As argued before, the upper floor of private houses belonged to the ground floor and do not represent multiple ownership, unless it is an apartment block. The presence of extra-mural architecture at Pompeii suggests that Pompeians also lived outside its town walls. Evidence for market gardens and animal husbandry within the walls of Pompeii however has been found. The agricultural produce included wine from small-scale vineyards, olive oil, nuts and fruits, and was sold on the markets of Pompeii. The presence of agricultural plots within the walled area supports a modest population density (Laurence 2007, 77-8). The urban make-up of the centres of the Pontine region, especially the presence of multi-storey buildings as found in Pompeii, remains to be proven. A population density of 120-200 persons/ha will be used for estimating the size of the population living in the main centres. This results in a population range of 21,000-35,500 for the Late Republican and 19,000-31,500 for the Early Imperial period (11-19 resp. 10-17 persons/km^2).

Medium and small villages seem to be absent in the settlement pattern. The average distance between the civic centres of the Augustan *regione* I (*Latium et Campania*), reported by Bekker-Nielsen is 11.0 km, with a range between the smallest and the largest distance of 5 to 21 km (Bekker-Nielsen 1989, 26, tab 6.4). Within his line of reasoning, these settlements can be classified as having a primitive or *polis*-type urbanisation (Bekker-Nielsen 1989, 65). This *regione* has the highest density of civic centres in Roman Italy. The theoretical radius of the hinterland, following Bekker-Nielsen's methodology, can be calculated as half the average intercentre distance multiplied by 1.25 to allow for overlapping hinterlands, forming polygonal areas (Bekker-Nielsen 1989, 29). This results in an average interdistance of 11.6 km for the Pontine region and a typical radius of the hinterland of 7.3 km for the Late Republican period up to the destruction of Norba (table 8.1) and an average interdistance of 12.7 km and a radius of 7.9 km for the period thereafter. This metric suggests that day-return trips to the civic centres were possible from all directions, theoretically reducing the functional need for lower order settlements. Does this observation also imply that the majority of the population lived in urban centres? The size of the urban to rural population depends on the rural population reconstruction of the countryside.

Table 8.2: Land systems and intensive surveys used for rural demographic estimates.

Land System	% of Pontine Region	Area (km^2)	GIA Survey	Survey Area (ha)
Alban Hills	20	370	Lanuvium	407
Lepine Margins	9	167	Norba/ Ninfa, Signia, Setia	1,101.5
Marine Terraces and the Astura Valley	30	555	Nettuno and Astura	816
Coastal Margins	7	130	Fogliano	300
Graben/Pontine Plain	13	240	Publication forthcoming	-
Volcano Lazale and Lepine Mountains	21	388	Hidden Landscape Project	-
Total	100%	1,850		2,624.5

Intensive rural field surveys
Archaeological enquiry in the Pontine region has a long tradition going back to the 1980's. The high quality publications by the Groningen Institute of Archaeology (GIA) are very relevant for the development of demographic estimates and comparative studies. The Pontine Region Project intensive field surveys cover a wide range of very diverse sample areas from different land systems. What are the differences in site densities for the different land systems and how do they compare to Witcher's modelled estimates? The identified land systems of the Pontine region are the Volcano Laziale (1), the Alban hills (2), the upper graben (3), the coastal zone (4), the Astura Valley (5), the Monti Lepini and Ausoni (6), the foothills (7), the lower graben (8) and (9) the marine terraces (figure 8.3). A graben is a depressed block of land bordered by parallel faults. The Pontine Marshes were a former lagoon that became filled-up with clay sediments (Attema and De Haas 2005, 11).

The volcanic land system of the Alban hills has highly fertile but poorly drained soils, which will have supported arable farming and offered possibilities for pasturing. The land system of the Lepine foothills consist of the Lepine mountains, the colluvial foot slopes, an alluvial cone, tuff hills and the alluvial Pontine plain. This land system was suitable for cereal farming and specialisation on olive culture (Attema and De Haas 2005, 101-2). The Pontine plain, consisting of the upper and lower graben, is a flat area between the monti Lepini to the northeast and the beach ridges to the southwest. It consists of a depressed area (former Pontine Marshes) and fluvio-colluvial areas. The land use, settlement pattern and density of the Pontine plain are currently under investigation. The Via Appia, constructed at the end of the fourth century BC, would have opened up the plain for potential agricultural exploitation and commercial activities. The Astura River runs from the Alban hills to the Tyrrhenian coast and has a dendritic drainage system upstream consisting of several small rivers. The Astura basin consists of the well-drained Astura Valley and the beach ridge area that extends to the northwest and southeast. The marine terraces of the coastal zone are an area with beaches, dunes and large lagoons, extending all the way along the Tyrrhenian coast from the Tiber delta to Terracina. This land system was especially suitable for olive cultivation (Attema and De Haas 2005, 103-5). Four rural settlement patterns of four land systems, covering ca. 1.4% of the total area, will be at the basis of the population estimates (table 8.2). The publication of the more recent fieldwork on the Pontine plain, which makes up a large portion of the agricultural potential of the region, is pending, as well as more recent work in the Hidden Landscape Project.

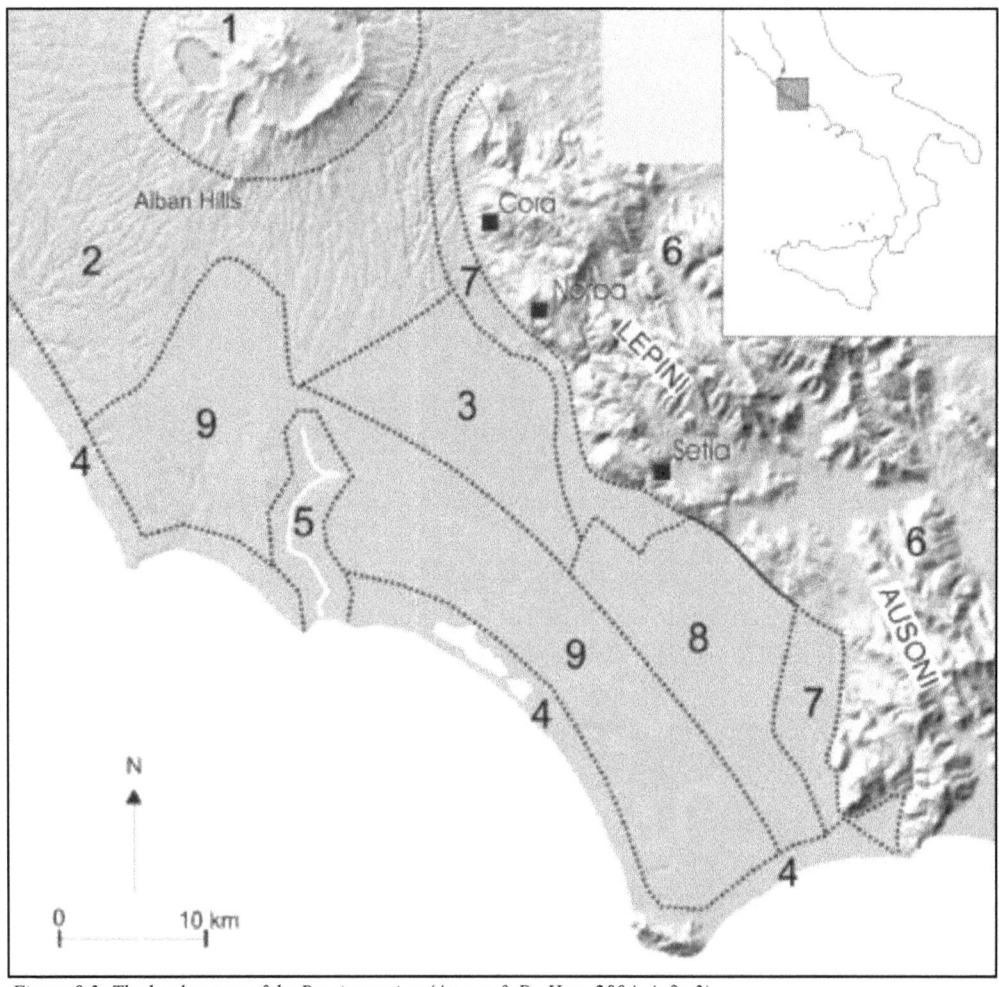

Figure 8.3: The land system of the Pontine region (Attema & De Haas 2004, 4, fig 3).

Table 8.3: Site typology for the Fogliano survey (Attema et al. 2005, 130).

Site	Scatter (m²)	Description
Small	< 1,050	No coarse or finewares, but only tile, *amphora* and *dolium*: probably a storage area
		Complete pottery assembly and building remains: farms
		Incomplete ceramic assemblage and building remains: could represent storage areas/outbuildings, farms or rural cemeteries
Large	2,500-7,800	Complete and often large ceramic assemblage, building remains and sometimes glass or metal finds: large farms
		Complete and large ceramic assemblage and building remains, glass, coins, marble and sculpture: *villa*
Very large	> 2 ha	Complete pottery assemblage, building remains. Can include evidence for metal working and pottery production: village
Roads		Presence of pavement stones
Tombs		Small size and occurrence of tiles and pottery
Indeterminate		Insufficient information or doubts about status

A detailed pottery classification that relates pottery sherds from the Lanuvium survey to well-defined pottery groups from stratigraphical context at Satricum has been developed (Attema 2000). This classification included local fabrics, coarse fabrics, and fabrics with volcanic inclusions. It excludes imported materials and finewares, such as black glaze wares and *terra sigillata*. Existing classifications for the latter two were used. The main criteria for judging sherds were the colour of the clay matrix and the sorting and types of mineral and other inclusions. This resulted in the identification of 114 ceramic reference types of which 60 were considered locally produced, representing 67% of the total number of sherds. The majority belong to storage vessels, cooking wares and roof tiles. The remaining 54 reference types relate to imported *amphorae* and jugs, to local or imported depurated pottery, black glaze and *terra sigillata* wares (Attema 2000, 416-7). Although a detailed classification of black glaze pottery exists, the Republican period, defined for this survey as 350 BC – 30 BC, has not been further sub-divided into Mid and Late Republican phases. The site typology has been based on the size of the scatter in combination with artefact attributes (table 8.3 for the Fogliano survey). The inter-walker distances varied between 2 and ca. 10 m, occasionally exceeding the latter (Attema and Van Leusen 2004, 165), creating different levels of survey intensity, which is a generally recognised bias (ch 2, fig 2.4). A site less then 10 m wide is not a significant occupation focus with the exception of vestigial pre- and proto-historic sites.

The Alban Hills land system (figure 8.4)

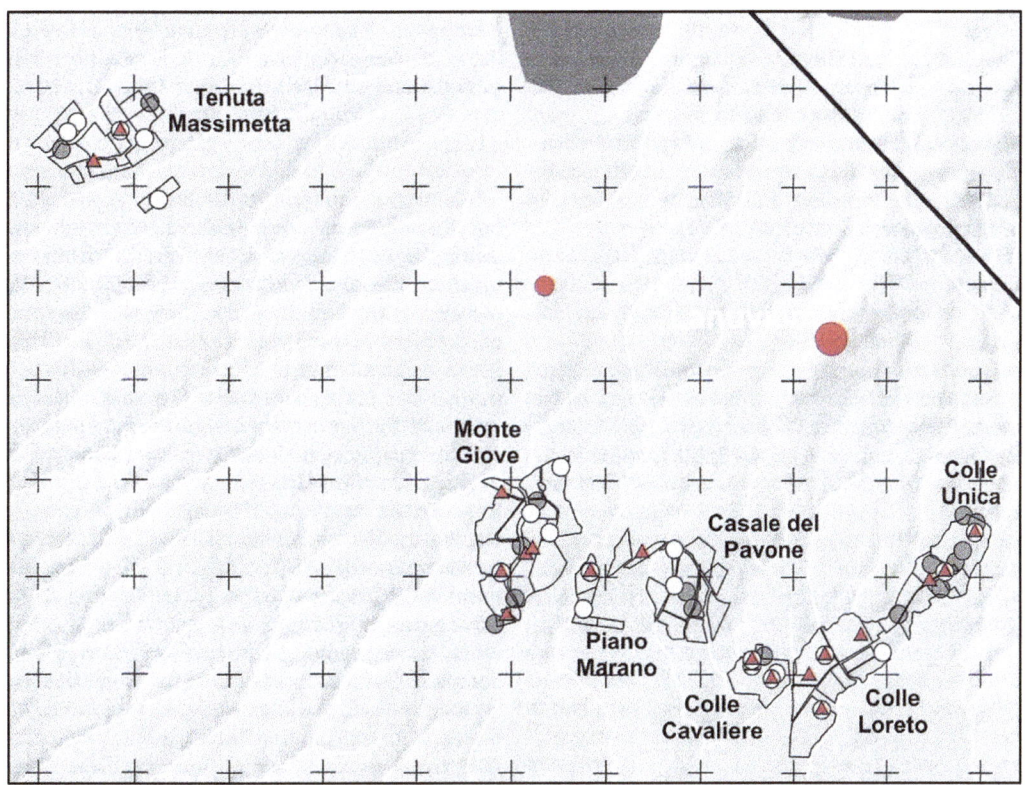

Figure 8.4: Lanuvium Survey – Distrubution of sites with Roman finewares: White circles: black glazed wares; triangles: terra sigillata wares; grey circles: no fine wares found (Attema & Van Leusen 2004, 187 fig 21).

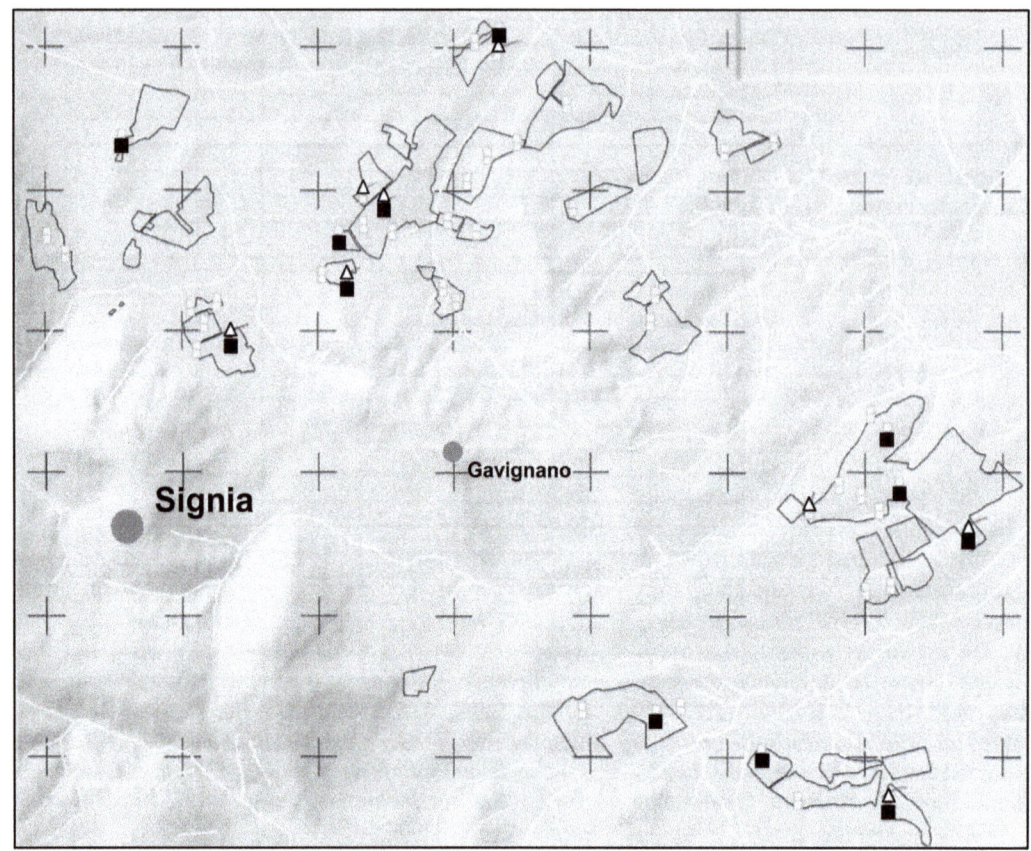

Figure 8.5: Signia Survey: Distribution of black glazed (white triangles) and terra sigillata (black squares) finewares (after Attema & Van Leusen 2004, 171, fig 8).

Lanuvium, originally a Latin city-state, became a Roman ally in the fifth century BC and a Roman *municipium* in the course of the fourth century BC. The field survey areas, covering 407 ha, were located around seven hills situated to the south and the west of the town (Attema and Van Leusen 2004, 180). For the Republican to Imperial periods 41 sites have been identified, which results in a site density of 10 sites/km². The survey results suggest a shift in settlement pattern from dispersed, with a high number of small farms, to a nucleated pattern with individual hill systems exploited from single *villa* sites (Attema and Van Leusen 2004, 185-7). Black glazed wares have been found at 22 sites and *terra sigillata* on 19 sites (figure 8.4), equating to a density of 5.4 resp. 4.7 sites/km². No segregation between farms and *villae* has been proposed, however, the earlier mentioned

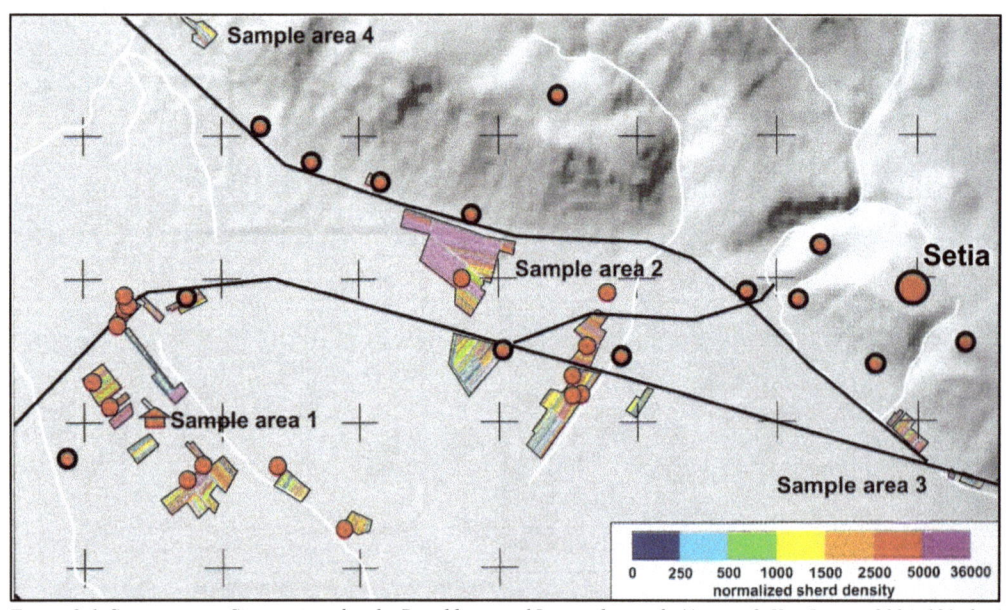

Figure 8.6: Sezze survey : Sites assigned to the Republican and Imperial periods (Attema & Van Leusen 2004, 180, fig 14).

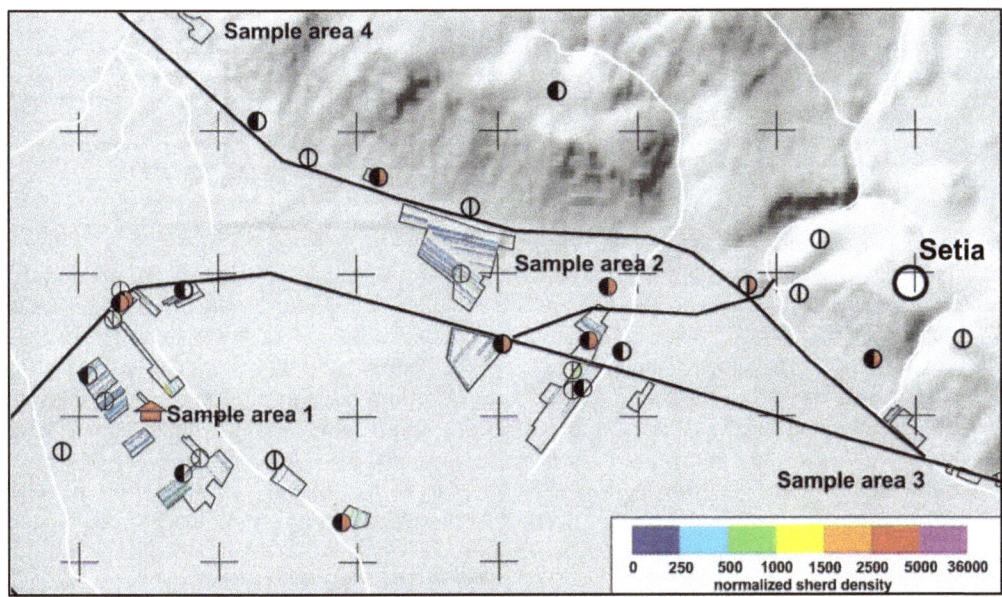

Figure 8.7: Sezze survey : The presence of black glazed wares (black) and terra sigillata (red) on identified sites (Attema & Van Leusen 2004: 181, fig. 15).

hypothesis could hint at 7 *villae* (1.7 *villae*/km^2), each located on an individual hill plateau. The number of sites associated with these *villae* that could be indicative for the remaining number of farms remains obscure.

The Lepine Margins land system (figure 8.5-8.9)
The fortified settlement of Signia, founded in 495 BC as a Latin *colonia*, is located on a hilltop overlooking the Sacco Valley, and is under modern-day Segni. The field survey covered transects (332 ha) over three landscape units; the foothills of the Monti Lepini, the tuff hills in the valley of the Sacco River (ancient river *Trerus*) and the Il Rio river valley, southeast of Segni (Attema and Van Leusen 2004, 167).

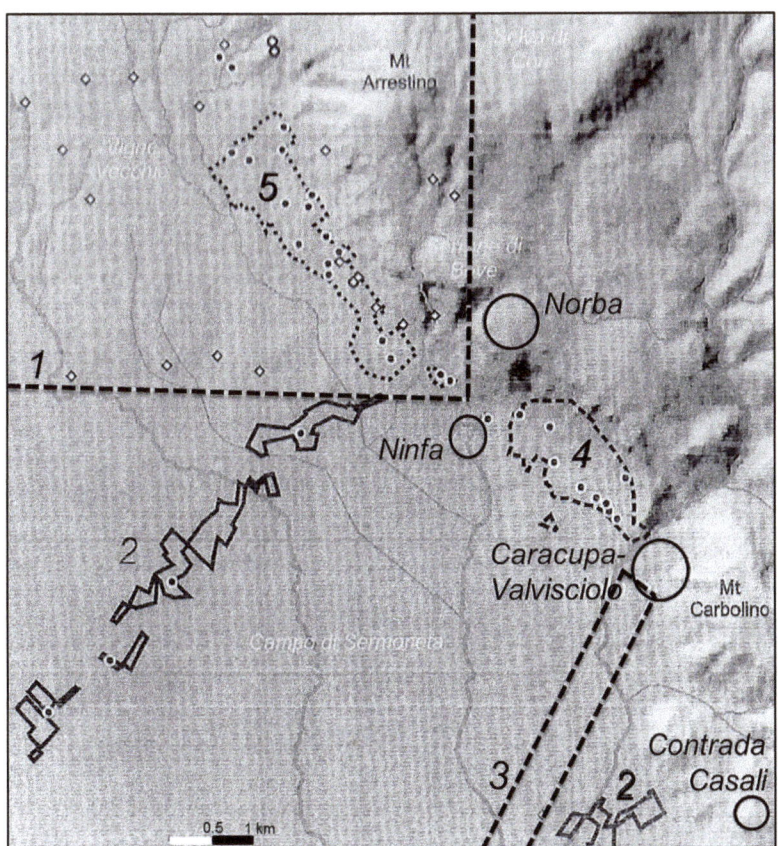

Figure 8.8: Survey areas around Norba: 1- Forma Italiae – Cora survey, 2- Agro Pontino Project, 3 – Pontine Region Project (Norba transect), 4 – Norba survey and 5 – Ninfa survey (after Van Leusen et al. 2005, 304, fig 3).

Table 8.4: Count of sites per type and site density for the foothills near ancient Norba.

Site type	Count		Density per km²	
	Republican	Early Imperial	Republican	Early Imperial
Farm	19	5	2.8	0.72
Platform *Villa*	7	5	1.0	0.72
Road Station/Hamlet	1	2		
Town	1	0		

The count of sites for the Late Republican and Early Imperial periods is 36, resulting in a density of 10.8 sites/km². This count refers to the presence of diagnostic sherds, regardless of the number of sherds per site. If a sherd threshold of 5 diagnostic sherds is used then the count is reduced to 27 sites (8.1 sites/km²). A number of sites possibly do not represent individual farms. A site typology that identifies farms and *villae* has not been presented, although the presence of a number of Roman *villae* is suggested in the publication (Attema and Van Leusen 2004, 173). Black glazed finewares have been found on 8 sites and *terra sigillata* finewares on 12 sites (figure 8.5) resulting in a site density for the Republican period of 2.4 sites/km², and 3.6 sites/km² for the Early Imperial period.

Ancient Setia (modern Sezze) is located on a hilltop of the Monte Lepini overlooking the Pontine plain. Four areas, covering 83.5 ha, were intensively field walked. Two are located on the alluvial plain and two on the slopes of the Monti Lepini. A high density of sherds from the Roman period was identified in all sample areas. Several 'platform' *villae* that were situated on the hill slopes have been dated to the Middle and Late Republic periods. Platform *villae* are wooden farm buildings built on earth-filled terraces contained by walls of heavy polygonal masonry containing finewares (Attema and De Haas 2004, 7). The sites that have been assigned to the Republican and Imperial periods have been graphically represented (figure 8.6). The sites with architectural remains have been highlighted with a heavy outline and have been interpreted as *villae*. Of special notice is their location along the lines of transport and communication. Several of the *villae* are outside of the actual sample areas, resulting in an over-estimation of the site density. If the sites that are located outside of the field walked areas are excluded then 15 farms and 3 *villae* are counted within the total sample area of 0,835 km². These counts result in a site density of 18 farms and 3.6 *villae* per km², and a ratio of farm to *villa* of 5. However, this density is for the combined Republican and Imperial periods. A further subdivision can be suggested based on the distribution and chronology of Roman finewares (figure 8.7). Black glazed pottery is too broad a type and no further refinements, which would allow the identification of the Late Republican sites, can be made. For the Republican period 7 farms and 3 *villae* can be identified, which brings the ratio of farms to *villae* to 2.3. For the Early Imperial period, these metrics are 4 farms and 2 *villae*, a ratio of 2. The site counts result in a site density of 8.4 farms and 3.6 *villae*/km² for the Republican and 4.8 farms and 2.4 *villae*/km² for the Early Imperial periods.

The area near Norba, close to modern-day Ninfa, has been subject to archaeological enquiry since the 1960's, first by Italian scholars and in the 1970's by the Universities of Amsterdam and Groningen (Voorrips *et al.* 1991), and more recently by the Groningen Institute of Archaeology (Pontine Region Project). The old and the more recent studies of the proto-historic to Roman settlements on the Lepine margins have been published in a site catalogue (Van Leusen *et al.* 2005). The publication does not provide the size of the areas covered by the surveys. Moreover, the area of the *Forma Italiae* survey, the Norba transect and the Agro Pontino Project are not fully shown on the map. This means that only sites that are within the defined intensively surveyed area should

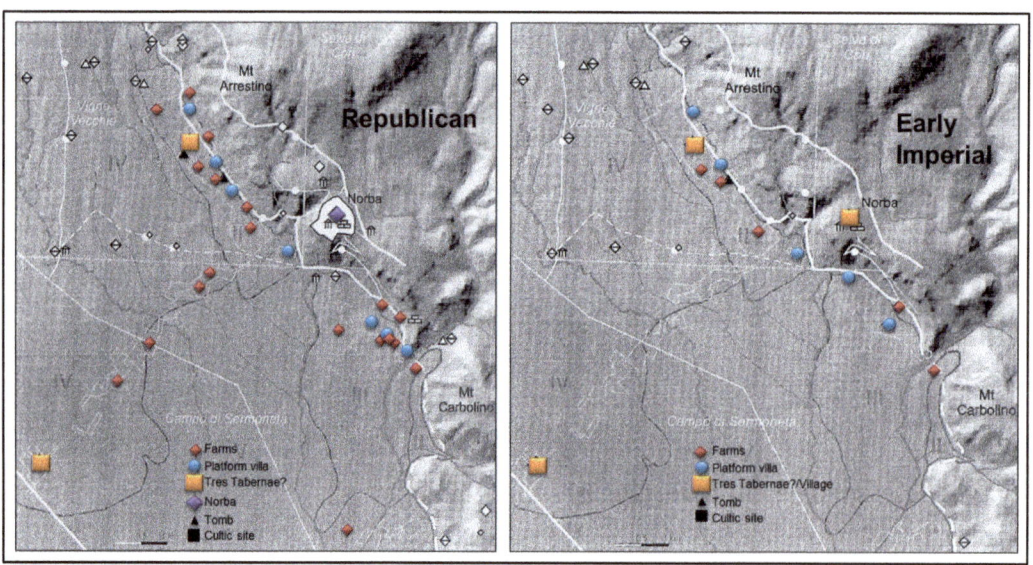

Figure 8.9: The Lepine foothills near ancient Norba (after Van Leusen et al. 2005, 319, fig 9, 321, fig 10).

Table 8.5: Site densities for the Fogliano area.

Site type	Count	Site Density (per km²)
Farm, incl. possible	6	2.0
Large farm	8	1.7
Villa	1	0.33
Village/Hamlet	2	0.67

be considered for site density calculations. The total area covered by the Agro Pontino Project (2), the Pontine Region Project (3), the Norba survey (4) and the Ninfa survey (5) totals ca. 686 ha (figure 8.8). The sites that are within these survey regions have been superimposed on the maps in the publication (figure 8.9).

The dating of the Republican sites has not been further refined. After its devastation in 81 BC by Sulla, Norba was abandoned, which explains the drop in the number of rural sites (table 8.4). The town remained occupied during the Early Imperial period, but was reduced in size to a small village or hamlet.

Coastal Margins land system (figure 8.10)

The results of the Fogliano survey, a marginal coastal zone consisting of a beach ridge complex located near the lago di Fogliano and the lago dei Monaci, have been published in *Palaeohistoria*. This publication includes detailed site and sherd catalogues (Attema et al. 2005). The term marginal refers to those landscape units that, based on their environmental characteristics, such as low fertility, inaccessibility, and distance from core areas, were not favoured for permanent settlement (Attema et al. 2002, 149). The archaeological investigation covered an area of 10 x 1 km, of which 300 ha have been intensively surveyed in blocs of 100 x 100 m (Van Leusen and Attema 1998, 31). The settlement pattern of the Republican period reveals the presence of two small villages or hamlets with a size above 2 ha and farms of varying sizes. The pollen assemblage indicate an intensification of farming activities in an increasingly drier environment, possibly caused by deforestation and olive cultivation (Attema et al. 2005, 133). The Fogliano region has been associated with fish breeding in the lakes (Attema et al. 2005, 135).

A coastal road, later known as the *Via Severiana*, opened the area and connected Antium with Circeii. The presence of road stations suggests travel and commercial activities. The maps for the Republican and the Early Imperial period have been combined, because the count and location of sites with habitation are the same (figure 8.10). As for the Potenza Valley, the data need to be grouped for later comparative analysis. This can be done by grouping the farms and large farms, the latter

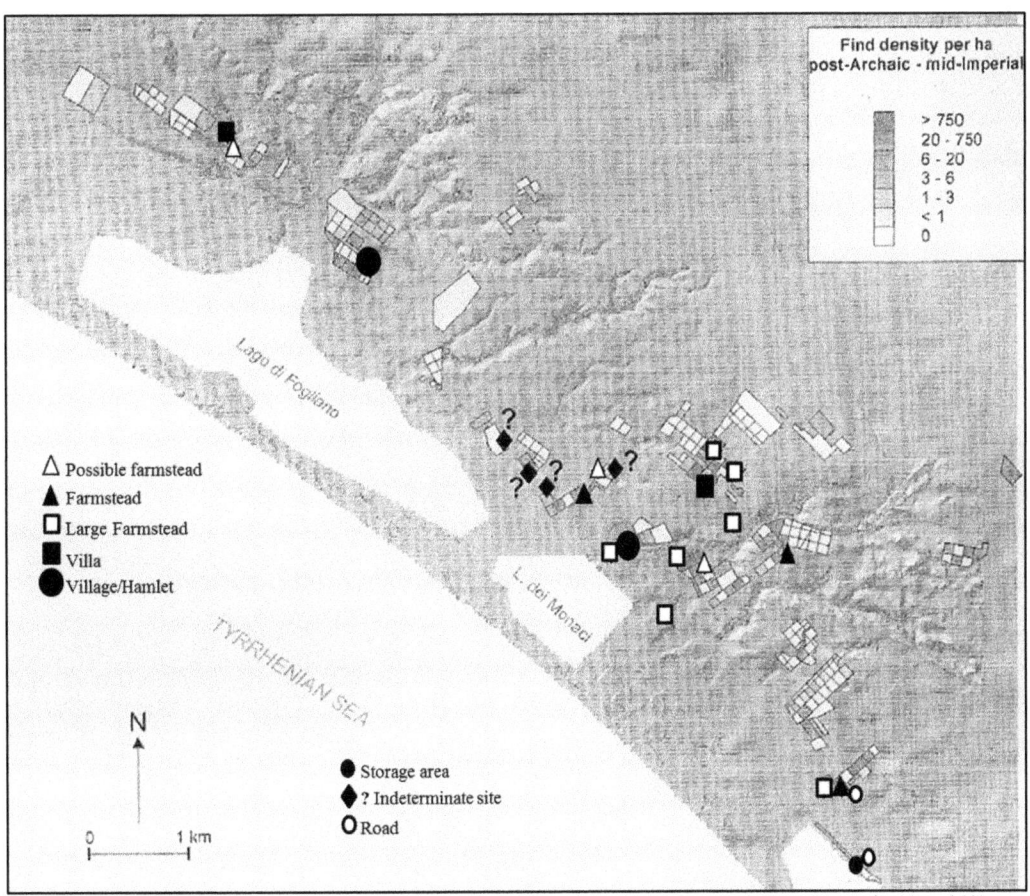

Figure 8.10: Republican and Early Imperial sites in the Fogliano area (after Attema et al. 2005, 136-7, fig 11 and 12).

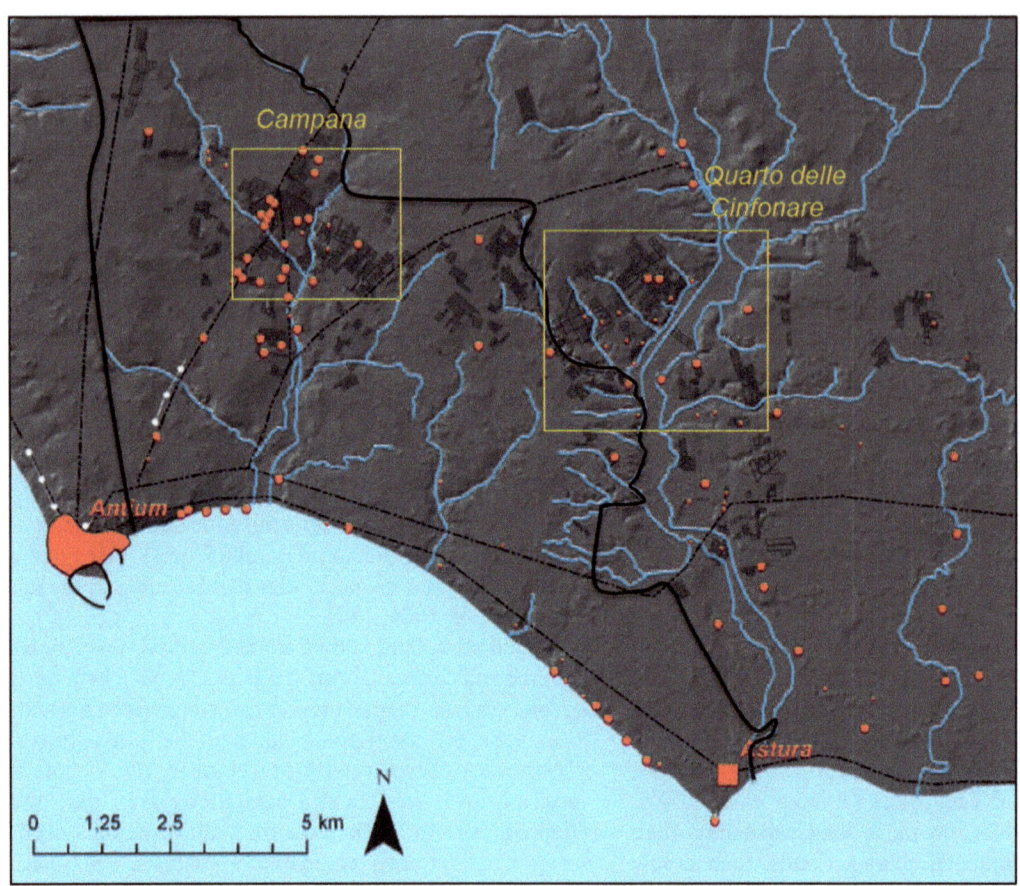

Figure 8.11: Late Republican and Early Imperial settlements from the Nettuno and Astura surveys, including the Forma Italiae identified sites (small dots: date uncertain; black dotted lines are roads; white lines are aqueducts) (after De Haas 2008, 26, fig 12). Campana and Quarto delle Cinfonare survey areas added by the author.

could represent simple *villae*, or by grouping the large farms and *villae*. In the former grouping, this results in a ratio of farms to *villae* of (14/1=) 14, and in the latter case of (6/9=) 0.67 (table 8.5).

The Marine terraces and Astura Valley land systems (figure 8.11)

The regions around modern-day Nettuno and the lower Astura Valley have been intensively surveyed in 2003 and 2005, covering an area of 816 ha. The first results have been published in *Palaehistoria* (Attema *et al.* 2008), *Digressus* (De Haas 2008), and in a book for the municipality of Nettuno, a sponsor of the surveys (Attema *et al.* 2009). Of further relevance is a recent case study describing the size of the rural population of the *ager* of Antium, which will be published in the 2nd volume of the *Oxford Studies on the Roman Economy* (Attema and De Haas forthcoming).[13] The GIA research consisted of revisiting the ceramic sites in the Astura Valley published in the *Forma Italiae* series (Piccarreta 1977) and newly conducted surveys. Recent human impact on the landscape is significant due to reclamations and the canalisation of the Astura and nearby Moscarello rivers, large-scale soil removal schemes, recent urbanisation and intensive ploughing (Attema *et al.* 2008,

415-7). During the 2003 Astura campaign, 560 blocks, covering ca. 155 ha have been intensively field walked. The observed site densities were low due to aforementioned changes in the landscape. A weakness of combining data from two different field surveys is that the site count cannot be related to site density because of differences in methodology and survey intensity. The GIA team tried to revisit 132 sites mentioned in the *Forma Italiae* publication from the 1970's. Recent building activities, levelling, or soil cleaning for intensive agriculture meant that 38 sites (ca. 30%) could not be revisited. Limited visibility resulted in not being able to identify 25 sites and landowners did not grant permission to enter their property in 25 cases. It has been suggested that 30-65% of the sites have been lost from the archaeological record since the published inventory (Attema *et al.* 2008, 429). This observation can be viewed as an indication of site recovery relative to a site count from the 1970s (statistical inference). This percentage is arguably higher as sites also disappeared from the archaeological record from antiquity to the 1970's. Moreover, a high portion of small rural sites tends to disappear and re-appear when resurveyed (archaeological inference). Statistical and archaeological inference are two interrelated variables that are importance for making past population reconstructions. The different area boundaries, the level of chronological detail, site typology and the inclusion of the *Forma Italiae* dataset into the analysis require a deconstruction

---

[13] I want to express my gratitude to Prof. dr. P. Attema and drs. T. de Haas of the Groningen Instute of Archaeology for sharing the draft publication.

of the available information from all publications to extract a dataset that refers to the intensive field surveys conducted by the GIA.

The publication for the community of Nettuno includes sites within the modern administrative boundaries (ca. 70 km^2), which means that the published site catalogue with site chronology covers a subset of the area under study. The publication in *Digressus* refers to the Campana and Quarto delle Cinfonare areas and includes a map with sites by chronological period, including the *Forma Italiae* dataset, but does not include site typology. The publication on the Astura Valley 2003 campaign also does not offer a site catalogue. Finally, the analysis of the demography of the *ager* of the *colonia* of Antium covers an area of 58 km^2 (Mid Republican period) and 236 km^2 (Imperial period), so expanding outside of the field walked area and that of the modern community (figure 8.11). An estimated 373 ha of the survey area is located outside of the area of the community of Nettuno. The site catalogue in *La Carta Archeologica* differentiates sites by period and certain from possible sites. The site density for the area covered by the GIA surveys in the Campana area results in significantly higher site densities compared to the area outside of this region covered in the *Forma Italiae* publication (table 8.6). This higher site density is probably a function of survey intensity and the datasets should not be combined or averaged. The site density of the Campana area is higher than the density of the Quarto delle Cinfonare area, which could be the result of favourable connectivity of the Campana region by the main road leading to the Alban hills and Bovillae. A cluster of sites located on the road suggests the presence of a nucleated settlement, a hamlet or small village. The dataset of the sum of certain and possible sites for the GIA surveyed areas is summarised in table 8.7.

The study of the settlement pattern of the *ager* of Antium, which overlaps with the GIA surveyed area of 443 ha, provides insight into the proposed site typology. In the publication, a variable recovery ratio for different site types and survey intensities has been introduced. The estimated share of *villae* and *villae maritimae* is ca. 20% in the Late Republican period and increased to 30% after 250 AD. It is suggested that these estates probably supplied Antium with cereals, wine and olive oil. The *villa maritimae* cluster around Antium, and on the coastal strip leading from Antium to the Astura River. Industrial and agricultural activities, including *amphora* and tile production suggests that these sites played a major role in wine and olive production, as well as possible fish breeding. An absence of *villa* sites was observed in the Astura Valley, which could suggest that these farms might be associated with the larger estates on the coast (Attema and De Haas forthcoming).

The recovery ratios for the high intensity surveyed areas, which have been proposed for the *ager* of Antium, are 80% for *villae* and 60% for farms (Attema and De Haas forthcoming). These recovery ratios are higher than the estimated 20-33% for the Albegna Valley (Cambi 1999, 117) and the 50% recovery ratio for the Cecina Valley (Ammerman and Terrenato 1996, 106). A rural population density of 17.5 persons/km^2 has been suggested for the *ager* during the Late Republican and Early Imperial periods, based on the certain and possible sites. The authors stressed that this population density should be interpreted as a minimum number and a higher density should be envisioned. If the suggestion of the estimated share of *villae* and *villae maritimae* of ca. 20% in the Late Republican period is accepted and ca. 25% is assumed for the Imperial Period then the ratio of farm to *villa* can be determined. Moreover, a further arbitrary refinement would be the acceptance of the suggested 60% recovery for farms and 80% for *villae* (table 8.8). The above methodology and suggested refinement does not

Table 8.6: Community of Nettuno – Site densities for the Late Republican and Early Imperial periods based on the Nettuno, Astura and the Formae Italiae Astura surveys.

		Count of Sites		Site Density (per km^2)	
		100-30 BC	30 BC-100 AD	100-30 BC	30 BC-100 AD
GIA Survey (4.43 km^2)	Certain	10	15	2.26	3.39
	Possible	12	4	2.71	0.90
Outside GIA Survey Region (65.57 km^2)	Certain	5	19	0.08	0.29
	Possible	11	9	0.17	0.14
Total (70 km^2)	Certain	15	34	0.21	0.49
	Possible	23	13	0.33	0.19

Table 8.7: Site counts and densities for the Nettuno and Astura surveys in the Late Republican and Imperial periods.

GIA Survey Area	Area (km^2)	Count of Sites		Site Density (per km^2)	
		100-30 BC	30 BC-100 AD	100-30 BC	30 BC-100 AD
Inside Nettuno Area	4.43	22	19	4.97	4.29
Outside Nettuno Area	3.73	17	17	4.56	4.56
Total	8.16	39	36	4.78	4.41

Table 8.8: Site count correction for the Nettuno and Astura surveys.

Site	Recovery	Count of Sites		Site Density (per km^2)	
		100-30 BC	30 BC-100 AD	100-30 BC	30 BC-100 AD
Farm	100%	31.2	27	3.82	3.31
Villa	100%	7.8	9	0.96	1.10
Farm	60%	52	45	6.37	5.51
Villa	80%	9.75	11.25	1.19	1.38

sufficiently address the issue that 30-65% of the sites have been 'lost' since the published inventory in the *Forma Italiae* publication due to human activity. In the GIA publication, the *Forma Italiae* dataset is used and corrected for survey intensity before the aforementioned multipliers are used, suggesting that surveys can be compared via standardisation. The dataset offers the opportunity to introduce a statistical inference recovery ratio and an archaeological inference recovery ratio. This suggestion obviously requires further thought, especially when comparing surveys from other regions of Italy that have been the subject of recent intensive surveys and more topographical fieldwork in the *Forma Italiae* series. Both the Potenza Valley and the Biferno survey datasets can be considered for such a study.

Land systems compared

A count and density of farms and *villae* by land system can be proposed by extrapolating uncorrected field survey data (table 8.9 and 8.10). The presupposition that needs to be challenged is that the intensively surveyed areas, covering ca. 1.4% of the total area, are representative for each studied land system, thus can be compared. This assumption is debatable because the dataset for the Alban Hills and the Lepine Margins is coming from urban hinterland surveys that are biased towards the major centres, potentially resulting in too high counts. A second bias comes from the close proximity of roads, such as for surveyed areas around Setia and Norba, and the Campana region. The high *villa* count for the Alban hills, for which 1.1% was intensively surveyed, is based on the hypothesis that clusters of sites could represent larger *villae* complexes. The coastal margins have the lowest density of *villae* and a surprisingly high density of farms compared to the other land systems, which suggest this area was less marginal than thought. The marine terraces and the Astura Valley also show a high density of farms. Without over-analysing the data it can be concluded that differences exist for the different land systems. To what extent this represents a true and significant difference remains a point for discussion. The introduction of guestimated site-specific recovery ratios will only magnify differences. A comparison of the density of *villae*, which has in principle the highest level of recovery, can be made, but assuming a certain fixed ratio of farms to *villae* exceeds the purpose of the enquiry.

Witcher used, in his *suburbium* model, an average site density of 1.5 farms and 0.2 *villae*/km^2 for the 50 to 100 km radii from Rome (Witcher 2005, 129-30). He excluded land above an elevation of 750 m elevation. On a comparison basis, the area that belongs to the Volcano Lazale and Lepine Mountains land system (ca. 21%) equates roughly to land with an altitude above 1,000 meters, so excluding this area from site density calculations will allow a rough comparison. For the Pontine region the density and ratio of farms and *villae* are higher than envisioned by Witcher. The Early Imperial site densities, without using site recovery factors, are 2.4 farms and 1.0 *villae*/km^2, calculated on the total area of the Pontine region. The site densities calculated on the area below 1,000 m altitude, 3.1 farms and 1.2 *villae*/km^2, should be compared against the model from Witcher. The density of *villae* in the Pontine region is a factor of 6 higher than envisioned by Witcher. His density of 0.2 *villae*/km^2 excluded land above 750 m and covers a large concentric area around Rome. The calculated uncorrected farm to *villae* ratio is 2.6 for the Pontine region compared to a factor of 7.5 for the *suburbium* model. The farm to *villa* ratio for the Pontine region comes closer to the dataset of Goodchild for the South Etruria surveys than the proposition from Witcher (Goodchild 2007, 107, fig 4.7) The discussion up to this point has referred to uncorrected data and introducing site specific recovery ratios would significantly impact site densities, the farm to *villae* ratio and the estimated size of the rural population.

The size of the rural population

In the absence of information on the average population that lived on a farm, the minimum and informed

Table 8.9: Extrapolated count for farms and villae for the different land systems of the Pontine region.

GIA Survey	Survey Area (ha)	Republican		Early Imperial	
		Farm	Villa	Farm	Villa
Lanuvium	407	1,364	636	1,091	636
Norba, Ninfa, Setia, Signia	1101.5	485	182	243	182
Nettuno and Astura	816	2,122	531	1,836	612
Fogliano	300	607	43	607	43
(Graben/Pontine Plain) Publication forthcoming	-	est. 799	est. 273	est. 742	est. 289
Hidden Landscape Project	-	?	?	?	?
Total		5,477	1,665	4,519	1,762

Table 8.10: Extrapolated site densities for farms and villae for the different land systems of the Pontine region.

Land System	Area (km^2)	Republican		Early Imperial	
		Farm	Villa	Farm	Villa
Alban Hills	370	3.7	1.7	2.9	1.7
Lepine Margins	167	2.9	1.1	1.5	1.1
Marine Terraces and the Astura Valley	555	3.8	1.0	3.3	1.1
Coastal Margins	130	4.7	0.3	4.7	0.3
Graben/Pontine Plain	240	3.3	1.1	3.1	1.2
Volcano Lazale and Lepine Mountains	388	?	?	?	?
Average Weighted Site Density		3.0	0.9	2.4	1.0
Average Weighthed Site Density <1,000 m altitude		3.7	1.1	3.1	1.2

Table 8.11: Rural population estimates for the Pontine region during the Republican period.

Parameter	Rural			Population Density (per km²)	
	Farm	Villa	Sum	< 1,000 m	Total Area
No of sites	5,477	1,665			
Min. Population/site	5	15			
Informed Estimated Pop./site	5.5	20			
Min. Pop.	27,385	24,975	52,360	36	28
Informed Estimated Pop.	30,124	33,300	63,424	43	34

Table 8.12: Rural population estimates for the Pontine region during the Early Imperial period.

Parameter	Rural			Population Density (per km²)	
	Farm	Villa	Sum	< 1,000 m	Total Area
No of sites	4,519	1,762			
Min. Population/site	5	15			
Informed Estimated Population/site	5.5	20			
Min. Population	22,595	26,430	49,025	34	27
Informed Estimated Pop.	24,855	35,240	60,095	41	32

population will be based on the work done by Bagnall and Frier. Based on Roman census figures for Roman Egypt a typical household size of 5.31 was established (Bagnall and Frier 1994, 66-8, 138-9) and for the Pontine region a range of 5 to 5.5 will be used. More problematic is the estimated population range for a typical *villa*. Information on the size distribution of *villae* is lacking, but it can be argued that the estimated *villae* population would depend on population pressure in the region and the size of the agricultural plot. Witcher used a minimum size of 15 people, a maximum of 50 and an informed estimated population of 25 people/*villa*. The high end would apply to large estates in regions with a low population density, such as Apulia, or sites like Settefinestre in the area of Cosa. For the Pontine region the minimum population of 15 people and an informed estimate of 20 people/*villa* will be used.

The size of the population that occupied farms and *villae* during the Republican period can be estimated between 52,360 and 63,424 people. The resulting rural population density is in the range of 36-43 persons/km² when calculated on the land area below an altitude of 1,000 m and 28-34 persons/km² when the mountainous areas are included (table 8.11). The same calculations can be made for the Early Imperial period (table 8.12), resulting in slightly lower population estimates and population densities, suggesting that a decline in the population living on farms is compensated for by an increase in the population associated with *villae*. The informed estimate for the population living in farms and villae during the Early Imperial period of 41 persons/km² is significantly higher than the 17 persons/km² assumed by Witcher

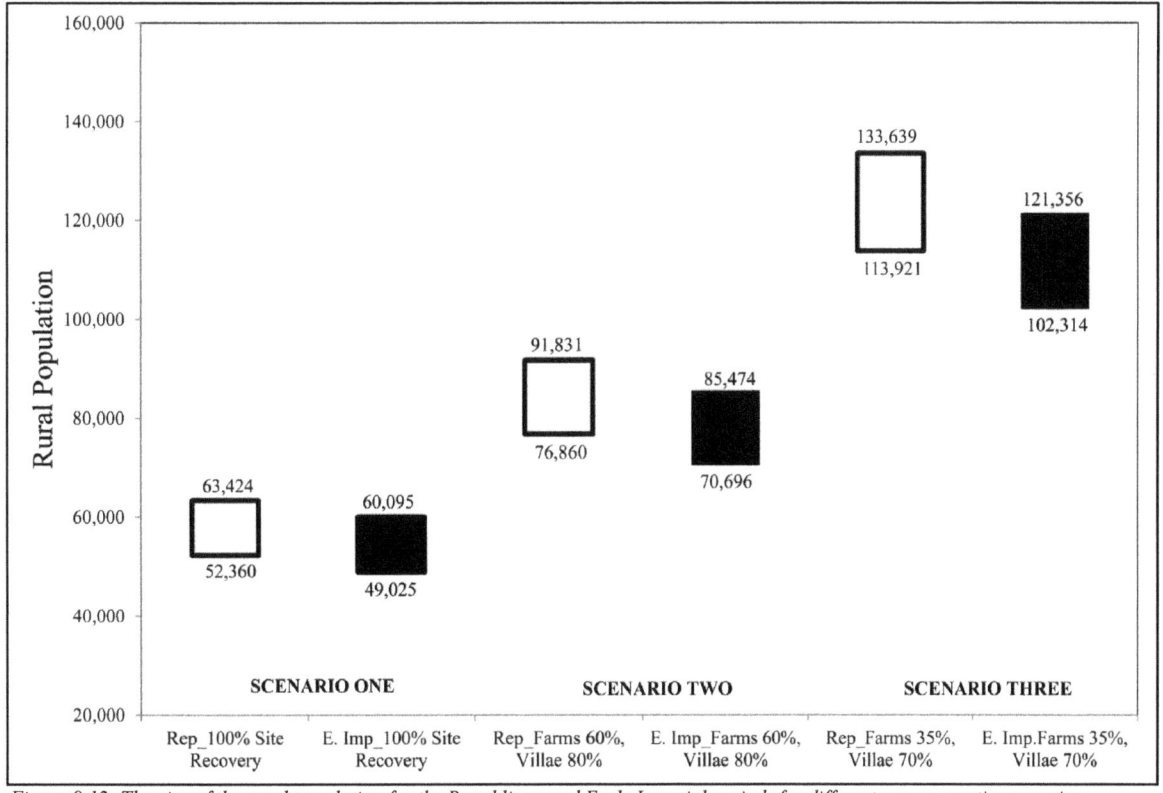

Figure 8.12: The size of the rural population for the Republican and Early Imperial periods for different recovery ratio scenarios.

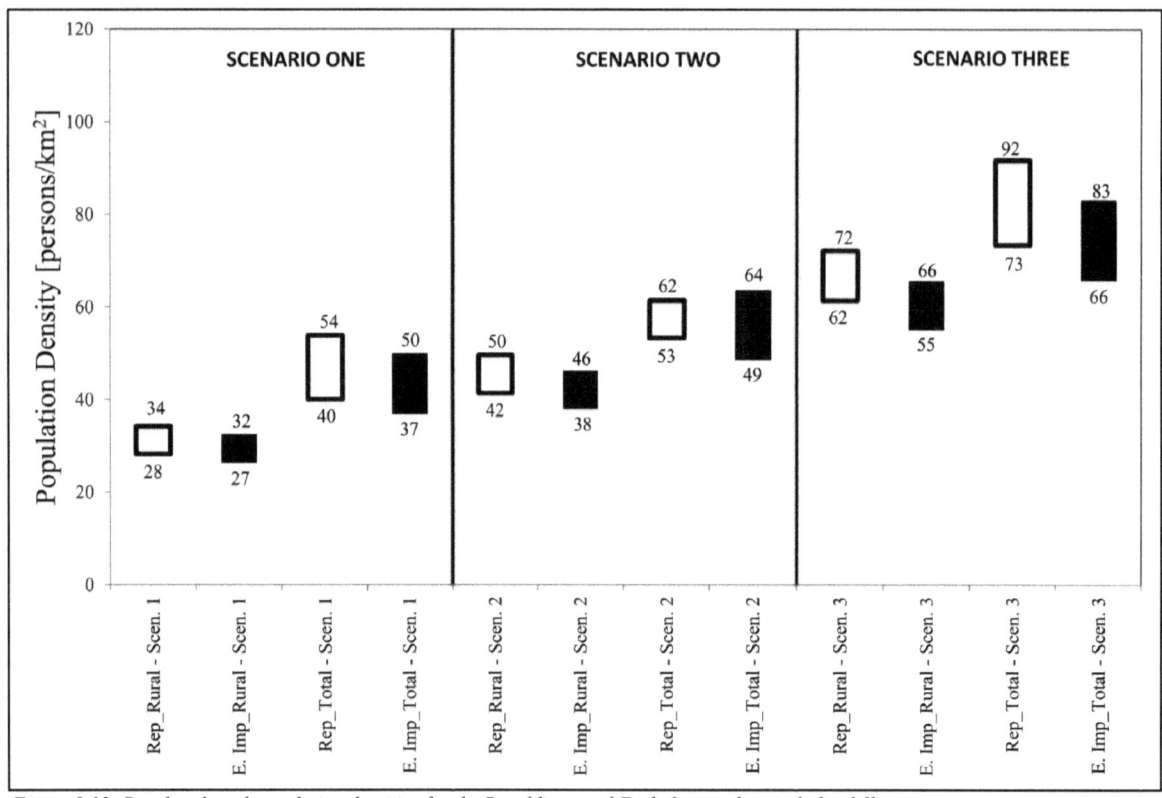

Figure 8.13: Rural and total population densities for the Republican and Early Imperial periods for different recovery ratio scenarios.

(Witcher 2005, 129). It needs to be stressed that the two numbers have been derived using a different methodology and although field survey based, different survey intensities lead to different statistical inferences, thus higher densities for the Pontine region. If a population estimate of 200 persons for the three road stations and the forum is accepted than these would add 800 persons to the rural population numbers (Witcher 2005).

The size of the total population
In the remainder of this chapter, different population reconstructions will be made based on three scenarios that focus on the estimated size of the rural and total population of the Pontine region during the Republican and Early Imperial periods. The first scenario assumes a 100% recovery of farms and *villae* for the surveyed areas, which would provide minimum ranges for the population size and densities. In the second scenario, the differentiated recovery ratios, which have been proposed for the *ager* of Antium (80% for villae and 60% for farms) will be used (Attema and De Haas forthcoming). Finally, the third scenario is built on the observation that an estimated 30-65% of the sites that were identified by the *Forma Italiae* survey disappeared from the site count since the published inventory due to human activity or problems accessing fields (Attema *et al.* 2008, 429). For this scenario, a recovery of 35% for farms and 70% for *villae* will be used. As a result, the ratio of the number of farms per *villa* changes as the count of farms receives a larger correction than *villae* (table 8.13).

The site density used by Witcher for the 50 to 100 km in his model of the *suburbium*, results in a ratio of 7.5 farms per *villa*. The third scenario, using a recovery ratio of 35% for farms and 70% for *villae* seems to best approach this arbitrary number, but also results in the highest total

Table 8.13: Ratio of farm to villae for the Republican and Early Imperial periods in the Pontine region.

	Republican Period	Early Imperial Period
100% Site Recovery (Scenario One)	3.3	2.6
Farms 60%, *Villae* 80% (Scenario Two)	4.4	3.4
Farms 35%, *Villae* 70% (Scenario Three)	6.6	5.1

Table 8.14: Level of urbanisation for the Republican and Early Imperial periods in the Pontine region

	Republican Period	Early Imperial Period
100% Site Recovery (Scenario One)	28-34%	27-34%
Farms 60%, *Villae* 80% (Scenario Two)	21-31%	21-27%
Farms 35%, *Villae* 70% (Scenario Three)	16-21%	15-20%

population. The introduction of different recovery ratios for farms and *villae*, which are site count multipliers, results in rural population estimates that are a factor 1.5 higher for the second and a factor of ca. 2.1 for the third scenario compared to the base case (figure 8.12). From a chronological perspective, the size of the rural population decreased from the Republican to the Early Imperial period, with a shift in rural population towards more people living in *villae*. Earlier in this chapter the size of the population living in the large settlements of the Pontine region was estimated in the range of 21,000-35,500 for the Late Republican and 19,000-31,500 for the Early Imperial period (11-19 resp. 10-17 persons/km^2).

The level of urbanisation can be established for the three rural population reconstructions. As the size of the rural population increases with the introduction of lower site recovery percentages the result will be lower urbanisation ratios (table 8.14). Because sites have been lost from the archaeological record, or not found during intensive field surveying, attention should focus on scenarios two and three. For the Early Imperial period this results in an urbanisation ratio of 21-27% for scenario two and 15-20% for scenario three.

Similar comparisons can be made by shifting attention from absolute population estimates to population densities for the three scenarios (figure 8.13). The use of differential rural recovery ratios leads to population estimates and densities that are a factor 1.3 higher for scenario two and a factor 1.7 higher for the third scenario versus the base scenario. The population density that Witcher estimated for the 50 to 100 km radii from Rome, for land below 750 m altitude, is 42 persons/km^2 for the Early Imperial period (Witcher 2005, 130). For comparison purposes, the densities from figure 8.13 need to be adjusted for cultivable land, which means a multiplier of 1.25. The total population density for scenario one would be 46-62 persons/km^2 and 61-80 and 82-104 persons/km^2 for scenario two and three. All three scenarios provide population density numbers that are above Witcher's average population density, but does this mean that higher recovery ratios should be considered for Witcher's dataset to account for lower survey intensity? The projected population densities for the Pontine region are realistic from a regional self-sufficiency perspective. The region seems to be well integrated into the economy of the Roman *surburbium* with good connectivity by road and water, making both scenario two and three as defendable. Both rural density and urbanisation ratios are comparable to the Potenza Valley presented earlier. However, a more scientific approach to determining differential site recovery ratios, including survey intensity, is urgently needed. A land system approach to estimating the rural population demonstrates relevant variations in farm and *villa* site densities and makes this a valuable addition to field survey methodology. An area for which very different site and population densities and underlying socio-economic structure are expected is the Biferno Valley.

9   Peopling the Rural Landscape: The Biferno Valley

The valley of the Biferno River is located in the Molise province, situated in south-central Italy and stretches from the Matese Mountains (Monti del Matese) to the Adriatic Sea near modern-day Termoli (figure 1.1). The Trigno River forms the northern boundary with the province of Abruzzo, and the Fortore River forms the southern boundary with Apulia. On the west, the region borders Campania. The Biferno River (*Tifernus* in antiquity) is 83.5 km long and has a catchment area of ca. 1,311 km^2. The Biferno Valley was part of Ancient Samnium. In literature, Samnium has been presented as a backward area, impoverished and thinly populated. Brunt suggested that the population consisted of primarily pastoralists, because much of the land was only suitable for stockbreeding with scarcely developed manufacturing and limited trade. Although vines and olives were cultivated, the principle crops from the arable soil were cereals, which were grown at low yields. Overall, the region has been described by Strabo, and based on the limited epigraphic record, as poor with a thin population density (Brunt 1987, 354-8). To what extent is this view sustainable? The field survey work directed by Graeme Barker started in 1974, continued through the 80's and was published in 1995. The title '*A Mediterranean Valley: Landscape Archaeology and Annales History in the Biferno Valley*' leaves little room to speculate on the theoretical framework (Barker 1995b). The size of the population at the time of the study was ca. 320,000 people (70 persons/km^2).

The Biferno Valley was part of a larger territory originally populated by Samnite tribes. The *Pentri*, who controlled the land from Bovianum, populated the upper part of the valley. The lower valley belonged to the *Frentani* with their leading settlement of Larinum. In the first half of the second century BC, the Romans expanded their control on the region via the foundation of the Latin *colonia* of Aesernia and a *praefectura* at Venafrum. The Latin *colonia* of Beneventum was located 50 km south of Bovianum in *Hirpini* territory (Barker 1995b, 182-3). The Latin *colonia* was assigned with a large territory, at the expense of the *Hirpini*, which separated the *Hirpini* from the *Caudini* tribe. The Romans also separated the *Hirpini* from the *Pentri* by a strip of territory, the *ager Taurasinus*. In 180 BC this territory was further populated with 47,000 Ligurian Apuani, women and children included, whom the consuls of the preceding year forcibly transferred from the region in the neighbourhood of Luna (northwest Italy) and located them in Ligures Baebiani and Ligures Corneliani (Salmon 1989, 227), which are to the southeast of the Biferno Valley. Pliny mentions both settlements as chartered towns in the second region (Afzelius 1942a, 61). The Biferno Valley came under Roman control after the Social War and as a result, the local Samnite population acquired Roman citizenship. A number of their settlements became Roman civic centres. Barker stressed the importance of mixed farming and pasturage, based on the ecology of the upper and lower valley, the former being more suitable for pasturage and the lower valley relying more on mixed farming, characterised by a polyculture incorporating cereals and legumes (Ikeguchi 1999, 20-1, 33). Cash crops were grown in the lower valley, of which the olive presses and amphorae sherds for transporting wine have been found. Long distance transhumance between Apulia and Samnium was a factor in the economy throughout the period. Wool production was an important feature of the Samnite agricultural economy. The archaeological evidence has shown that the region was much better connected with immediate and the far-flung hinterlands of the Mediterranean than originally thought (Barker 1995b). A main access route from Venafrum via Aesernia to Beneventum crossed the head of the valley by Bovianum and Samnite Saepinum. The valley itself was not an important crossroad and the main artery of the lower valley was probably the road running along the Adriatic Sea. The principal lines of communication during the Roman period, as mentioned in itineraries, passed across rather than along the valley, continuing the earlier Samnite pattern. The coastal road bent inland from the port of Sipontum, leading via Teanum Apulum to Larinum, before reaching the coast again at Histonium. At the head of the valley, the Aesernia-Beneventum road passed through Bovianum and Saepinum. The *Tabula Peutingeriana* documents a road connecting Larinum with Bovianum along the eastern valley watershed. During the Roman period a network of minor roads was in use (Barker 1995b, 183, 213-4).

Nucleated settlements

Pliny mentions four civic centres: the *municipia* of Larinum, Fagifulae, Saepinum and the *colonia* Bovianum. The region was reorganised under Augustus. Larinum and its territory fell within *regione* II Apulia, and the rest of the valley within *regione* IV Samnium. Roman Bovianum received a veteran colony, probably between 48-27 BC. The site of Saepinum (12 ha intramural) is well preserved and partially excavated, but little is known of the archaeology of the other main settlements. Fagifulae showed up during the field survey as a small one-hectare scatter, suggesting the very moderate size of this settlement (Barker 1995b, 213-7), but the small size of the scatter raises doubt on the identification of the site as Fagifulae. Inscriptions have attested the presence of *severi Augustales* taking care of the Emperor cult for all three *municipia* leaving little doubt on the existence of Fagifulae (Ross Taylor 1914). Barker suggests that Bovianum was probably larger than Saepinum and Fagifulae smaller. In the lower valley, Larinum remained the dominant settlement and obtained *municipium* status, probably in the late 80's BC. The settlement possessed an amphitheatre and signs of imperial architecture.

The average distance between the civic centres of southern Samnium and northern Apulia, reported by Bekker-Nielsen, are 15.8 (range: 8-27 km), and 23.3 km (range: 19-37 km) (Bekker-Nielsen 1989, 25). Within his line of reasoning the urban pattern can be classified as

Table 9.1: Interdistance between for the civic centres of the Biferno Valley.

Civic Centre	Nearest Centre	Distance (km)	2nd Nearest Centre	Distance (km)	Avg. Distance (km)	Avg. Radius (km)
Bovianum	Saepinum	14.5	Aesernia	24.0	19.3	12.0
Larinum	Teanum Apulum	25.5	Fagifulae	27.0	26.3	16.4
Saepinum	Bovianum	14.5	Fagifulae	26.8	20.7	12.9
Fagifulae	Terventum	17.0	Bovianum	25.3	21.2	13.2
			Average		21.8	13.6

colonial, however, the settlement pattern shows strong continuity from the previous Samnite period. The addition of the large civic settlements in close proximity to the Biferno Valley into the locational analysis can help to create a better understanding of the settlement pattern. The interdistance between the civic centres of the Biferno Valley varies between 17 and 27 and a typical radius of the hinterland, following Bekker-Nielsen's methodology (Bekker-Nielsen 1989, 29), is 13.6 km (table 9.1). This radius suggests that the rural population had a service centre within a day-return travel distance. The estimated size of the hinterland based on the constructing of Thiessen polygons is 970 km^2 for Larinum; 632 km^2 for Fagifulae; 454 km^2 for Saepinum and 443 km^2 for Bovianum; with an average hinterland of ca. 625 km^2. Barker also identified lower order settlements, such as villages, road stations and hamlets that functioned as central places. An inscription from Larinum and an early Antonine inscription suggest a *pagus-vicus* settlement organisation. The five lower-valley communities, which probably should be viewed from a central place perspective, have their names preserved are Gereonium, Sicalenum, Cliterna, Buca and Uscosium (Barker 1995b, 227). Geronium is also mentioned on the *Tabula Peutingeriana*, an itinerarium showing the road network in the Roman Empire, and was located south of Larinum. Sicalenum could be identified with site C317. Site A198 has been proposed, based on a 7 ha scatter and limited excavation work, as the possible location of Cliternia. Both Strabo and Pliny mention the settlement of Buca. Uscosium appears only in the mid to late Roman Antonine itinerary, located between Histonium and Larinum, and possibly identified as site B102. This site had a 16 ha scatter, artefacts suggesting significant architecture, a cistern from the first or second century AD, sunken *dolia*, and large-scale pottery and tile production. Nearly all these sites show continuity from the Samnite period to Late Antiquity (Barker 1995b, 230).

Stek argues in his PhD dissertation (Stek 2008) on sanctuary and society in Central-Southern Italy (third to first centuries BC) that the *pagus-vicus* system should not be viewed as a remnant of a pre-Roman settlement pattern, but also needs to be seen as having a legal and administrative function during the Roman period. In the Roman context, *pagi* might be a territorial division, and *vici* small villages, both the result of and shaped by Roman intervention. He identified two consequences of

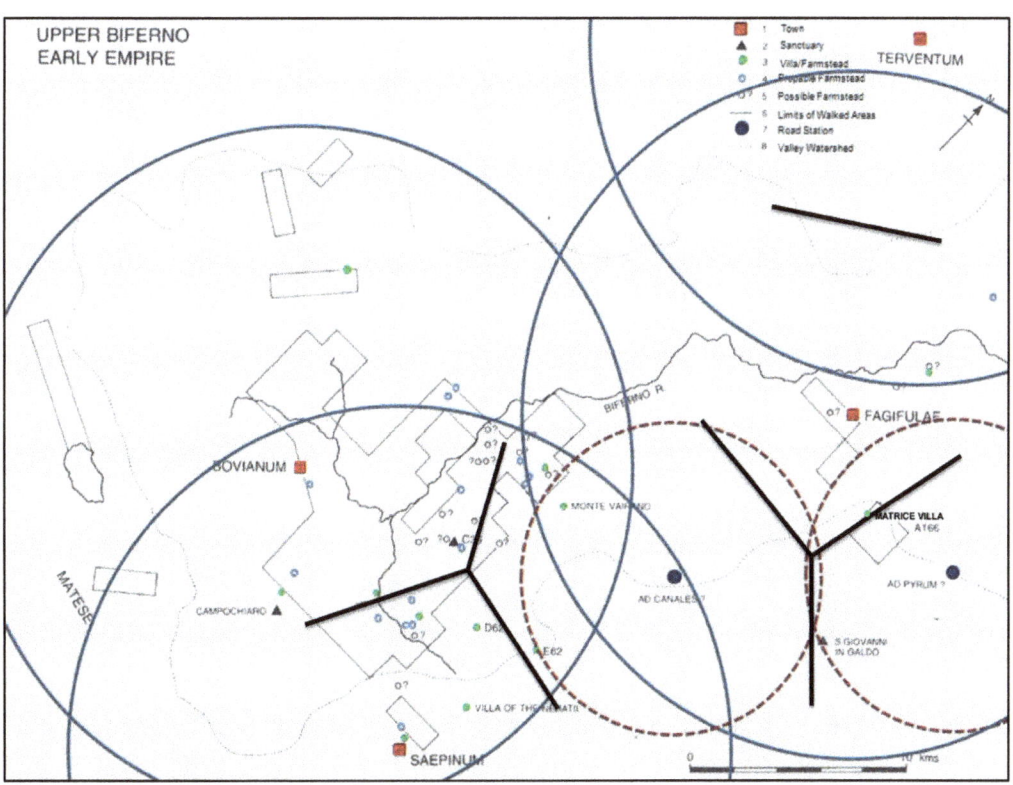

Figure 9.1: The upper Biferno Valley in the Early Imperial period with 15 km radii for civic centres and 7 km for lower order nucleated settlements (after Barker 1995b, 186, fig 72). Thiessen lines have been added between towns and vici.

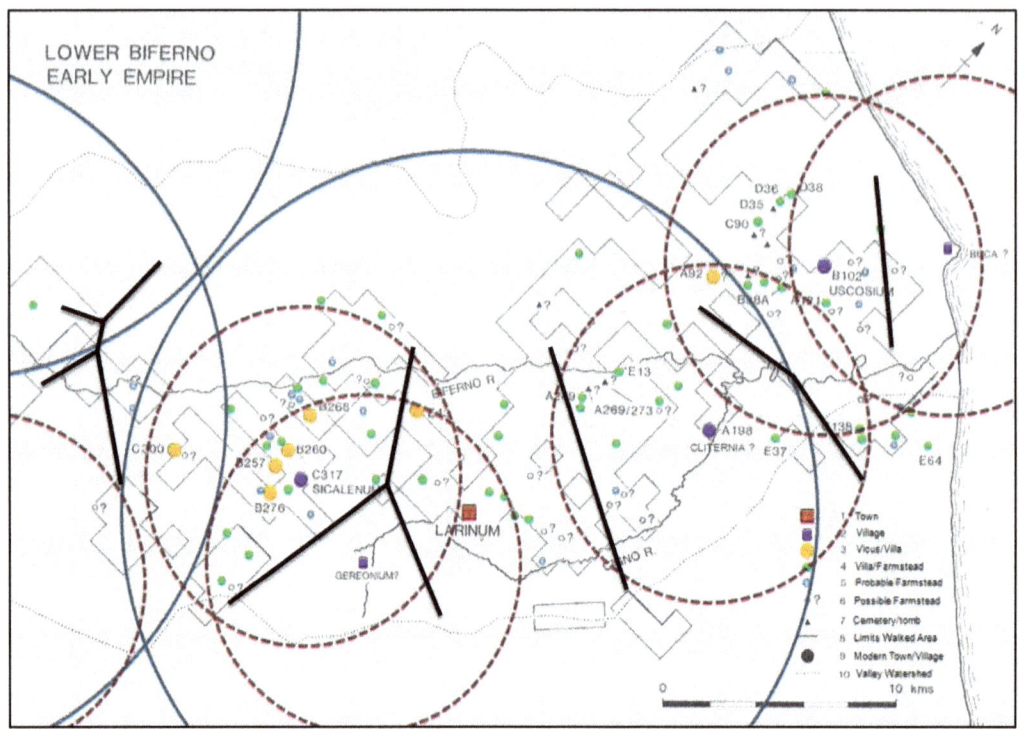

Figure 9.2: The lower Biferno Valley in the Early Imperial period with 15 km radii for civic centres and 7 km for lower order nucleated settlements (after Barker 1995b, 228, fig 86). Thiessen lines have been added between towns and vici.

this discourse: when epigraphic sources suggesting *pagi* or *vici* are absent then a more neutral terminology, such as dispersed settlement organisation or village-farm pattern of settlement, should be used. Secondly, when a *pagus-vicus* structure is attested in literary sources then this should be viewed from an institutional perspective and has implications for ideas on the cultural Romanisation of Italy and Roman religious influence on the countryside (Stek 2008, 273-4). Of special interest in this argument is the suggestion that for the Roman period *vici*, just like *coloniae* and *municipia*, can be positioned within a legal and administrative context, but probably as a second tier in the civic hierarchy. However, the minimalist view that only those *vici* that are attested in literature can be viewed as true *vici*, versus the non-attested ones being nucleated settlements, limits the interpretation of the settlement system for the Roman period, and might be an artificial construct. How the hinterland of these 'civic' villages should be interpreted is open to debate, but very relevant, especially for Cisalpine Gaul and other regions of Italy for which the landscapes are being perceived as empty based on the restricted density of *coloniae* and *municipia*. Villages that could have been civic in nature and significant in size, could have filled the gaps in the landscape. The attested five lower order settlements of the lower valley are all located within the theoretical hinterland of Larinum, which measured 970 km^2, resulting in a typical size of the village hinterlands that exceeds subsistence farming requirements and does not create the perception of an empty landscape. The same is valid for the hinterland of Fagifulae. The *Tabula Peutingeriana* list two road stations, Ad Canales and Ad Pyrum. Both have been identified in the upper part of the valley in the hypothetical hinterland of Fagifulae (Barker 1995b, 217).

A method often employed in functional locational analysis is the plotting of circles around the nucleated settlements. In this case, 15 km radii circles have been drawn around the civic centres and 7 km radii around the second order nucleated settlements (figure 9.1 and 9.2). All the civic centres have, based on a farmer's day-return radius, overlapping hinterlands; so none of them was isolated. However, Larinum was poorly connected to the coastal region. The villages of Cliternia, Uscosium and Buca filled this gap in the settlement pattern. The only settlement for which the size of the centre has been determined is Saepinum. The intra-mural area is 12 ha, suggesting that the civic centres of the region were small, even relative to the Potenza Valley. As the size of the other settlements is unknown, or expected to be in the same range as Saepinum, there is no opportunity to look at the rank-size distribution. Saepinum is well preserved and partially excavated: a forum- basilica complex with temples; theatre; *macellum*; baths; houses, shops, workshops and an aqueduct have been identified. The *macellum* at Saepinum is mentioned in an inscription of Augustan date, and is the smallest of those surviving in Italy. There may have been more of these small market buildings catering for a limited trade or a restricted selection of goods. The market is in the shape of a trapezium and measures only 14 by 17 metres, housing six shops.

The presence of second and third order settlements in the Biferno Valley suggests a different settlement hierarchy compared to the Potenza Valley, which possessed civic centres, one road station and hamlets. The small size of

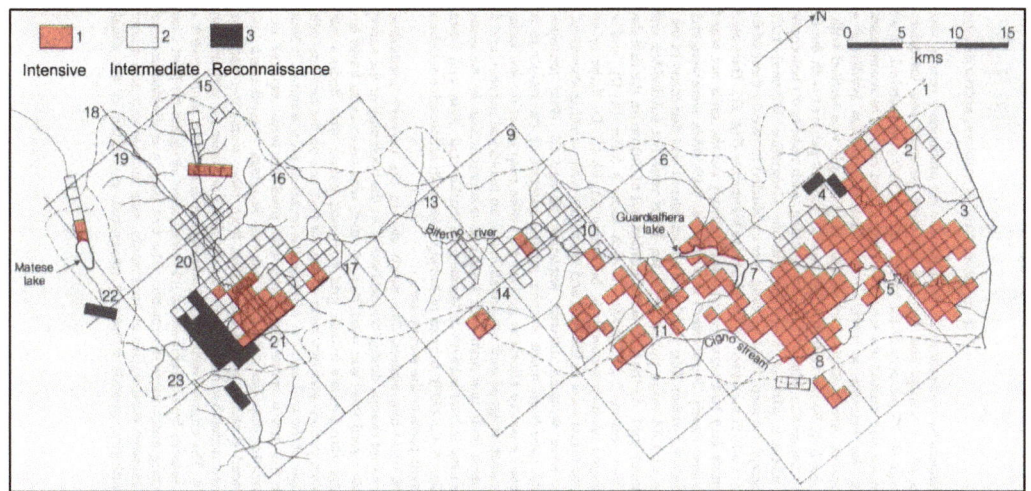

Figure 9.3: The Study Area of the Biferno Valley Survey (after Barker 1995b, 43, fig 21).Intensive areas are highlighted in red.

the civic centres in the Biferno Valley can be indicative for the rural setting and nature of the economy highlighted by Brunt. If towns are small and not so distinct from *vici*, the pattern may be more of equal Thiessen territories than of large town territories within which smaller *vici* catchments are nested. Thiessen lines have been added between both catagories in figure 9.1 and 9.2 and appears to make a much clearer pattern than hierarchical set of catchements as shown in the blue and red circles.

Rural field survey
The study area is rectangular shaped and covers an area of ca. 2,250 km^2 of which 400 km^2 (18%) have been field surveyed in a grid of ca. one km^2 blocks (figure 9.3). The data are biased towards the lower valley, which represented 45% of the sample. The upper and middle valley represented 30 and 25% of the surveyed area. Three levels of survey intensity has been used corresponding to the surveying of all accessible land (intensive); of 50-75% of the unit (intermediate); and reconnaissance work, representing 40, 50 and 10% of the study sample. Ploughed fields were targeted for field walking within the units. The blocks that have been surveyed at intermediate levels or by reconnaissance were predominantly located in the upper valley. A weakness in Barker's publication is the absence of the exact area that has been field walked. Population reconstructions for the Pontine region and Potenza Valley surveys have been based on accurately established areas. This hinders, together with the use of three levels of survey intensity, site density calculations and rural population reconstructions for the Biferno Valley. If the assumption is made that half of the intermediate and reconnaissance, representing 60% of the 400 km^2 survey area, was actually surveyed, then a conservative rural site multiplier of at least 1.5 could be envisioned. A second correction factor that compensates for survey intensity will be discussed further in the chapter.

Barker created three levels of certainty for sites in his analysis of the field survey: certain, probable and possible, and different categories of sites based on surface scatter. Category A (large) sites have a scatter above 7,500 m^2; category B (medium) sites a scatter between 7,500 and 1,000 m^2, category C (small) sites less than 1,500 m^2 and finally category D sites, which are sporadic or only contained individual finds. Category A sites would represent small villages; category B a site with plain buildings, possibly *villae* or large farms and category C would include farms and agricultural store

Table 9.2: Villae and farms in the Biferno Valley.

	Upper Valley	Lower Valley	Sum of Sites	Density (site/km^2)
Certain	11	56	67	0.168
Probable	15	20	35	0.088
Possible	17	33	50	0.125
Certain + Probable				0.255
Villae	4	14	18	0.045
Farms				0.21

Table 9.3: Population reconstruction for the Biferno Valley (Witcher 2008, 293).

	Sporadic	Domestic Site	Farm	*Villa*	Village/*Villa*	Village	Towns	Total
Sites identified	19	34	34	14	2	5	3	
Total number of sites (x5)	95	170	170	70	10	25	3	
Persons per site type	1	2	8	25	50	100	2500	
Total population per site type	95	340	1,360	1,750	500	2,500	7,500	14,045
% of total population	1%	2%	10%	12%	4%	18%	53%	

Table 9.4: Reassesment of Witcher's reconstruction of the size of the population of the Biferno Valley.

	Farm	Villa	Village	Road Station	Small Town	Pop Density
No of sites	710	152	5	2	4	
Informed estimated population per site	8	25	100	200	1,500	
Informed estimated total population	5,680	3,800	500	400	6,000	5.9
% of total	35%	23%	3%	2%	37%	

buildings. Barker recognizes that some of the smaller Samnite scatters with poor datable finds could actually be Late Republic and point to veteran settlement, especially in the territories of Bovianum and Saepinum (Barker 1995b, 185, 224, 232-5). The outcome of the field survey in terms of the above mentioned criteria are summarised in table 9.2. The calculated uncorrected site density for the Early Imperial period is 0.21 farm/km^2 and 0.045 villa/km^2, a ratio of farm to villa of ca. 5. Core sampling and elaborate geophysics surveys were conducted at selected sites to confirm the interpretation of sites discovered during field walking (Barker 1995b, 51-4).

The size of the population
Witcher made a reconstruction of the population density for the Biferno Valley in the Early Imperial period (table 9.3) based on the published site catalogue (Barker 1995a). He estimated a rural population density of 3.4 persons/km^2 and a total population density of 7.4 persons/km^2 (Witcher 2008b, 292-3). This low population density suggests an empty rural landscape focussed on pastoral activities. Saepinum has been excluded from his estimate, probably because it was located outside of the catchment area of the valley. However, this has been compensated by the use of a debatable population size of 2,500 persons for the remaining three large settlements resulting in a high degree of urbanisation for the valley. If the intra-mural area of Saepinum (12 ha) would be indicative for the size of Bovianum, Larinum and Fagifulae then a population of 1,500 would be more realistic. Moreover, the settlement of Fagifulae showed up during the field survey as a small one-hectare scatter, which means that the scatter is either not Fagifulae or the settlement was relatively small with a population size that would be more appropriate for a village. As noted earlier, these comments agree with the possible merger of towns and *vici* into a single class of local centres.

An informed population size of 5.5 people for a farm and 20 people for a *villa* was used for the Potenza Valley, the *suburbium* of Rome and the Pontine region. These parts of the Italian peninsula were more densely populated compared to the Biferno Valley. Yntema suggest, based on observations in funerary contexts made during the Oria Survey, that at least 8-10 persons, basically three generations, could have lived at one farm in this part of Italy at the same time (Yntema 2008, 379, ft 17). For the Biferno Valley larger families, such as described by Yntema could have occupied a farm. The same rationale can be applied for *villae*, which could be larger estates. An informed estimated population per site of 8 people for a farm and 25 for a *villae* will be used in population reconstructions.

A rural site multiplier of 1.5 was argued earlier in this chapter based on the three levels of survey intensity and the surface area covered by each. When the count of certain and probable farms are used, and a multiplier of 1.5 for farms and *villae*, then a total population estimate of 16,380 people (7.3 persons/km^2) can be calculated of which 37% lived within the 4 small towns (table 9.4). An alternative reconstruction of Witcher considers a site recovery ratio, but as a heuristic device for arguing which conditions would fit a low count model, with an Early Imperial Italian population of ca. 6-7 million, and which conditions a high count scenario with an estimated population of ca. 12-14 million. In the high count scenario the consequence is that survey fails to recognize the majority of sites, hence undercounts the people living outside of the major centres (Witcher 2008b, 294-5). Is it possible to draw on a comparative high intensity field survey in close proximity to the Biferno Valley to estimate the recovery ratio?

An intensive field survey has been conducted in 2004 and 2005 as part of a PhD study, around the Samnite sanctuary of San Giovanni in Galdo, located in the higher part of the Tappino Valley, ca. 6 km south of the Matrice *villa*. The aim of the field survey was to reconstruct the ancient landscape surrounding this Samnite sanctuary and to provide chronological depth (Stek 2008, 8). Moreover, a reinterpretation of the so-called *pagus-vicus* pattern of settlement has been presented in this study that augments the Biferno Valley publication. An area of 1.5 km^2, covering different landscapes, such as hilltops, slopes, river valleys and terraces was surveyed in units of ca. 50 by 100 m at 10 m intervals between the walkers. Sites have been revisited and selective geophysical research conducted. The area around the sanctuary was surveyed more intensively in a grid of 10 by 10 m (Stek 2008, 104-5). The field survey resulted in a high site density for the Hellenistic and Roman periods. The poverty of clearly diagnostic sherds for the Late Republican and Early Imperial periods hindered the development of a more detailed chronology. One large *villa* from the Imperial to late Roman period, with visible structures and abundant ceramics (site G7), has been identified, and a village has been suggested for a cluster of sites (G2, G3, G17-G20) which was visible as a 10 ha scatter. The size of the scatter per period has not been reported (Stek 2008, 113). The other sites that have been assigned to the Roman period could be interpreted as small farms, but a function as outbuildings cannot be excluded. The sanctuary itself has a significant Roman phase, especially for the first and second century AD (figure 9.4). A density of 4 possible farms and 0.67 *villa*/km^2 can be calculated for the 1.5 km^2 survey area. A site that is very similar to San Giovanni in Galdo is a small sanctuary in the upper part of the Biferno Valley, ca. 7 km north of Saepinum and ca.

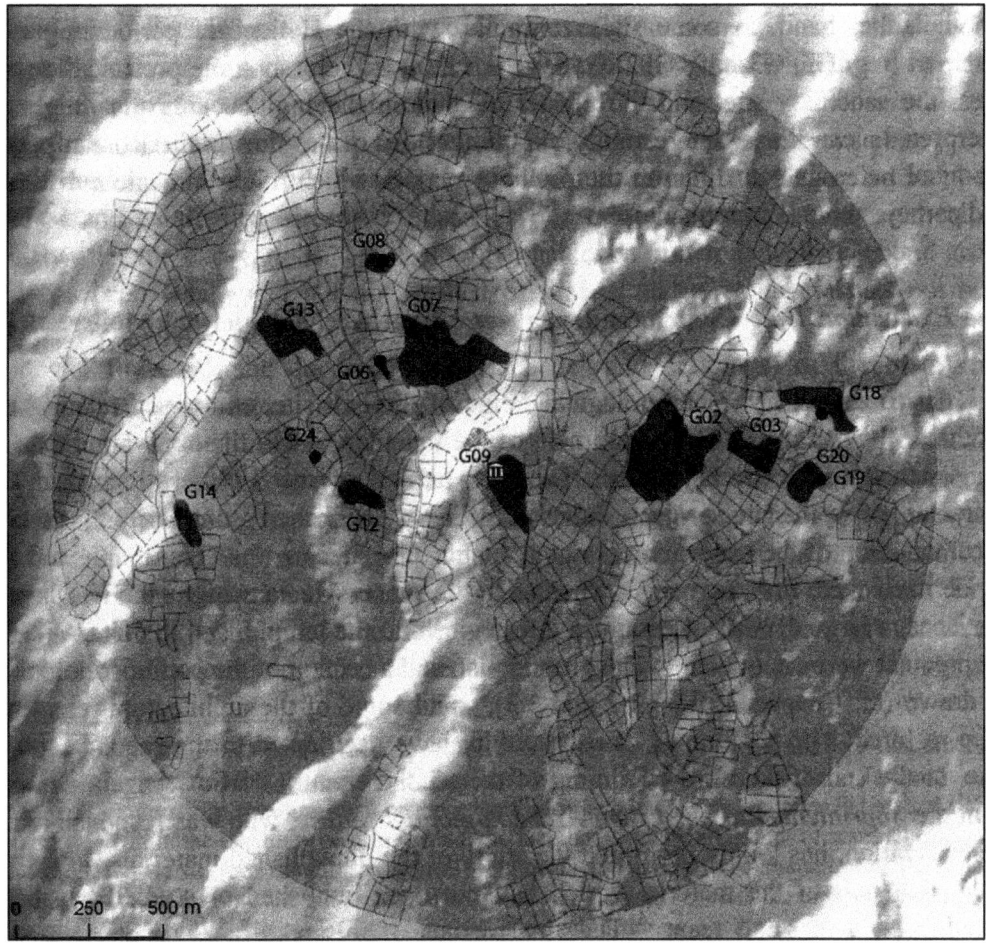

Figure 9.4: The Roman Imperial sites (Stek 2008, 119, fig 5.18).

7 km east of Bovianum. Barker refers to the sanctuary as Site C36. Around this sanctuary, a cluster of sites was identified that was interpreted as a village rather than a cluster of farms from the Samnite period. The size of the scatter has not been confirmed by geophysics. This possible village seems to have been deserted during the Imperial Period (Barker 1995b, 217). An area within the survey grid needs to be identified that approaches the survey area surrounding the sanctuary of San Giovanni in Galdo. The latter covers ca. 7.1 km², of which 1.5 km² has been intensively surveyed. The area demarcated in the square around the sanctuary of C36 is ca. 9.2 km² (figure 9.5).

Stek identified seven possible farms from the Hellenistic period (fourth to first century BC), which would equate to a site density of 4.67 farms/km² for the survey area

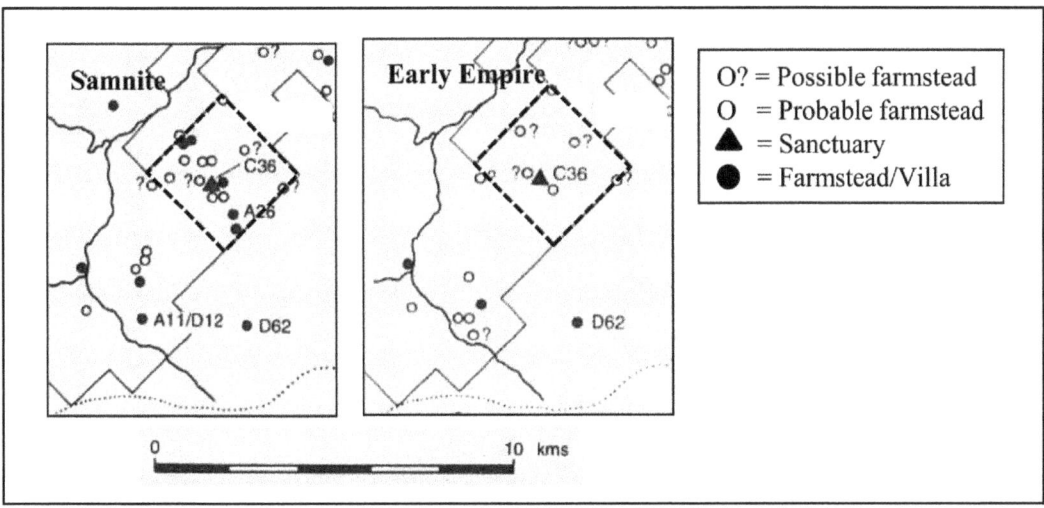

Figure 9.5: Survey area around sanctuary C36 (after Barker 1995b, 186 and 228, fig 12 and fig 86).

Table 9.5: Revised population reconstruction for the Biferno Valley including correction factors.

	Farm	Villa	Village	Road Station	Small Town	Total
No of sites	3,905	304	5	2	4	
Informed estimated population per site	8	25	100	200	1,500	
Informed estimated total population	31,240	7,600	500	400	6,000	45,740
% of total	68%	17%	1%	1%	13%	

around the sanctuary of San Giovanni in Galdo (Stek 2008, 111, fig 6.7). The site density during the Samnite period, for the 9.2 km^2 surrounding the sanctuary of C36, calculates to 1.7 sites/km^2 when the certain, probable and possible farms are included in the calculation. However, this includes the sites belonging to the presumed village. If the 7 sites that represent the village, located southeast of the sanctuary of San Giovanni in Galdo are taken into consideration, and the burial area G22 is excluded, then a total site density of 9.3 sites/km^2 can be established. Under the assumption that both areas would have the same settlement pattern and site density during the Samnite period, a ratio between the two densities of 5.5 can be established, which includes statistical, but excludes archaeological inference. The implications to demographic reconstructions are significant, as the use of this multiplier on top of the 1.5 argued earlier would increase the count of farms and *villae*, thus the size of the rural population even further. This factor 8.25 comes not unexpected and can be explained from Barkers own description and method. Although a plausible analogy for the Samnite period can be debated, the Early Imperial period shows a significant drop in site density around sanctuary C36 that could be indicative for a different historical trajectory related to the areas proximity to Roman Saepinum and Bovianum. The count of farms shows a decline in the Early Imperial period, which may have been absorbed in larger estates, and the possible development of sheep stations has been suggested by Garnsey, whereas Lloyd suggested large scale pasturage and cultivation of cereal and fruits. A shift from mixed farming to large-scale pasturage could have occurred (Ikeguchi 1999, 22).

A more refined view, such as that given for the Pontine region, would assume a different recovery ratio for farms compared to *villae*, however this would be guesswork as there are no data at hand for making this assessment. For the sake of the argument, a recovery ratio for *villae* of 50% will be assumed. The revised population reconstruction would result in a total population of 45,740 people (20 persons/km^2) of which 13% lived in the four small towns (table 9.5). The calculated uncorrected site density for the Biferno Valley of 0.21 farm/km^2 and 0.045 *villa*/km^2 for the Imperial period could be corrected to 1.7 farm/km^2 and 0.14 *villa*/km^2.

Discussion

The reassessment of the size of the rural population of the Biferno Valley sheds a different view on other surveys that resulted in low rural site densities, such as the suburbium of Rome, or high densities, such as the Potenza Valley Survey and the Pontine Region. It puts the spotlight on survey methodology and the accuracy of publications, especially with respect to survey intensity and the actual area surveyed. A very relevant study by Witcher describes the theoretical challenges and archaeological implications on the use of legacy survey data within GIS based on two case histories (Witcher 2008a). One of the case histories describes the area around Larinum and tries to merge the metadata from the Biferno Valley Survey and the *Forma Italiae* Survey (De Felice 1994). The Larinum survey covered a ca. 100 km^2 block. Within the area walked in both surveys, ca. 51 (25%) of the sites were identified in both surveys. Moreover, for the overlapping areas, 97 sites were not recorded by the Biferno Valley survey and 59 sites were not identified by the *Forma Italiae* survey. Increased survey intensity could explain the former, resulting in a site recovery percentage, but not the latter. A possible explanation discussed by Witcher refers to the variable accessibility to fields, the changing surface visibility and the nature of the archaeological record itself, due to erosion of surface material and the appearance and disappearance of small sites. Additional insight can be obtained from studying the site distribution based on the number of occupations clarifying which sites were part of a long-term settlement pattern and which sites were single phase and short-lived (Witcher 2008a).

The integration of survey data has been studied, as part of a PhD dissertation by Gkiasta, for the Island of Crete and more specifically for the region of Siteia. The integration of survey data is, according to Gkiasta, hindered by difficulties in functional site classification, also from a chronological perspective (sites can shift from one functional category to another), inconsistencies in publications of a project or the absence of publications, and variable chronological precision (Gkiasta 2008, 199). Moreover, specific criteria for site definition and site function have not been agreed among archaeologists and vary with time, region, and period of study. In the last two decades, there seems to be a convergence to a minimum level standardization, but this is very much the prerogative of the leader of the survey. She, unfortunately, does not discuss the demographic implications, which can be very significant. Farinetti has recently published a parallel exercise for Boeotia Central-Greece (Farinetti 2011).

10 Discussion and Conclusions

The study and reassessment of published intensive field surveys that cover different landscapes and regions on the Italian peninsula has not only been challenging, but also very rewarding in terms of new insights into regional differences, and areas of commonality in how the landscape was structured and on demography. The challenge for this chapter is to synthesise the de- and reconstruction of intensive field surveys, for which the original research questions were often different and focussed on long term chronological developments for the region of study. Comparative studies are a relatively young area of scientific focus, primarily because there first need to be enough high quality regional studies available (Gkiasta 2008; Ikeguchi 1999; Alcock 1993; Wilkinson 2003; Bintliff 1997a). The question of the validity of the comparison then quickly becomes critical. The research questions that have been formulated in this comparative study thus cover theoretical and methodological challenges as well as questions on the nature of the regional variations, the implications for how Roman society could be viewed, and even the nature of Roman urbanism. The latter can be contrasted with the current understanding of the Greek World. However, the intention of the discussion and conclusion chapter is not to be exhaustive. Discussions with scholars from different backgrounds, and the constant stream of publications have always resulted in new perspectives, which make the topic lively, and very interesting to study. Instead of summarizing what others have said about the topic, which has been covered in depth in the individual chapters; this summary will try to focus on personal observations and judgements that offer room for debate. The research questions that were formulated in the introduction section focus on how the archaeological data are structured, the validity of making regional comparisons, the use of historical and contemporary analogies as heuristic devices, the outcome of the comparative study, and finally if new insights have been obtained. The individual case studies all resulted in a dataset that provides a *birds-eye view* of the settlement pattern, settlement hierarchy, and demography, which can be used for comparisons. The word *birds-eye view* is used because there are boundaries and limitations to making landscape and demographic reconstructions and comparing regions. This high-level understanding is, in the current situation, still subject to debate.

The opportunistic answer to the closed question 'if published intensive field surveys can be used for making a case for regional variations' is yes, quickly followed by 'but'. This 'but' refers to the problems that have been encountered in doing this comparative study; the intentional and unintentional biases and how they limit interpretive comparisons. From these biases, follow areas for consideration for future intensive field surveys.

Bias one - incomplete nucleated settlement pattern
For any given intensive field survey studied, a detailed study of the complete settlement pattern is absent or incomplete. This results in a distorted picture of the landscape, which is the result of current archaeological enquiries and practices. Time, money and research questions direct archaeological fieldwork to specific discourses, which do not provide a total picture, as might be considered necessary for studying the landscape, as to how this translates into demographic estimates and the distribution of the regional population.

A delicate divide along the line of the urban-rural dichotomy and/or town and country has been observed. For the nucleated settlements, the focus has been on the top of the settlement hierarchy, an area where traditional excavation practices often focus on public buildings and elite houses. The focus for the bottom of the settlement hierarchy has been on the identification of farms and *villae*, and sites versus off-site, which is the working territory of field survey archaeology. The top of the settlement hierarchy, represented by the *municipia* and *coloniae* are well described in literature, however the size and urban make-up of these centres are less well known and understood. The nucleated settlements, without *municipium* or *colonia* status, representing unofficial small towns, villages, road stations and hamlets are seldom a specific area of enquiry and form a blind spot in our knowledge. This situation is not unique to Roman Italy. The incomplete record of villages is also known from Greece (Farinetti 2009, 230) and Roman Britain (Brown 1995; Burnham 1995).

Locational and rank-size analysis can help to identify gaps in the settlement pattern, where, from a functional perspective, a nucleated settlement could be expected, but archaeological verification of these settlements would be required to close this gap. Survey archaeology has been focussing primarily on farms and *villae*, and a study of the lesser civic and other nucleated settlements is often lacking from publications. Although the majority of the road stations are well attested in ancient road maps, such as the *Tabula Peutingeriana*, they are seldom excavated, apart from a few exceptions (Johnson et al. 2004). The category of villages (*vici*) forms another gap in current knowledge. The chapter on the empty landscape of Cisalpine Gaul tried to explore the village dimension, attempting to estimate the number of villages that are not attested for in literature or from the archaeological record. The outcome of the study remains a hypothetical construction until archaeological enquiry offers clarification, not only for Cisalpine Gaul, but also for the Greek and Roman World alike. The Potenza Valley Survey identified hamlets that, although it can be debated if they are actually part of the *extra-mural* settlements belonging to the nearest civic centre, do offer a new perspective on the rural landscape. This perspective, one in which a significant percentage, ca. 15-20% of the rural population could have been living in hamlets, consisting of 5-15 farms, spread over the landscape with infill of farms and *villae*, would provide a different view of the organisation of the landscape. Site typology often ignores this category and the sites are treated separately, potentially creating excessive high farm and *villae* densities, and not as a part of a widespread pattern of small nucleated settlements.

Bias two - The size and urban make up of civic centres
The scarcity of data for civic centres, especially for the make-up and variations in the size and density of the inhabited area from a chronological perspective, can result in a distortedly static picture and consequent population estimate. This has shown to be a special concern for the centres that are located in the extended *suburbium* of Rome, where population from a wide distance migrated to the main centre, which could have left the intra-mural area of large centres relatively empty. The opposite scenario should also be considered; overpopulated centres with extramural habitation. The debate on the inhabited area and chronology of civic centres can be extended to villages and road stations. Because the civic centres function as population sinks in demographic reconstruction, extra caution should be taken because their size can make a difference between a low or high degree of urbanisation for a region.

Bias three - Transect size and location
Current field survey research design and practices focuses on transects that are 'doable', not only in terms of accessibility, visibility (ploughed fields), and landscape features, but also in size and required resources. A relatively small team with a limited budget will be forced to make trade-offs. If the unit of study is a river valley then only a small percentage of the total area can practically be surveyed and the question can be asked if these transect areas are representative for reconstructing the landscape and local demography of the whole region or valley? Moreover, transects are typically located in the immediate hinterland of large settlements, covering agricultural land where a high density of sites can be expected, resulting in high population densities which are then extrapolated over a larger area. Current practice could suffice for obtaining a chronological view, from an *Annales* or micro-region perspective. A disadvantage of selective partial survey coverage is that nucleated settlements that are not part of the literary record (*vici* and hamlets) for which the location is unknown, will be overlooked. None of the surveys made use of control transects for which the location was randomly determined. The data from the control transect can be used to adjust the size/population numbers and densities.

Bias four - Sample/transect versus actual field walked area
A distinction between the size of a sample/transect and the actual field walked area is often lacking in the older publications, unintentionally leading to underestimates of site and population densities. This data probably exist in the GIS metadata files and could be revisited in future research. This bias will be further elaborated on in the discussion of the outcome of the comparative study.

Bias five – Site recovery multipliers
The use of site recovery ratios for farms and *villae*, which goes beyond ground-cover correction factors and interwalker distance, seems to have received wide acceptance. These site multipliers are used very loosely and further refinements, based on region, survey intensity, landscape or type of sites have been theorized. The rationale behind recovery ratios is perfectly legitimate, but the impact on rural population densities and how Roman society could be described can be significant when such an approach is accepted. This study forms no exception. The methodological implications, especially with respect to research design and survey practices, remain an epistemological weakness of the archaeological discipline. Personal beliefs on what the population density could have been, possibly instigated by population statistics from more recent periods, are used to make a position plausible. The challenges of how to establish a defendable and falsifiable recovery ratio cannot be resolved in this study. Besides site typology and occupation chronology, much more thought and effort should be dedicated to developing a practical methodology that separates statistical from archaeological inference. As the reconstruction of the landscape and demography requires input of the number of sites by type, it will be vital to understand how many sites have disappeared from the archaeological record, or invisible in a particular year, and how many sites can still be identified in sufficient quality of information by improving survey practices! Sites being on the brink of getting 'lost' from the archaeological record, because of the introduction of mechanized farming, were driving a lot of the rescue survey work done by Ward-Perkins in the Tiber Valley (Potter 1979). For statistical and archaeological inference a key issue is that a sample is taken from an unknown population of different types of sites with an unknown distribution. The use of the word 'sample' is misleading, as the location and size of transects are not randomly chosen, but hand-picked based on research aims and presuppositions of the survey team (*bias three*). Geophysical prospection has become a popular alternative to time consuming excavations. The method is used for intra- and extra mural surveys around large settlements to determine the urban make-up and the density and extent of occupation. These techniques have also been used for obtaining floor plans of *villae*. Little experimenting has been done to evaluate if these methods would be of value, or even suitable, in assessing recovery ratios, specifically statistical inference. Knowledge on changes in the landscape can be factored into reconstructions. Digital Elevation Modelling was used in the Pontine region for determining changes in landscape due to sedimentation, erosion or agricultural activity, which could reveal areas where sites once existed, buried under metres of sedimentation, or bulldozed to the sides of agricultural plots. It is obvious that a combination of methods needs to be used for studying the important dimension of site recovery.

Bias six – site typology and site population
Many scholars already commented on the artificial nature of site typology, and elaborated on the continuum of

different types and forms, and how meaning is given to the size of scatters and the presence of certain types of building materials and diagnostic finds. A key element to making demographic estimates that must be better researched is the number of inhabitants and social organization per site-type. It has been argued that high site and population densities would result in low site populations for farms and relatively moderate population per *villae*. In other regions, with a lower population pressure and different agricultural practices higher site population densities for farms and *villae* are envisioned. It is not quite clear if this argument is supported by archaeological or historical evidence. Witcher has tried to capture this dimension in his extended *suburbium* model, but more detailed enquiry should allow more narrow ranges depending on region and the estimated area of the land under cultivation.

Bias seven – The integration of metadata from different surveys

The integration and comparison of intensive field surveys with overlapping geography poses an additional challenge. In the Pontine region, the sites identified by the *Formae Italiae* team were revisited, but the area was not intensively (re-)surveyed for undiscovered sites. A view on the potential issues of combining field survey data has been discussed for the Biferno Valley and the Larinum Survey. The latter had a significant overlap with the region surveyed by Barker, but the Larinum Survey ignored the older dataset. The comparison of the metadata suggests that, although an overlap exists, two different populations of sites were identified. This can partially be explained by survey intensity and biases, and begs for more investigation and maybe small scale resurveying to expand our understanding.

The second research question focused on the use, validity and limitations of ethnographic and historical analogies. In the absence of sufficient archaeological data, historical or contemporary analogies are used as heuristic devices for exploring ranges for the variables that are used for demographic estimates. This unfortunately takes away the potential uniqueness of the individual settlement or micro-region, and the split between people living in nucleated settlement and in the rural landscape that might have existed. As a heuristic device, analogies can provide a first hypothesis that can trigger further research. Analogies should not be confused with scientifically obtained data from the archaeological record. These first hypotheses often start their own life and find their way into publications easily. The Latin *colonia* of Cosa is often used as a contemporary analogy, but how exemplary was Cosa, or even Pompeii for the Roman World on the Italian peninsula? Was Italy covered with little Cosa- or Pompeii-like civic centres? Most likely not. Cosa was even a failure with marginal existence and a declining population numbers into the Imperial period. The same can be argued for analogies that are based on those Roman *coloniae* for which the number of initial settlers and the walled area are known. Historical analogies have also been used, especially in cases where there are no intensive field survey publications available.

A key weakness of such an approach is that an assumption needs to be made on the size (range) of the rural population using an urbanisation ratio and an arbitrary population threshold. As archaeological evidence is lacking this presupposition cannot be challenged. What if both archaeological and literary sources would be available, would the data make sense? Ginatempo and Giorgi described the challenges when making a reconstruction of the settlement pattern and demography of medieval settlements in Italian Tuscany based on comparing the available literary sources and archaeological data (Ginatempo and Giorgi 1999). A settlement hierarchy became visible from the thirteenth century onwards, driven by the documentation of territorial rights of the major centres. It was not until the fifteenth century that demography was recorded. The merger of the two data sources is not without problems, especially the interpretation of an increase in the number of sites compared to the recorded size of the population. Regional studies like these are exceptional and have the potential to provide more insights into how a case for a (regional) historical analogy can be build.

The arbitrary population threshold that defines when a settlement can be classified urban is often treated as a tipping point, referring to the occupational structure of the Medieval or Early Modern town. For the Roman World, the occupational structure of towns is lacking, making this not a useful criterion. In opposition to a potentially complete settlement system for the Early Modern period, there is an incomplete settlement system for the Roman World. The logic focuses on the civic centres, under the assumption that large settlements are civic centres. This may all sound very sceptical, but not intended as such. If analogies are used for investigating ranges, and the assumptions are clearly articulated then they can provide a defendable position that can be falsified on key elements or by new research.

The remainder of the chapter will focus on creating a comparative perspective for the regions of study, and will discuss the archaeological implications (research objective 3). The data from the Early Imperial period will be used because this period has more and better quality data available and covers a limited, archaeologically well-defined, period. The civic centres played a dominant role in all the regions and surveys that have been discussed. This is related to gaps in the settlement hierarchy in terms of villages, road stations and hamlets and provides a distorted functional picture and distribution of the population (*bias one*). A comparative view of the distribution of civic centres and typical size can be provided for the civic centres (table 10.1). Although the size of the regions, the number of centres and the landscapes vary, the size of a typical *municipium* or *colonia* can be considered relatively small, in the 12-30 ha range with a modest population size per centre; 1,200-4,500 at a population density in the 100-150 people/ha range. The centres of the inner *suburbium* and the Pontine region, especially the former Latin and Etruscan city-states, have a larger walled area, but their inhabited area, during the Late Republican and Early Imperial periods can be debated (*bias two*). The typical

Table 10.1: Average size and hinterland for the civic centres for the Early Imperial period.

Region	Municipia and Coloniae	Average Size (ha)	Avg. Hinterland (km^2)	Avg. Interdistance (km)	Avg. Radius (km)
Cisalpine Gaul	78	ca. 30	1,815	28.0	17.5
Potenza Valley	4	17	153	10.3	6.4
Inner Suburbium	33 excl. Rome	26 excl. Rome	223	11.2	7.0
Outer Suburbium	39	ca. 23	344	14.7	9.2
Pontine Region	8	ca. 20	225	12.7	7.3
Biferno Valley	4	ca. 12	625	21.8	13.6

size of the hinterland, established via the construction of Thiessen polygons, indicates that the area under immediate control of the Roman civic centres was in a 150-225 km^2 range for the inner *suburbium*, the Pontine region, and the Potenza Valley. A bivariate statistical analysis for the extended *suburbium* in a 100 km radius from Rome suggests that the size of the hinterland is very much structured by landscape. A spatial ordering of centres that was driven on the agricultural potential of the immediate hinterland would make sense for a pre-industrial society. The rugged mountainous areas of Cisalpine Gaul, which covers ca. 50% of the area, could not have supported the same dense settlement and population density, skewing the average size of the hinterland upwards. The geographic boundaries of this region do not provide an equal basis for comparison versus the catchment area of a river valley. The same can be argued for parts of the area within the extended, outer *suburbium* that covers the Apennine Mountains. Bekker-Nielsen reported an average interdistance for the centres located in the fertile Po Valley, on the *Via Aemilia* corridor, of 15.3 km (Bekker-Nielsen 1989, 25), which was within a peasant day-return trip. The other, more remote areas would require infill with lower order nucleated settlements that functioned as central places, or a different socio-economic organisation based on more isolated settlements with poor interconnectivity. Following this landscape centred rationale, the relatively large average size of the hinterland of the small civic centres of the Biferno Valley could be envisioned to have been linked to the agricultural potential of this region. The infill of the landscape with lesser order settlements, *vici* and road stations, provided farmers with central places within a day return distance. In summary, looking at table 10.1, the two exceptional non-marketable radii (Cisalpine Gaul and Biferno Valley) confirm the likelihood that *vici* filled the servicing gaps in these regions.

The study of urbanism and demography is strongly influenced by conventions. Both Bairoch and De Vries took a 3,000 people population threshold value in their demographic studies. However, this value was instigated by the available literary sources and does not mean that centres with less than 3,000 people do not have functional traits, such as marketing and services, jurisdiction, administration, elite presence, and a social organisation that can be associated with urban life. The present study did not aim at resolving the urban-rural dichotomy or aiming at defining criteria for urban in a Roman context, but a lower level for functioning local nucleations was clearly present in Roman Italy in, for example, the Biferno Valley. Hypothetically sites of 10 ha or ca. 1,000 people might represent a threshold above which such foci can be recognised.

The establishment and comparison of rural population densities has been shown to be challenging and problematic. Although the precise site-typology varied by survey team, a high-level comparison, without the use of site recovery ratios, can be proposed for site densities of farms and *villae* derived from the published intensive field surveys (table 10.2). The base case would be the inner *suburbium* of Rome, which was believed to have been the most densely populated region of Roman Italy. Witcher modelled an idealised two farms and one *villae*. The Pontine region and the Potenza Valley show a significantly higher site density of farms compared to the inner *suburbium* (0.63 farm/km^2). For farms, this is a factor of 3.8 for the Pontine region and a factor of 8.3 higher for the Potenza Valley. This difference compared to the survey information used by Witcher is significant and requires further discussion as to why.

The first explanation is that the data represent a genuine difference in which the rural landscape of the Potenza Valley was at least as densely settled as the Pontine region, and the Pontine region would have had a higher density of farms and *villae* compared to the area north of Rome (South Etruria). If this outlook is accepted then the *suburbium* model, as postulated by Witcher, in which the population density decreased with increased distance to Rome, can be questioned. Moreover, the Italian peninsula would have had pockets of high population density, such as the Potenza Valley and areas with very low density, such as the Biferno Valley.

The alternative explanation considers differences in survey methodology, landscape and at micro-region level. Farm and *villae* densities have been extrapolated from the

Table 10.2: Uncorrected densities of farms and villae for the Early Imperial period.

Survey Region	Survey Intensity Ranking (1-5)	Study Area (km^2)	Surveyed Area (km^2)	% of Study Area	Farm Density (sites/km^2)	Villae Density (sites/km^2)
Potenza Valley	1	400	10.72	2.7%	5.2	1.0
Inner Suburbium	5	5,415	(1,638.5)	30.3%	0.63	0.72
Outer Suburbium	4	9,051	(494)	5.5%	-	-
Pontine Region	2	1,850	26.245	1.4%	2.4	1.0
Biferno Valley	3	2,250	400 / 267	17.8% / 11.9%	0.21 / 0.32	0.045 / 0.068

survey data. The size of the surveyed areas, the relative location of these areas to civic centres, and survey intensity can skew results (*biases three and four*). The published survey areas have been a subset of the total study areas, but do these survey areas equate to the actual field walked areas or to the ploughed fields within these survey areas? For the Potenza Valley Survey and the Pontine region this difference has been explicitly made in the publications and resulted in high rural site densities that covered a relatively low percentage of the total study area (2.7% and 1.4%). The Biferno Valley Survey publication covers a reported survey area of 400 km^2. A close study of the publication arbitrarily narrows this down to 267 km^2, covering still an impressive 11.9% of the study area. Doubt has been expressed in this study over the intensity of the Biferno Valley Survey, confirmed by Stek's analysis of an adjacent area. The dataset that Witcher used for his extended *suburbium* model has been based on a collection of published surveys and suggests impressive 30.3% coverage of the area of the inner *suburbium*. It is not clear though if this 30.3% coverage refers to the survey or the actual fieldwalked area. A study of the raw metadata for the Biferno Survey and the surveys used by Witcher for the *suburbium* model would be required for further refinements.

All investigated surveys have a strong rural hinterland component (*bias four*); areas where high densities can be expected and with sufficient agricultural potential to support the civic centre. This bias cannot be filtered out and future research designs should consider using randomly picked control areas outside of these rural hinterlands. Not all field surveys have been conducted at the same survey intensity and a ranking can be suggested for each region that has been discussed (table 10.2). High survey intensities can be argued for the Potenza Valley and the Pontine region and lower survey intensity for the inner and outer *suburbium* as well as the Biferno Valley.

Simulations with the use of recovery ratios have been made in the case history chapters (*bias five*). As argued earlier, the underlying rationale for obtaining a realistic multiplier, per site-type, landscape or region, including the separation between statistical and archaeological inference has not been sufficiently studied by archaeologists. The same can be argued for the population per site type (*bias six*). Population densities ranges can be calculated using an estimated 5-8 person for each farm and 15-25 persons for a *villae* (table 10.3). Population estimates for the Potenza Valley offer a very limited playing field for correction factors, unless an economy is envisioned that relied on food imports for the population, which can be considered an unlikely scenario from a geo-political perspective. A recovery ratio of 18% (12% after correction for survey area) was arbitrarily established in this study for the Biferno Valley, which would result in a total population density of ca. 20 persons/km^2. An assumed differentiated recovery ratio of 35% for farms and 70% for *villae*, for the Pontine region would result in a hypothetical total population density in the range of 66-83 persons/km^2. Finally, a recovery ratio for the inner *suburbium* was not hypothesised in the individual chapter. If a rural population density in the same range as for the Potenza Valley would be assumed then a differentiated site recovery of 35% for farms and 70% for villae, which was also used for the Pontine region, could be considered realistic for the inner *suburbium*.

The high level view on demography, settlement pattern and hierarchy that emerges for the Late Republican-Early Imperial Roman Itlay considers the majority of the population, in the range of 75-90%, living in the countryside. Moderately sized civic centres of 12-30 ha in size were spaced at regular intervals, depending on landscape, facilitating a day-return trip, essential for the marketing needs of the people living in the countryside. *Vici* filled the servicing gaps in those regions with exceptional non-marketable radii, such as Cisalpine Gaul and the Biferno Valley. The size of the hinterland of the civic centres, excluding Cisalpine Gaul and the Biferno Valley, was in the 150-225 km^2 range. A working hypothesis on the function of the civic centres would consider them as service centres. These centres would have had market facilities, small-scale industry, imported goods from trade, legal services, entertainment and the presence of local elites that could afford a certain level of public display, resulting in limited urban architecture. A banding-servicing view has been envisioned for the towns and market centres that could reflect different levels of servicing for local, sub-regional and regional centres. The nature of the Roman civic centres can be contrasted with the situation in Classical Greece. Hansen estimated that ca. 80% of all *poleis*, representing small and medium sized centres, had a maximum territory of 200 km^2 and a population of a few thousands (Hansen 2006, 28-9). Bintliff has argued, based on seven Greek surveys, that 70-80% of the population lived within the *polis* walls. This implies that the Greeks must have been farmers for which the majority lived in the *polis* centre and walked every morning to their fields in the hinterland (Bintliff 1997b; Bintliff 2002a). The typical size of the hinterland of Greek *poleis* (ca. 200 km^2) is in the same ballpark range as for the inner *suburbium*, the Pontine region and the Potenza Valley.

The differences between Greek and Roman urbanism could have political and socio-economic origins. There was more power associated with the Roman class system in the Roman World and the average Roman citizen was not politically involved and was instead tied to the elite

Table 10.3: Estimated rural and total population densities for the Early Imperial period (incl. recovery ratios).

Region	Site Recovery	rural Population Density (persons/km^2)	Total Population Density (persons/km^2)	Urbanisation Ratio
Potenza Valley	100%	63-89	84-111	19-26%
Pontine Region	Farms 35%, *Villae* 70%	55-66	66-83	15-20%
Biferno Valley	12%	ca. 18	ca. 20	ca. 13%

by the clientele system. Politics was an urban phenomena and was focussed on the resident elite. Moreover, territorial empire building and the *Pax Romana* would have reduced the need for protection from wars resulting in 75-90% of the population living in the countryside, so a low urbanisation ratio. The Greeks had a different concept of the citizen community, which was built on exclusiveness and fierce rivalry existed between the *poleis*. For the citizens of a *polis* it would thus have been ideal to live in the centre, resulting in a relative high level of urbanisation. In the pre-Roman periods on the Italian peninsula, the balance could have been pushed towards the urban end and the Greek model of urbanisation, which shifted towards the rural end and the Roman model with a low level of urbanisation that extended to the Medieval and Early Modern periods.

Abstract

In this study, published intensive field surveys from different geographies on the Italian peninsula have been revisited with the aim of developing a better understanding of regional differences in demography, settlement pattern, landuse and how Roman society could have functioned. The field surveys/regions that have been subject to in-depth enquiry are Cisalpine Gaul, the Potenza Valley, the *suburbium* of Rome, the Pontine region and the Biferno Valley. The focus has been on the Late Republican to Early Imperial period. Models and interpretive concepts have been assessed that originate from archaeology, social geography and ethnography using archaeological evidence.

The following seven biases hinder the interpretation and comparison of field survey information; (1) an incompletely identified nucleated settlement pattern; (2) questions on the size and urban make up of civic centres; (3) the precise size and location of field walked transects; (4) the reported sample/transect size versus actual field walked area; (5) the use of site recovery multipliers; (6) site typology and site population and (7) the integration of metadata from different surveys.

The establishment and comparison of the demographic dimension have been shown to be challenging and problematic. The base case would be the inner *suburbium* of Rome, which was believed to have been the most densely populated region of Roman Italy. A bivariate statistical analysis for the *suburbium* of Rome suggests that the settlement patterns of the main centres are structured by landscape and have Archaic antecedents.

Not all field surveys have been conducted at the same survey intensities and a ranking has been suggested for each region. High survey intensities can be argued for the Potenza Valley and the Pontine region and lower survey intensities for the inner and outer *suburbium* as well as the Biferno Valley. The underlying rationale for obtaining a realistic multiplier, per site-type, landscape or region, including the separation between statistical and archaeological inference has not been sufficiently studied by archaeologists.

The high-level view on demography, settlement pattern and hierarchy considers the majority of the population, in the range of 75-90%, living in the countryside. Moderately- sized civic centres of 12-30 ha in size were spaced at regular intervals, depending on landscape, facilitating a day-return trip, essential for the marketing needs of the people living in the countryside. *Vici* filled the servicing gaps in those regions with exceptional non-marketable radii. The size of the hinterland of the civic centres, excluding Cisalpine Gaul and the Biferno Valley, was in the 150-225 km^2 range. A working hypothesis on the function of the civic centres would consider them as service centres. A banding-servicing view has been envisioned for the towns and market centres that could reflect different levels of servicing for local, sub-regional and regional centres. The contrast between Greek and Roman urbanisation ratios offers very fruitful insights for future research in the functioning of these two civilisations.

Bibliography

Afzelius, A., (1942a). Areal und Bevölkerung des römischen Bundes im Jahre 225 v. Chr. , in *Aarsskrift for Aarhus Universitet* Copenhagen, 15-135.

Afzelius, A., (1942b). Die Römer erobern Italien, in *Aarsskrift for Aarhus Universitet* Copenhagen, 136-96.

Alcock, S. E., 1993. *Graecia Ccapta : the landscapes of Roman Greece,* Cambridge: Cambridge University Press.

Ammerman, A. J. & N. Terrenato, 1996. Visibility and Site Recovery in the Cecina Valley Survey, Italy. *Journal of Field Archaeology,* 23(1), 91-109.

Attema, P., 2000. Ceramics of the First Millennium BC from a Survey at Lanuvium in the Alban Hills, Central Italy: Method, Aims and First Results of Regional Fabric Classification. *Palaeohistoria,* 39/40, 413-39.

Attema, P. & T. De Haas, (forthcoming). Rural Settlement and Population Extrapolation: A Case Study from the Ager Antium, Central Italy (350 BC - AD 400), in *Oxford Studies on the Roman Economy*.

Attema, P., T. De Haas & G. Tol, 2009. *Nettuno, il Territorio Dalla Preistoria al Medioevo. La Carta Archeologica* Groningen: Institute of Archaeology, University of Groningen.

Attema, P., T. C. A. De Haas & M. La Rosa, 2005. Sites of the Fogliano Survey (Pontine Region, Central Italy), Site Classification and a Comment on the Diagnostic Artefacts from Prehistory to the Roman Period. *Palaeohistoria,* 45/46, 121-96.

Attema, P., E. van Joolen & M. Van Leusen, 2002. A Marginal Landscape: Field Work on the Beach Ridge Complex near Fogliano (South Lazio). *Palaeohistoria,* 41/42, 149-62.

Attema, P. & M. Van Leusen, (2004). The Early Roman Colonization of South Lazio; a Survey of Three Landscapes, in *Centralization, Early Urbanization and Colonization in First Millennium BC Italy and Greece. Part 1: Italy*, ed. P. Attema Leuven: Peeters, 165-95.

Attema, P. A. J. & T. De Haas, (2004). Villas and farms in the Pontine region between 300 BC and 300 AD: a landscape archaeological approach, in *Roman villas around the Urbs. Interaction with landscape and environment*, eds. B. Santillo Frizell & A. Klynne Rome: Swedish Institute in Rome, 1-16.

Attema, P. A. J. & T. De Haas, (2005). Villas and farms in the Pontine region between 300 BC and 300 AD: a landscape archaeological approach, in *Roman villas around the Urbs. Interaction with landscape and environment*, eds. B. Santillo Frizell & A. Klynne Rome: Swedish Institute in Rome, 97-112.

Attema, P. A. J., H. Feiken, T. C. A. De Haas & G. W. Tol, 2008. The Astura and Nettuno Surveys of the Pontine Region Project (2003-2005). 1st Report. *Palaeohistoria,* 49/50, 415-516.

Bagnall, R. S. & B. W. Frier, 1994. *The demography of Roman Egypt,* Cambridge: Cambridge University Press.

Bairoch, P., J. Batou & P. Chevre, 1988. *La population des villes européennes de 800 è 1850,* Genève: Libraire Droz.

Barker, G., 1995a. *The Biferno Valley Survey. The Archaeological and Geomorphological Record,* London: Leicester University Press.

Barker, G., 1995b. *A Mediterranean Valley. Landscape Archaeology and Annales History in the Biferno Valley,* London: Leicester University Press.

Barker, G. & T. Rasmussen, 1998. *The Etruscans,* Oxford: Blackwell Publishers.

Becker, J. A., M. Mogetta & N. Terrenato, 2009. A New Plan for an Ancient Italian City: Gabii Revealed. *American Journal of Archaeology,* 113, 629-42.

Bekker-Nielsen, T., (1989). The Geography of Power. Studies in the Urbanization of Roman North-West Europe, in *BAR International Series 477* Oxford.

Bintliff, J., 1997a. Regional Survey, Demography, and the rise of Complex Societies in the Ancient Aegean: Core-Periphery, Neo-Malthusian, and Other Interpretive Models. *Journal of Field Archaeology,* 24(1), 1-38.

Bintliff, J., (1999). Settlement and Territory, in *The Routledge Companion Encyclopedia of Archaeology*, ed. G. Barker London: Routledge, 505-45.

Bintliff, J., (2002a). Going to Market in Antiquity, in *Zu Wasser und zu Land. Verkehrswege in der Antiken Welt*, eds. E. Olshausen & H. Sonnabend Stuttgart: Franz Steiner Verlag, 209-50.

Bintliff, J., (2006). City-country relationships in the 'Normal Polis', in *City, Countryside, and the Spatial Organization of Value in Classical Antiquity*, eds. R. M. Rosen & I. Sluiter Leiden: Brill, 13-32.

Bintliff, J., (2007). Emergent Complexity in Settlement Systems and Urban Transformations, in *Historische Geographie der Alten Welt. Grundlagen, Erträge, Perspectiven. Festgabe für Eckart Olshausen aus Anlass seiner Emeritierung*Hildesheim: Georg Olms Verlag 43-82.

Bintliff, J. & A. Snodgrass, 1988. Off-Site Pottery Distributions: A Regional and Interregional Perspective. *Current Anthropology,* 29(3), 506-13.

Bintliff, J., P. Howard & A. Snodgrass, 1999. The Hidden Landscape of Prehistoric Greece. *Journal of Mediterranean Archaeology,* 12(2), 139-68.

Bintliff, J., P. Howard & A. Snodgrass, 2007. *Testing the hinterland. the work of the Boeotia Survey*

Bintliff, J. F., *(1989-1991) in the southern approaches to the city of Thespiai*, Cambridge: Oxbow Books.

Bintliff, J. F., (1994). Territorial behaviour and the natural history of the Greek Polis, in *Grenze und Grenzland. Stutgarter Kolloquium zur historischen Geografie des Altertums*, eds. E. Olshausen & H. Sonnabend Stutgard: Franz Steiner Verlag, 207-49, Tafel 19-73.

Bintliff, J. L., (1997b). Further considerations on the population of ancient Boeotia, in *Recent Developments in the History and Archaeology of Central Greece*, ed. J. L. Bintliff Oxford: BAR Int. Series, 231-52.

Bintliff, J. L., (2002b). Rethinking Early Mediterranean Urbanism, in *Mauerschau, Bd. 1. Festschrift für Manfred Korfmann*, ed. R. Aslan Tübingen: Verlag Bernhard Albert Greiner, 153-77.

Bintliff, J. L. & A. M. Snodgrass, 1985. The Boeotia Survey, a Preliminary Report: The First Four Years. *Journal of Field Archaeology*, 12, 123-61.

Bispham, E., 2007. *From Asculum to Actium. The Municipalization of Italy from the Social War to Augustus*, Oxford: Oxford University Press.

Boatwright, M. T., D. Gargola & R. J. A. Talbert, 2004. *The Romans from Village to Empire*, Oxford: Oxford University Press.

Brandizzi Vittucci, P., 2000. *Antium. Anzio e Nettuno in epoca romana*, Rome: Bardi Editore.

Brown, A. E., (1995). Roman small towns, medieval small towns and markets, in *Roman Small Towns in Eastern England and Beyond*, ed. A. E. Brown Oxford: Oxbow Books, 1-6.

Brunt, P. A., 1987. *Italian Manpower 225 B.C.–A.D. 14*, Oxford: Oxford University Press.

Burnham, B. C., (1995). Small towns: the British perspective, in *Roman Small Towns in Eastern England and Beyond*, ed. A. E. Brown Oxford: Oxbow Books, 7-17.

Cambi, F., (1999). Demography and Romanization in Central Italy, in *The Archaeology of Mediterranean Landscapes 1, Reconstructing Past Population Trends in Mediterranean Europe* eds. J. Bintliff & K. Sbonias Oxford, 115-27.

Caroll, G. R., 1982. National City-size distributions: what do we know after 67 years of research? *Progress in Human Geography*, 6(1), 1-43.

Cavanagh, W., (2002). The Laconia Survey: An Overview, in *The Laconia Survey. Continuity and Change in a Greek Rural Landscape* London, 421-37.

Cavanagh, W., 2009. Settlement Structure in Laconia and Attica at the End of the Archaic Period: The Fractal Dimension. *American Journal of Archaeology*, 113(3), 405-21.

Cavanagh, W. & R. R. Laxton, 1995. The rank-size dimension and the history of site structure from survey data. *Journal of Quantitative Anthropology*, 5, 327-58.

Cherry, J. F., J. Brennet & E. Mantzourani, 1991. *Landscape archaeology as long-term history : northern Keos in the Cycladic Islands from earliest settlement until modern times.*, Los Angeles.

Christaller, W., 1933. *Die zentralen Orte in Süddeutschland: eine ökonomisch-geographische Untersuchung über die Gesotzmässigkeit der Verbreitung und Entwicklung der Siedlungen mit städtischen Funktionen*, Jena: Gustav Fischer.

Clark, D., 1982. *Urban Geography*, London: Chroom Helm Ltd.

Clark, P., 2009. *European Cities and Towns 400-2000*, Oxford: Oxford University Press.

Coarelli, F., 1993. *Lazio*, Rome: Laterza and Figli.

Coarelli, F., (2008). Lexicon Topographicum Urbis Romae. Suburbium. Volume 5, ed. A. La Regina Rome: Quasar, 17-21.

Conolly, J. & M. Lake, 2006. *Geographical Information Systems in Archaeology*, Cambridge: Cambridge University Press.

Conventi, M., 2004. *Città romane di fondazione*, Rome.

Cornell, T. J., 1995. *The Beginnings of Rome. Italy from the Bronze Age to the Punic Wars (c. 1000-264 BC)*, London: Routledge.

Cornell, T. J., (2000). The City-States in Latium, in *A Comparative Study of Thirty City-State Cultures*, ed. M. H. Hansen Copenhagen: C.A. Reitzels Forlag, 209-28.

De Felice, E., 1994. *Larinum*, Florence: Firenze.

De Haas, T. C. A., 2008. Comparing settlement histories in the Pontine Region (southern Lazio, central Italy): surveys in the coastal landscape near Nettuno. *Digressus*, 8, 1-32.

De Ligt, L., 1990. Demand, Supply, Distribution: The Roman Peasantry between Town and Countryside: Rural Monetization and Peasant Demand. *Münstersche Beiträge zur Antiken Handelsgeschichte*, IX(2), 24-56.

De Ligt, L., 1991. The Roman Peasantry Demand, Supply, Distribution between Town and Countryside. II: Supply, Distribution and a Comparative Perspective. *Münstersche Beiträge zur Antiken Handelsgeschichte*, X(1), 33-77.

De Ligt, L., (2008). The Population of Cisalpine Gaul in the time of Augustus, in *People, Land, and Politics. Demographic Developments and the Transformation of Roman Italy, 300 BC-AD 14* eds. L. d. Ligt & S. J. Northwood Leiden: Brill, 139-83.

De Ligt, L. & S. J. Northwood (eds.), (2008). *People, Land, and Politics. Demographic Developments and the Transformation of Roman Italy, 300 BC-AD 14* Leiden: Brill.

De Vries, J., 1984. *European Urbanisation 1500-1800*, London: Routledge.

Drennan, R. D. & C. E. Peterson, 2004. Comparing archaeological settlement systems with rank-size graphs: a measure of shape and statistical confidence. *Journal of Archaeological Science*, 31, 533-49.

Duncan-Jones, R., 1982. *The Economy of the Roman Empire: Quantitative Studies.*, Cambridge: Cambridge University Press.

Falconer, S. E. & S. H. Savage, 1995. Heartlands and Hinterlands: Alternative Trajectories of Early Urbanization in Mesopotamia and the Southern Levant. *American Antiquity,* 60(1), 37-58.

Falconer, S. E. & S. H. Savage, 2003. Spatial and Statistical Inference of Late Bronze Age Polities in the Southern Levant. *Bulletin of the American Schools of Oriental Research,* 330, 31-45.

Farinetti, E., (2009). Boeotian Landscapes. A GIS-based study for the reconstruction and interpretation of the archaeological datasets of ancient Boeotia, (Leiden, unpublished PhD thesis University Leiden).

Farinetti, E., (2011). Boeotian Landscapes. A GIS-based study for the reconstruction and interpretation of the archaeological datasets of ancient Boeotia, in *BAR International Series 2195* Oxford.

Fentress, E., 2003. *Cosa V: An intermittent town. Excavations 1991-1997,* Michigan.

Fentress, E., (2009). Peopling the Countryside: Roman Demography in the Albegna Valley and Jerba, in *Quantifying the Roman Economy: Methods and Problems*, eds. A. Bowman & A. Wilson Oxford: Oxford University Press, 127-61.

Finley, M. I., 1985. *The Ancient Economy,* Berkeley: University of California Press.

Frayn, J. M., 1993. *Markets and Fairs in Roman Italy. Their Social and Economic Importance from the Second Century BC to the Third Century AD,* Oxford: Clarendon Press.

Garnsey, P., (1998). Where did Italian Peasants Live?, in *Cities, Peasants and Food in Classical Antiquity: Essays in Social and Economic History*, ed. W. Scheidel Cambridge: Cambridge University Press, 107-33.

Ginatempo, M. & A. Giorgi, (1999). Documentary Sources for the History of Medieval Settlements in Tuscany, in *The Archaeology of Mediterranean Landscapes 1, Reconstructing Past Population Trends in Mediterranean Europe* eds. J. Bintliff & K. Sbonias Oxford: Oxbow Books, 173-93.

Gkiasta, M., 2008. *The Historiography of Landscape Research on Crete,* Leiden: Leiden University Press.

Goodchild, H., (2007). Modelling Roman Agricultural Production in the Middle Tiber Valley, Central Italy, in *Institute of Archaeology and Antiquity* Birmingham: University of Birmingham, Unpublished PhD Dissertation.

Hansen, M. H., 2006. *The Shotgun Method. The Demography of the Ancient Greek City-State Culture,* Columbia: University of Missouri Press.

Hansen, M. N., (2004). The concept of the consumption city applied to the Greek polis, in *Once again: Studies in the ancient Greek polis,* ed. T. H. Nielsen Stuttgart, 9-47.

Harrison, T. P., 1997. Shifting Patterns of Settlement in the Highlands of Central Jordan during the Early Bronze Age. *Bulletin of the American Schools of Oriental Research,* 306, 1-37.

Haselgrove, C., (1985). Inference from Ploughsoil Artefact Samples, in *Archaeology from The Ploughsoil. Studies in the Collection and Interpretation of Field Survey data,* eds. C. Haselgrove, M. Millett & I. Smith Sheffield: University of Sheffield.

Hayes, J. W., 1997. *Handbook of Mediterranean Roman Pottery,* Norman, Oklahoma: University of Oklahoma Press.

Horden, P. & N. Purcell, 2000. *The Corrupting Sea. A Study of Mediterranean History*: Blackwell Publishing.

Ikeguchi, M., 1999. A Comparative Study of Settlement Patterns and Agricultural Structures in Ancient Italy: A Methodology for Interpreting Field Survey Evidence. *Kodai. Journal of Ancient History,* 10, 1-59.

Johnson, P., S. Keay & M. Millett, (2004). Lesser Urban Sites in the Tiber Valley: Baccanae, Forum Cassii and Castellum Amerinum, in *Papers of the British School at Rome* London, 69-99.

Johnston, R. J., D. Gregory, G. Pratt & M. Watts, 2000. *The Dictionary of Human Geography,* Oxford: Blackwell Publishing.

Jongman, W. M., 1988. *The Economy and Society of Pompeii,* Amsterdam: Gieben.

King, E. M. & D. R. Potter, 1995. A Heterarchical Approach to Lowland Maya Socioeconomies. *Archeological Papers of the American Anthropological Association,* 6(1), 17-32.

Kolb, C. C., 1985. Demographic Estimates in Archaeology: Contributions from Ethnoarchaeology on Mesoamerican Peasants. *Current Anthropology,* 26, 581-99.

Kron, J. G., (2008). The Much Maligned Peasant. Comparative Perspectives on the Productivity of the Small Farmer in Classical Antiquity, in *People, Land, and Politics. Demographic Developments and the Transformation of Roman Italy, 300 BC-AD 14* eds. L. de Ligt & S. J. Northwood Leiden: Brill, 71-119.

Kunow, J., 1988. Zentrale Orte in der Germania Inferior. *Archäologisches Korrespondenzblatt,* 18, 55-67.

Laurence, R., (1998). Land transport in Roman Italy: costs, practice and the economy, in *Trade, Traders and the Ancient City,* eds. H. Parkins & C. Smith London: Routledge, 129-48.

Laurence, R., 2007. *Roman Pompeii. Space and Society,* London: Routledge.

Mandelbrot, B. B., 1982. *The Fractal Geometry of Nature.,* New York: W.H. Freeman and Company.

Mari, Z., (2008). Lexicon Topographicum Urbis Romae. Suburbium. Volume 5, ed. A. La Regina Rome: Quasar, 145-6.

Mattingly, D. & R. Witcher, (2004). Mapping the Roman World: The Contribution of Field Survey Data, in *Side-by-Side Survey. Comparative Regional*

Studies in the Mediterranean World, eds. S. E. Alcock & J. F. Cherry Oxford: Oxbow Books, 173-86.

Morley, N., 1996. *Metropolis and hinterland. The city of Rome and the Italian economy 200 B.C.-A.D. 200,* Cambridge: Cambridge University Press.

Morley, N., (2008). Urbanisation and Development in Italy in the Late Republic, in *People, Land, and Politics. Demographic Developments and the Transformation of Roman Italy, 300 BC-AD 14* eds. L. de Ligt & S. J. Northwood Leiden: Brill, 121-37.

Moscatelli, U., 1988. *Trea*: Firenze.

Musgrave, P., (1995). The small towns of northern Italy in the seventeenth and eighteenth centuries: an overview, in *Small towns in early modern Europe*, ed. P. Clark Cambridge: Cambridge University Press, 250-70.

Osborne, R., (2004). Demography and Survey, in *Side-by-Side Survey. Comparative Regional Studies in the Mediterranean World*, eds. S. E. Alcock & J. F. Cherry Oxford: Oxbow Books, 163-72.

Patterson, H. (ed.) (2004). *Bridging the Tiber. Approaches to Regional Archaeology in the Middle Tiber Valley,* London.

Patterson, H., H. DiGiuseppe & R. Witcher, (2004). Three South Etrurian 'Crisis': First Results of the Tiber Valley Project, in *Papers of the British School at Rome* London, 1-36.

Pelgrom, J., (2008). Settlement Organisation and Land Distribution in Latin Colonies before the Second Punic War, in *People, Land, and Politics. Demographic Developments and the Transformation of Roman Italy, 300 BC-AD 14* eds. L. de. Ligt & S. J. Northwood Leiden: Brill, 333-71.

Peña, J. T., 2007. *Roman Pottery in the Archaeological Record,* Cambridge: Cambridge University Press.

Perkins, P., (1999). Etruscan Settlement, Society and Material Culture in Central Coastal Etruria, in *BAR International Series 788* Oxford.

Piccarreta, F., 1977. *Astura*: Firenze.

Potter, T. W., 1979. *The Changing Landscape of South Etruria,* London: Palgrave Macmillan.

Purcell, N., (1987). Town in Country and Country in Town, in *Ancient Roman villa gardens*, ed. E. B. MacDoughall Washington: Dumbarton Oaks, 187-203.

Rathbone, D., (2008). Poor Peasants and Silent Sherds, in *People, Land, and Politics. Demographic Developments and the Transformation of Roman Italy, 300 BC-AD 14* eds. L. de Ligt & S. J. Northwood Leiden: Brill, 305-31.

Renfrew, C. & E. V. Level, (1979). Exploring Dominance: Predicting Polities from Centres, in *Transformations. Mathematical Approaches to Culture Change*, eds. C. Renfrew & K. L. Cooke London: Academic Press, 145-67.

Ross Taylor, L., 1914. Augustales, Seviri Augustales, and Seviri: A Chronological Study. *Transactions and Proceedings of the American Philological Association,* 45, 231-53.

Ruschenbusch, E., 1985. Die Zahl der griechischen Staaten und Arealgrösse und Bürgerzahl der "Normalpolis". *Zeitschrift für Papyrologie und Epigraphik,* 59, 253-63.

Salmon, E. T., 1969. *Roman colonization under the Republic,* London: Thames & Hudson.

Salmon, E. T., 1989. The Hirpini: "ex Italia semper aliquid novi". *Phoenix,* 43(3), 225-35.

Savage, S. H., 1997. Assessing Departures from Log-Normality in the Rank-Size Rule. *Journal of Archaeological Science,* 24, 233-44.

Sbonias, K., (1999). Introduction to Issues in Demography and Survey, in *The Archaeology of Mediterranean Landscapes 1, Reconstructing Past Population Trends in Mediterranean Europe* eds. J. Bintliff & K. Sbonias Oxford: Oxbow Books, 1-20.

Sheppard, E., 1982. City Size Distributions and Spatial Economic Change. *International Regional Science Review,* 7(2), 127-51.

Sisani, S., 2006. *Umbria Marche,* Rome: Laterza and Figli.

Spelman, E., 1758. *The roman antiquities of Dionysius Halicarnassensis, translated into English; with notes and dissertations. Volume 2,* London: Eighteenth Century Collections.

Spivey, N. & S. Stoddart, 1990. *Etruscan Italy,* London: B.T. Batsford.

Stek, T. D., (2008). Sanctuary and Society in Central-Southern Italy (3rd to 1st centuries BC). A study into Cult Places and Cultural Change after the Roman Conquest of Italy, in *Faculty of Humanities* Amsterdam: University of Amsterdam.

Storey, G. R., 1997. The population of ancient Rome. *Antiquity,* 71, 966-78.

Sumner, W. M., 1989. Population and Settlement Area: An Example from Iran. *American Anthropologist,* 91, 631-41.

Talbert, R. J. A. (ed.) (1985). *Atlas of Classical History,* London: Routledge.

Talbert, R. J. A. (ed.) (2000). *Barrington Atlas of the Greek and Roman World* Princeton: Princeton University Press.

Traill, J. S., 1986. *Demos and trittys. Epigraphical and topographical studies in the organisation of Attica,* Toronto: The Coach House Press.

Ullman, E., 1941. A Theory of Location for Cities. *The American Journal of Sociology,* 46(6), 853-64.

Van Leusen, M., (2002). Pattern to Process. Methodological Investigations into the Formation and Interpretation of Spatial Patterns in Archeaeological Landscapes, in *Groningen Institute of Archaeology* Groningen: University of Groningen.

Van Leusen, M. & P. Attema, 1998. Kern en periferie in het RPC-project (2): De Fogliano-survey in de

Pontijnse regio (midden-Italië). *Paleo-Aktueel,* 10, 31-5.

Van Leusen, P. M., T. C. A. De Haas, S. Pomicino & P. A. J. Attema, 2005. Protohistoric to Roman Settlement on the Lepine Margins near Ninfa (South Lazio, Italy). *Palaeohistoria,* 45/46, 301-45.

Verdonck, L. & F. Vermeulen, 2004. A Contribution to the Study of Roman Rural Settlement in Marche. *Picus,* 24, 161-229.

Vermeulen, F., (2008). Functional Zoning and Changes in the Use of Space in the Roman Town of Potentia. An Integrated Survey Approach, in *Thinking About Space. The Potential of Surface Survey and Contextual Analysis in the Definition of Space in Roman Times,* eds. H. Vanhaverbeke, J. Poblome, F. Vermeulen, M. Waelkens & R. Brulet. Leuven: Brepols, 233-49.

Vermeulen, F. & C. Boullart, 2001. The Potenza Valley Survey: Preliminary Report of Field Campaign 2000. *BaBesch,* 76, 1-18.

Vermeulen, F., M. D. Dapper, P. Combre, B. M. D. Vliegher, P. Monsieur, C. Boullart, T. Goethals, H. Verreyke, G. Verhoeven & etc., 2003. The Potenza Valley Survey: Preliminary Report on Field Campaign 2002. *BaBesch,* 78, 71-106.

Vermeulen, F., M. D. Dapper, B. Music, P. Monsieur, H. Verreyke, F. Carboni, S. Dralans, G. Verhoeven, L. Verdonck, S. Hay, M. Sterry, P. D. Paepe & S. D. Seranno, 2009. Investigating the impact of Roman urbanisation on the landscape of the Potenza Valley. A Report on Fieldwork in 2007. *BaBesch,* 84, 91-116.

Vermeulen, F., S. Hay & G. Verhoeven, (2006). Potentia: An Integrated Survey of a Roman Colony on the Adriatic Coast, in *Papers of the British School at Rome* London, 203-36.

Vermeulen, F., P. Monsieur, C. Boullart, H. Verreyke, G. Verhoeven, M. D. Dapper, T. Goethals, R. Goossens & B. M. D. Vliegher, 2005. The Potenza Valley Survey: Preliminary Report on Field Campaign 2003. *BaBesch,* 80, 33-64.

Verreyke, H. & F. Vermeulen, 2009. Tracing Late Roman Rural Occupation in Adriatic Central Italy. *American Journal of Archaeology,* 113, 103-20.

Von Thunen, J. H., 1875. *Der isolirte Staat in Beziehung auf Landwirtschaft und Nationalokonomie,* Berlin: Hermann Schumacher-Zarchlin.

Voorrips, A., S. H. Loving & H. Kamermans (eds.), (1991). *The Agro Pontino Survey Project,* Amsterdam.

Wallace-Hadrill, A., 1994. *Houses and Society in Pompeii and Herculanium,* Princeton: Princeton University Press.

Wilkinson, T. J., 2003. *Archaeological landscapes of the Near East,* Tucson: University of Arizona Press.

Wilson, A., (2008). Villas, horticulture and irrigation infrastructure in the Tiber Valley, in *Mercator placidissimus. The Tiber Valley in Antiquity,* eds. H. Patterson & F. Coarelli Rome: Quasar, 731-68.

Witcher, R., 2005. The extended metropolis: Urbs, suburbium and population. *Journal of Roman Archaeology,* 18, 120-38.

Witcher, R., (2006a). Broken Pots and Meaningless Dots? Surveying the Rural Landscapes of Roman Italy, in *Papers of the British School at Rome* London, 39-72.

Witcher, R., 2006b. Settlement and Society in Early Imperial Etruria. *Journal of Roman Studies,* 96, 88-123.

Witcher, R., 2008a. (Re)surveying Mediterranean Rural Landscapes: GIS and Legacy Survey Data. *Internet Archaeology,* (24).

Witcher, R., (2008b). Regional Field Survey and the Demography of Roman Italy, in *People, Land, and Politics. Demographic Developments and the Transformation of Roman Italy, 300 BC-AD 14* eds. L. de Ligt & S. J. Northwood Leiden: Brill, 273-303.

Yntema, D., (2008). Polybius and the Field Survey Evidence from Apulia, in *People, Land, and Politics. Demographic Developments and the Transformation of Roman Italy, 300 BC-AD 14* eds. L. de Ligt & S. J. Northwood Leiden: Brill, 373-85.

Zanker, P., 1998. *Pompeii. Public and Private Life,* Cambridge: Harvard University Press.

www.ingramcontent.com/pod-product-compliance
Lightning Source LLC
Chambersburg PA
CBHW061545010526
44113CB00023B/2802